Personal Finance Workbook For Dummies®

Sheryl's Favorite Web Sites

Purpose	Web site(s)
Credit	www.annualcreditreport.com (the free credit report site)
Financial calculators	www.choosetosave.org/calculators
General financial news and resources	www.marketwatch.com
Insurance information	www.iii.org (Insurance Information Institute); www.insure.com (for all major types of insurance covered)
Legal resources	www.nolo.com (Legal info, downloadable forms, and books)
Locate an advisor	www.cfp.net/learn/ (Certified Financial Planners Board of Standards); www.napfa.org/consumer/planners/ (fee-only financial advisors); www.garrettplanning network.com (hourly-based, fee-only financial advisors); www.iiaba.net/agentlocator/findagent.aspx (Independent Insurance Agent Organization); www.findlaw. com (to find a lawyer); www.CPAdirectory.com (CPA locator)
Mortgages and interest rates	www.bankrate.com
Privacy	www.donotcall.gov
Rating services	www.jdpower.com (J D Power & Associates for free ratings); www.consumerreports.org (full ranking details requires subscription)
Investing	www.morningstar.com

Getting on the Fast Track to Financial Freedom

Managing your personal finances involves a *balance* between what you need and want today and what you'll need and want in the future. Always going for the instant gratification leads to constant dissatisfaction! Instead, plan ahead by using the following tips:

- Write down your goals! Be specific and revisit them annually.
- Save at *least* the first 10 percent of your income.
- Set up your savings and investing to occur automatically.
- Don't miss out on free money from your employer's retirement plan matching contribution or the phenomenal benefits of the Roth IRA.
- Don't use credit if you can't pay cash. Credit cards are convenience tools, not loans. If you can't afford it today, you can't afford to pay twice as much over time. Going into debt gives others control of your financial freedom.
- Before spending money, always ask yourself, "How will this affect my net worth?"

Remember: Nobody will watch out for your money *better* than you, and *everybody* wants a piece of what you have!

For Dummies: Bestselling Book Series for Beginners

Personal Finance Workbook For Dummies®

Cheat Sheet

Financial Advisor Acid-Test Questions

You, the client, have the right to ask any questions you feel are appropriate to help you select the right advisor for you. If you're trying to figure out whether an advisor is worth your hard-earned dollars, be sure to ask the following questions:

- **How and how much are you paid?** Advisors are required to tell you *how* they're paid but not *how much.* If an advisor quotes their compensation as a percentage, ask her to convert that compensation into dollars and get it in writing. Don't settle for the common brush off response, "I'm paid by the company." The advisor doesn't get paid by the company if she doesn't sell you some sort of an insurance or investment product. And if the advisor can't or won't tell you how much she'll be compensated if you work with her, she's definitely getting paid commissions and likely doesn't want to tell you how much.

- **Are you a fiduciary?** A fiduciary has a *legal* responsibility to put her client's interest above all others. If you're seeking professional, objective financial advice, don't settle for anything less than a fiduciary.

These are my acid-test questions. Starting with these questions saves you a lot of time because asking them eliminates the overwhelming majority of advisors. Now you can concentrate your search for an advisor based on her qualifications, experience, and expertise. Refer to the Financial Advisor Interview Questionnaire in Chapter 20 for the remainder of the questions I recommend you ask of any prospective advisor.

2007 Retirement Plan Contribution Limits

401(k), 403(b), and 457 plans	$15,500
401(k), 403(b), and 457 plans	$5,000
IRA – Roth and Traditional	$4,000
IRA – Roth and Traditional*	$1,000

* If you're 50 or better, you may make a larger maximum contribution.

2007 Roth IRA Qualification Limits

Maximum Contribution	Maximum Income (AGI)
100%	Less than $99,000 for singles
100%	Less than $156,000 for married couples*
Phase-out	Between $99,000 and $114,000 for singles
Phase-out	Between $156,000 and $166,000 for married couples*
Not eligible	More than $114,000 for singles
Not eligible	More than $166,000 for married couples

*Must file tax return jointly

For Dummies: Bestselling Book Series for Beginners

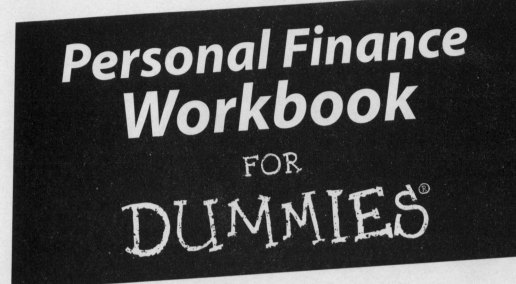

Personal Finance Workbook

FOR DUMMIES®

Personal Finance Workbook

FOR

DUMMIES®

by Sheryl Garrett, CFP®

Wiley Publishing, Inc.

Personal Finance Workbook For Dummies®

Published by
Wiley Publishing, Inc.
111 River St.
Hoboken, NJ 07030-5774
www.wiley.com

Copyright © 2008 by Wiley Publishing, Inc., Indianapolis, Indiana

Published by Wiley Publishing, Inc., Indianapolis, Indiana

Published simultaneously in Canada

For general information on our other products and services, please contact our Customer Care Department within the U.S. at 800-762-2974, outside the U.S. at 317-572-3993, or fax 317-572-4002.

For technical support, please visit www.wiley.com/techsupport.

Wiley also publishes its books in a variety of electronic formats. Some content that appears in print may not be available in electronic books.

Library of Congress Control Number: 2007936458

ISBN: 978-0-470-09933-9

Manufactured in the United States of America

10 9 8 7 6 5 4 3 2 1

WILEY

About the Author

Sheryl Garrett, CFP® and founder of The Garrett Planning Network, Inc., has been dubbed "The All-American Planner," possibly because of her zealous mission to "help make competent, objective financial advice accessible to all people" and partly because she's just an all-American gal from Kansas.

Growing up in a working-class family and even setting out to get her first job at age 8, Sheryl was (and is) a consummate schemer and planner, which made financial planning a great fit for her. In 1998, Sheryl struck out on her own and designed her financial advisory shop to service clients in a way that she'd want to receive services. Sheryl's fresh approach — working with clients on an hourly, as-needed, fee-only basis — has evolved into an international network of independent financial advisors and a charitable foundation that is helping Sheryl fulfill her personal mission.

As a consumer advocate, Sheryl has been honored to work with the House Subcommittee on Financial Services regarding predatory lending regulation and the United States' need for financial literacy and Social Security reform. She also enjoys her involvement with the financial planning departments at Kansas State University, The University of Missouri, and Texas Tech University, as well as the Kansas Counsel on Economic Education. Most recently, Sheryl has become ignited by her work "going after the bad guys" by consulting and testifying as an expert witness in lawsuits against financial advisors who rendered inappropriate financial advice.

Sheryl has also authored or served as a technical editor on more than a dozen books and a couple monthly magazine columns. These books include *Garrett's Guide to Financial Planning* (National Underwriter), *Just Give Me the Answer$* (Dearborn Trade), *Money Without Matrimony* (Dearborn Trade), as well as this book, *Personal Finance Workbook For Dummies* (Wiley).

Sheryl has been interviewed on CNNfn, Bloomberg, ABC World News Now, Fox-TV, NPR's *All Things Considered* and *Marketplace,* and in *Business Week, Newsweek, Time, Forbes, Kiplinger Personal Finance, Money, Smart Money, MarketWatch, U.S. News & World Report,* the *New York Times, USA Today,* and the *Wall Street Journal.* For four straight years, Sheryl was recognized by *Investment Advisor* magazine as "One of the Top 25 Most Influential People in Financial Planning."

Dedication

I dedicate this book to everyone who believes that knowledge is power — power to change things for the better and power to make a positive difference in our lives and the lives of those whom we love.

I have an extra-special dedication to my daughter Claire. Although we haven't met yet, this book has kept me preoccupied during the long wait for our forever family. Hurry home, baby — Momma's getting restless!

Author's Acknowledgments

Because of the love and devotion of my family, staff, and colleagues in the Garrett Planning Network, I have the freedom and support to carry out my life's work, which involves my passion to help make competent, objective financial advice accessible to all people. The *For Dummies* folks share this vision.

Thank you, Eric Tyson, for allowing me the honor to serve as technical editor of *Personal Finance For Dummies* and for suggesting that I write this workbook. Your support and confidence is most appreciated. And thank you, Randy Gardner, for helping me not disappoint you when you call me the greatest financial planner in the world. Without your technical review, comments, and suggestions, I might have embarrassed both of us. Also, many thanks to Mike Baker, Kelly Ewing, Sarah Westfall, and the great team behind the scenes at Wiley Publishing for all their hard work.

But most of all, thank you — the reader — for taking the initiative to achieve financial success!

Publisher's Acknowledgments

We're proud of this book; please send us your comments through our Dummies online registration form located at www.dummies.com/register/.

Some of the people who helped bring this book to market include the following:

Acquisitions, Editorial, and Media Development

Project Editor: Kelly Ewing

Acquisitions Editor: Mike Baker

Copy Editor: Sarah Westfall

General Reviewer: Randy Gardner, LLM, MBA, CPA, CFP

Editorial Manager: Michelle Hacker

Editorial Supervisor and Reprint Editor: Carmen Krikorian

Editorial Assistants: Erin Calligan Mooney, Joe Niesen, Leeann Harney

Cover Photos: © Jamie Grill/Corbis

Cartoons: Rich Tennant (www.the5thwave.com)

Composition Services

Project Coordinator: Erin Smith

Layout and Graphics: Carrie A. Cesavice, Stephanie D. Jumper, Julie Trippetti, Christine Williams

Anniversary Logo Design: Richard Pacifico

Proofreaders: Jessica Kramer, Penny Stuart

Indexer: Sherry Massey

Publishing and Editorial for Consumer Dummies

Diane Graves Steele, Vice President and Publisher, Consumer Dummies

Joyce Pepple, Acquisitions Director, Consumer Dummies

Kristin A. Cocks, Product Development Director, Consumer Dummies

Michael Spring, Vice President and Publisher, Travel

Kelly Regan, Editorial Director, Travel

Publishing for Technology Dummies

Andy Cummings, Vice President and Publisher, Dummies Technology/General User

Composition Services

Gerry Fahey, Vice President of Production Services

Debbie Stailey, Director of Composition Services

Contents at a Glance

Table of Contents

Introduction

Do the terms *personal finance* or *money management* dredge up feelings of inadequacy, confusion, discomfort, or fear in you? If so, you're not alone. Many people dread anything that relates to money for many reasons. Perhaps you find yourself lacking adequate income to support your lifestyle, or you're swimming in debt. You may love to just stop thinking about money for a while, but unfortunately, you just can't get away from it.

Enter *Personal Finance Workbook For Dummies.* I wrote this book to help you purge any negative feelings you've had regarding your personal finances, and I promise that no matter where you find yourself, you can improve your financial situation. All you need is to be informed, motivated, and dedicated; you can do it, and this workbook can help.

Personal finance isn't rocket science, but because so much misinformation and so many self-serving nut cases are out there, differentiating all the great stuff from the garbage can be quite a chore. The financial services industry, the media, and many authors benefit by keeping you dazed and confused. Others would prefer to lead you dreaming of how easy it will be to retire in style, on the beach somewhere, in better shape than you've ever been in your life — if you only hire them or buy their magazine, book, or too-good-to-be-true system. However, I chose to keep it good and simple.

I crammed *Personal Finance Workbook For Dummies* with the tools and strategies you need to make smarter decisions about your personal finances. As an informed money manager, you're empowered to save money, simplify your life, and achieve your most cherished financial life goals, so invest a little time on your personal finances. I promise you'll be forever glad you did.

About This Book

Personal Finance Workbook For Dummies is designed for you to use as a hands-on workbook for all the major subjects involving your personal finances. If you're like most people, you really don't want or don't have the time to read an entire book cover to cover — let alone, work through an entire workbook on personal finances. If I've just described you, just turn to the Index or the Table of Contents and zero in on the issue you currently have questions about. Zone in on the chapter or section that addresses your specific need at this time. Then refer back to this workbook each time you have additional questions or areas about your personal financial lives that you'd like to improve.

But, if you're a nerd like me and just enjoy this stuff, proceed step by step through the entire workbook! By working through this book page by page, you can develop a comprehensive financial plan for yourself.

This workbook can help you develop your own personal financial plan or simply get the answers to your personal financial questions. However, due to the nature of this workbook, you won't find a lot of text providing definitions or explanations about all things personal finance. Should you desire or need to augment your knowledge gained in this book — no worries. I recommend checking out *Personal Finance For Dummies* by Eric Tyson, also published by Wiley, or you can use some of the great resources I've included all throughout this workbook.

Conventions Used in This Book

While writing this workbook, I used a few conventions throughout its pages in order to make your life just a bit easier. Here's what you can expect:

- ✔ I use *italics* when I define a word or phrase that's important to understanding a topic. And when I get especially excited, I may throw in some italics for a little extra emphasis.

- ✔ When you see text in **bold,** you can expect it to be either a step in a numbered list or a key word in a bulleted list.

- ✔ All Web addresses appear in monofont.

- ✔ When this book was printed, some Web addresses may have needed to break across two lines of text. If that happened, know that I haven't put in any extra characters (such as hyphens) to indicate the break. So, when using one of these Web addresses, just type in exactly what you see in this book or on the Cheat Sheet and ignore the line break.

Foolish Assumptions

Don't be afraid, but I have some preconceived ideas about you, my dear reader. In order to provide the tools and advice you need, I made some of the following assumptions:

- ✔ You passed fourth-grade math. You need a few basic math skills to work through some of the exercises in this workbook; however, I added instructions and examples to make it as easy as possible to complete the exercises. And, unlike your fourth-grade math class, the results of these homework assignments can have an immediate positive impact on your finances.

- ✔ You don't want to become victim of self-serving sales pitches, struggle to make ends meet, or become a bag lady. You want to become empowered to achieve financial security.

- ✔ You have *some* interest in taking a more active and productive role in managing your personal financial life, or at least want to make sure that you don't do anything really stupid or get ripped off in the scary and dangerous world of financial products and services.

- ✔ You want to create your own financial plan in order to meet your life goals.

- ✔ You have access to the Internet. Although Internet access isn't a requirement, you can enjoy the tips I share regarding my favorite Web sites for gaining additional information, products, or services, for everything you need to manage your personal finances.

- ✔ You're no idiot! In fact, you're so smart you realize that to really get ahead in life financially, you've got to get educated and stay involved. With a little time, energy, persistence, and determination, you can achieve what you really want in life.

How This Book Is Organized

Personal Finance Workbook For Dummies is organized into six distinct parts, each covering a major area involving your personal finances. The following summarizes what you can find in each part.

Part I: Getting on the Road to Financial Fitness

The chapters in this part help you get focused and motivated to achieve your financial dreams. You can use the worksheets and tips in these chapters to begin to simplify and better manage your current financial life so that you can achieve what matters most to you. If you can measure it, you can manage it. If you can manage it, you can achieve it. This part gets you started.

Part II: Getting the Most Out of Your Money

In this part, I get into the when's and how's to use credit to your advantage. I provide you tools to help you get the most out of your money when grocery shopping, entertaining, or paying your taxes and provide hands-on suggestions to get your family onboard with your financial plans.

Part III: Thinking about the Future

What do you want out of your financial life — to have a comfortable home, to be able to educate your kids, to retire someday, or at least have that choice? What about planning for what you leave behind? Part III focuses exclusively on how best to approach each of these major life goals and how you can deal with the many options and opportunities available to you.

Part IV: Building and Managing Wealth

To achieve the goals most important in your financial life, you need to discover and continue to develop your knowledge of specific investments and investment strategies that are most appropriate for your goals, options, and comfort with risk. I help you determine the right way to invest your money to get the biggest bang for your buck, yet keep it simple, highly effective, and easy to manage.

Part V: Protecting Your Assets

In one quick instant, all you have worked for, all you dream about, could be wiped out. In this part, I help you understand the risks you face and show you ways to determine and obtain exactly what you need and how to get it at the best price. You may need more appropriate insurance or guidance from a professional financial advisor. I help you determine just exactly what types of insurance coverages you may need and how to obtain that coverage. I also provide specific questions and tips that I encourage you to use when considering hiring a financial advisor. And I'm sure that you can benefit from the tips I share about protecting your privacy.

Part VI: The Part of Tens

A landmark of the *For Dummies* books, the Part of Tens highlights my top ten lists for trimming your expenses, getting your financial life organized, and avoiding getting ripped off.

Icons Used in This Book

As you flip through this workbook, you see a lot of icons, which are there to draw your attention to specific issues or examples. Check them out:

This icon alerts you to common pitfalls and dangers that you must be on the lookout for when managing your personal finances.

If you don't read anything else, pay attention to this icon, which points out information that I just had to stress because it is *that* important to your financial well being.

If you're looking for a time-saving tool or insider suggestion that you can utilize immediately, the text marked by the Tip icon has what you want.

This icon directs you to an example (shocker, right?) that illustrates a particular point or exercise.

Where to Go from Here

If you're just beginning to get your financial house in order, I suggest you start at the beginning; it's a very good place to start. (I'm hearing Julie Andrews singing.) However, if you feel that your current financial plan is working and you're ready to take it to the next level, zone in on the areas of your financial plan that need attention now and refer to that chapter or section of the workbook. If you're here for a specific topic, such as insurance or investments, feel free to flip to that chapter at any time or look it up in the index or table of contents.

Remember, you don't have to read the book cover to cover. If you've always wanted to start on the last page, go for it! It's your workbook and your financial future you're planning! Work it however it works best for you!

Part I

Getting on the Road to Financial Fitness

The 5th Wave   By Rich Tennant

"I ran an evaluation of our last pie chart. Apparently, it's boysenberry."

In this part . . .

You explore your current financial situation, examine some primary factors that got you there, and discover what you really want to achieve in your life financially. You can discover tricks to help take the drudgery out of personal money management, streamline your financial records, improve your credit rating, and find out what truly matters most in your life. If you're wanting to get financially fit, this part can get you well on your way.

Chapter 1

Exploring Money in Your Life

•••

In This Chapter

▶ Understanding attitudes when it comes to money

▶ Reflecting on the messages you learned as a child

▶ Recognizing what obstacles stand in the way of your financial progress

•••

*B*efore you begin making concrete financial plans, you should explore your history with money. What messages were you taught, consciously or unconsciously, about money when you were growing up? How have these messages affected the way you make money management decisions now? If you're in a long-term relationship, what lessons did your spouse or partner learn, and how does your loved one's money history affect your financial plans together? In this chapter, I help you delve into and analyze your financial history.

Exploring Your Attitudes about Money

I'm sure you've heard people say that they're "frugal" or "good savers." However, I find these statements to be less common than "I'm a bad money manager," "I don't know how to manage money," "It's too confusing," "I'll never get ahead," or "I'll have to work 'til I drop."

Your thoughts about money influence your actions. Positive thoughts lead to positive money management behaviors. Negative thoughts lead to financial ruin.

Try to maintain a spirit of open mindedness when you think about your finances, because your thoughts become reality. For example, if you think you'll never have financial security, you may very well give up before you even begin to try. However, if you remain open to making changes in your financial habits, you're more likely to succeed. Which reality do you want? You have the opportunity now to make changes that affect your financial life forever.

Each of us, at one time or another, has experienced discomfort, stress, anxiety, or the feeling of ignorance about money. However, these attitudes and feelings change. Exploring your current attitudes about money is an important step in improving your financial education and situation.

To help you figure out your current frame of mind when it comes to money, I've included Worksheet 1-1. To use this worksheet, determine how often the statements fit you — frequently, sometimes, or never? In the blank provided, write **F** for frequently, **S** for sometimes, and **N** for never. Don't spend a lot of time mulling over the answer — just a few seconds on each question. And because your attitudes can and do change, respond to these questions as you feel right now — and go with your gut.

Worksheet 1-1   Attitudes about Money Quiz

_____   I hate to open the mail, because all I ever receive is bills.

_____   I'll never have enough money.

_____   When I'm feeling down or bored, I go shopping.

_____   My spouse/partner/kids spend money faster then I can bring it in.

_____   I don't want my kids to go without things they want, like I had to when I was growing up.

_____   If I have cash in my wallet or purse, I'll spend it.

_____   How can I save for retirement when I can barely make ends meet now?

_____   I can't or won't be able to help my kids pay for college.

_____   In the event of a financial emergency, I don't know how I could come up with the money.

_____   My employer has a retirement plan, but I'm not participating because I can't afford to.

_____   If I want something, I buy it, even if I have to use credit.

_____   I'm not out of money until I'm out of credit.

_____   I will postpone making a purchase if I don't have the cash right now.

_____   I use a list when I shop and only buy those items on my list.

_____   My family will be financially okay if something happens to me.

_____   I expect my income to increase enough to allow me to pay off credit-card debt in the very near future.

_____   I feel stress when I think about my financial commitments.

_____   I am ashamed of my wardrobe, car, and/or home.

_____   I know how much money is in my checking account.

_____   I save every month.

_____   My parents had to "_do without._" I will not.

_____   I hope to retire by 65 or before.

_____   My income has increased steadily for years, and there is no limit to my earning potential.

_____   My lack of money makes me feel inadequate around my friends.

_____   I am the one my friends/family turn to when they need money.

_____   I have lied about money to people I care about.

_____   I'm tired of not having _enough_ money all the time.

_____   I have been financially burned before (ex-spouse, financial advisor, deadbeat friend, or family member), and I won't let it happen again.

_____   I feel knowledgeable about my ability to manage money.

_____   I make minimum monthly payments on my credit-card debt.

After completing Worksheet 1-1, you should have a pretty good picture of your attitude and feelings when it comes to money. But to take it a step further, spend a few minutes writing about your current attitudes and feelings about money; see Worksheet 1-2 as an example and use the space provided in Worksheet 1-3. This exercise can help you become more thoughtful and aware of how your thoughts and attitudes toward money may have evolved and how those thoughts and attitudes are affecting your financial life today.

Worksheet 1-2 **Example Reflection**

> I don't know much about money management. I feel like I ought to know, but I don't. We save a little each month, and we pay extra toward our credit-card balances each month. And I'm very happy to say that the balances are finally starting to go down. Unfortunately, I feel like I am nagging my family every time I turn around. They think I'm becoming a miser. My dad was a miser and didn't live long enough to enjoy it. My mother and I would have loved to have had a few niceties like clothes that were in fashion, a newer car, and a larger house. But my dad said we couldn't afford it. When it came to money, Dad's only communication was "No."
>
> I don't want to turn into my dad, but I do want our family to be financially secure.

Worksheet 1-3 **My Reflections**

_____

_____

_____

_____

_____

_____

_____

Taking Stock of Your Financial History

Your financial history consists of the lessons and messages you heard about money while growing up. Much of what you are today you owe to your upbringing — whether good or bad. So it makes sense to reflect on the messages you received and how they may be impacting your money-management decisions today.

Your parents or primary caregivers may have been somewhat or very secretive about their personal financial situation; however, what they said and how they acted can reveal a lot.

Worksheet 1-4 helps you reveal your financial history. Check off each statement that you heard (or anything darn close to it) from a parent or primary caregiver growing up.

Worksheet 1-4   Figuring Out Your Financial History

❏ Money burns a hole in my pocket.

❏ Live for today. You never know what tomorrow will bring.

❏ Don't carry cash. You'll either spend it, or someone will clunk you over the head and take it.

❏ If you want something, you have to work very hard to get it.

❏ You'll never amount to anything.

❏ It is easier for a camel to pass through the eye of a needle than for a rich man to enter the kingdom of heaven.

❏ If you want something, you must be willing to sacrifice.

❏ You don't appreciate how hard I work to put food on the table.

❏ If you can't afford to pay cash for something, you shouldn't buy it.

❏ Neither a lender nor a borrower be.

❏ You can accomplish anything you desire in life.

❏ Women don't make as much money as men.

❏ Invest in yourself.

❏ Diamonds are a girl's best friend.

❏ Your mother or father can't manage money.

❏ Your mother or father hides or lies about purchases.

❏ The rich get richer on the backs of working class people like us.

❏ I can't afford to pursue the career of my dreams.

❏ If we would have only waited longer before having kids. . .

❏ Save it for a rainy day.

Read through the statements in Worksheet 1-4 that you checked off and spend a few minutes reflecting on the messages you heard as a child and how these messages may have affected your current attitudes and feelings about money. Ask yourself the following questions about each of your parents or primary caregivers. (You can use Worksheet 1-5 as an example if you get stuck.) Write your reflections in Worksheet 1-6.

✔ Were they spenders or savers? Do you know?

✔ Did they talk about money around you?

✔ Did they fight about money?

✔ What lessons did you learn about money from them?

Many of the messages listed in Worksheet 1-4 are somewhat or very negative belief statements. Of those that you checked, which do you find potentially negative, and what effect do you feel these messages may have had on you growing up?

Some people are hoarders, and others are overspenders. Being extreme — on either end of the spectrum — isn't healthy. Balance is key. You can't spend everything today, or you won't have anything for tomorrow. You also shouldn't put off everything you'd like to do until tomorrow because tomorrow may never come. Finding the appropriate balance with your time, energy, and money will lead to the best outcome.

Worksheet 1-5   Example Reflections on Financial Origins

Example #1:
My father was a good provider — financially speaking. Unfortunately, he wasn't home as much as I would have liked him to be because he was constantly working. I regret not having more time with him while I was growing up. I don't know whether he worked to better provide for his family, or because he felt he had to, or maybe he was just a workaholic. He grew up in a very poor family. He never felt we were saving enough.

Example #2:
My mother would like to spend more money than she does. However, my father keeps a tight grip on the purse strings in our family. I remember a few occasions when my mother bought a new dress or pair of shoes, and she hid them from my father in the back of their closet. She'd tell me, "By the time I wear them, Dad won't realize that they are new." And my father may have been too much of a hoarder. When he was growing up, his family was broke. I know he didn't want that for us.

Worksheet 1-6   Reflections on My Financial Origins

_____

_____

_____

_____

_____

_____

_____

Identifying What or Who May Be Holding You Back

What unhealthy behaviors or characteristics do you feel you may have picked up from your parents or primary caregivers growing up? Using Worksheet 1-8, reflect on ways of thinking that you may have picked up and how those messages or behaviors you witnessed may be affecting you now. (If you'd like to see an example of this type of reflection, you can check out Worksheet 1-7.) For example, do you find that you follow in your "tightwad" father's footsteps or resent the fact that you weren't allowed to buy things that you wanted to when you were younger and have made up for it — in spades — in your adulthood?

Worksheet 1-7   Example Reflection of Unhealthy Behaviors Learned When Growing Up

My father felt very strongly that if you want to achieve financial security you have to be willing to sacrifice time with family. He felt his job was to make money and be a good provider. I got the feeling that money was more valuable than his family. I missed my father. I wanted more time with him when I was growing up. You can't replace that with any amount of money. I will never let that happen to my kids.

From my mother, I learned that if she wanted something but ought not to buy it, she could so long as Dad didn't know about it. She definitely wouldn't endorse lying, but that is exactly what I learned when it came to her relationship with my dad and money. "What he doesn't know won't hurt him," she used to say. I'd like to have a more understanding, collaborative partnership with my spouse, rather than it being so one-sided as it was with my parents.

Throughout my childhood, it became apparent to me that people judge you by how much money they think you have. I care about what others think of me. But I have to really try not to spend my money on things that will impress "them."

Worksheet 1-8   Unhealthy Behaviors Learned Growing Up

_____

_____

_____

_____

_____

_____

_____

You may hold a grudge, feel taken advantage of, or have animosity toward people in your financial life. You may also have regrets about decisions you've made. So in addition to the messages you received growing up, what other people or issues do you feel may be keeping you from realizing your full potential financially? Use Worksheet 1-9 as a guide to get you thinking (and writing) about what or who may be holding you back from your financial goals.

Thus far, you've been focusing on the messages you learned growing up. In Worksheet 1-9, I'd like you to focus for a moment on other people in your life and how your relationship with them may be affected by money.

Worksheet 1-9   Who or What Is Holding You Back?

Spouse/partner (if so, how?):

_____

_____

_____

_____

Children and family responsibilities (if so, how?):

_____

_____

_____

_____

Education and/or career (if so, how?):

_____

_____

_____

_____

Other(s) (if so, how?):

_____

_____

_____

_____

By becoming more aware of your beliefs and attitudes about money and recognizing how these beliefs influence your relationship with others and with money, you can discover who or what may be holding you back and possibly how to work through these challenging issues. The first step is awareness.

Dealing with the Subject of Money

Sharing your financial goals, objectives, quirks, and hang-ups about money with the people in your life is the best way to overcome perceived or real issues impeding your personal and your family's financial success. However, money is the last taboo subject for most people, and you likely don't talk about your personal finances with others.

Worksheet 1-11 is designed to help stimulate healthy and meaningful dialogue with your spouse/partner, kids, parents, friends, and employer. See Worksheet 1-10 for some examples to jump-start your thinking. Focus on positive, healthy interactions that you've had in the past. Where might you benefit from having these types of conversations now?

Worksheet 1-10   Example Meaningful Money Discussion

My daughter recently started her first "real" job. She asked me for advice regarding whether she should sign up for her retirement plan at work. I don't know much about investing or retirement plans. However, I do know that I regret not participating in my employer's retirement plan when I first started working. Because I didn't, I have not saved anywhere near the amount of money I should have by now. So I encouraged my daughter to start saving now. The biggest regret I have about my financial decisions is that I didn't start saving a lot sooner. Hopefully, I have helped my daughter avoid the same mistake I made, by being open and honest with her about my mistakes and regrets. Heck, if you can learn from your mistakes and that knowledge helps someone else, all is not lost.

Worksheet 1-11   My Reflections on Meaningful Money Discussions

With your spouse or partner:

_____

_____

_____

_____

With your children:

_____

_____

_____

_____

With your parents:

_____

_____

_____

_____

With your friends:

_____

_____

_____

_____

With your employer:

_____

_____

_____

_____

With others:

_____

_____

_____

_____

Many people avoid talking about money, but trouble brews when couples or families ignore the topic. You should discuss issues, such as your desires as to what you want to do with your annual bonus or tax refund, because your spouse or partner may have very different ideas about using this money. Communication and compromise are required. Remember, you are in financial partnership with your spouse. Collaborate on your financial plans together.

You and your spouse/partner are not only romantic and domestic partners; you are also financial partners.

Using Worksheet 1-12, determine some financial discussions you may need to have — perhaps with your loved ones or even your employer. Be specific about what needs to be addressed and why.

Worksheet 1-12   Financial Discussions You Need to Have

With your spouse or life partner:

_____

_____

_____

_____

With your children:

_____

_____

_____

_____

With your parents:

_____

_____

_____

_____

With your friends:

_____

_____

_____

_____

With your employer:

_____

_____

_____

_____

With others:

_____

_____

_____

_____

Now that you have identified some key conversations that need to take place, consider how and when you should approach these people about the issues you raised. Address these issues as soon as possible. The longer you wait, the more resentment and animosity can fester. Nip potential problems in the bud.

Chapter 2

Getting Your Financial House in Order

▶ Determining what financial records you need to keep, how to keep them, and for how long

▶ Assessing your current financial status and monitoring your progress

▶ Figuring out your net worth and getting your credit score

Money isn't just affected by your attitudes, emotions, or beliefs. You do have to consider the cold, hard facts of your finances. Whether you're a millionaire or living paycheck to paycheck, this chapter helps you deal with the numbers surrounding money in your life.

Organizing Your Financial Records

Do you have stacks of unopened bills? Do you stress out at tax time trying to find all your required documents? Do you have financial records that you don't know what to do with? And are you lacking a system for managing all this mess? Well, you aren't alone. Most people could use a thorough financial house cleaning right now and a little regular maintenance to keep their financial records in good shape.

Getting organized takes time, but you'll be very glad if you do it. Imagine no more late payments and fees merely because you misplaced a credit-card bill, tax records that you can organize in minutes rather than hours, and critical information or documents ready at a moment's notice.

Organization truly isn't that hard, although it does take time. So if you're ready to put an end to the mess, then the following steps can walk you down the path of organization:

1. **Gather all your financial documents, paperwork, bills, and unopened mail.**

2. **Set up a filing system (refer to Worksheet 2-1).**

   You can use this worksheet as a guide to organize your personal files. For most of the primary subjects listed in Worksheet 2-1, you need only one file. (I prefer hanging files, which you can purchase at any office-supply store.) In this worksheet, the name of each file is in bold type. You may find that fewer or more files are necessary depending on your personal situation, preferences, or number of documents you have for a particular file. I also outline in this worksheet how long you should retain these documents for your records.

3. **Separate your paperwork into four stacks: Bills To Be Paid; To Do/Read; File; and Shred.**

4. **Place the Bills To Be Paid stack into your new Bills Due file; place the papers in your To Do/Read stack into your new To Do or Read files; file all items in your File stack in their appropriate files (see Worksheet 2-1); and shred the remaining papers.**

Every time you retrieve the mail or obtain additional paperwork from work, from the bank, and so on, immediately follow Steps 3 and 4.

Worksheet 2-1   Financial Records Filing System

✔ **Advisors:** Keep a list of names, addresses, and phone numbers of the important people in your financial life (refer to Worksheet 2-2).

✔ **Auto:** Be sure to include the following for each vehicle:

- Title: Keep as long as you own the vehicle.

- Maintenance Records: Keep as long as you own the vehicle.

✔ **Bank Accounts:** This file includes both your checking and savings accounts. For each account, be sure to include the following in the file:

- Current Monthly Statement: Keep until next statement is received.

- Historic Monthly Bank Statements: Keep until account is reconciled.

✔ **Bills Due:** Immediately upon opening mail, file bills due in this file. After you've paid the bills, the file will be empty again.

✔ **Contracts:** Keep the following contracts as long as they are in force:

- Legal Agreements

- Employment Contracts

✔ **Credit Cards:**

- Current Monthly Statements: Keep until you receive the next statement.

- Historic Monthly Statements: Keep until account is reconciled, at a minimum. However, if you purchased an item that is under warranty through your credit-card company, or it may be a tax-deductible expense, keep the record indefinitely. If in doubt, keep.

- Credit Report: Obtain a copy of your credit report for both you and your spouse at least annually. Retain the report until the new report is received and compared with the prior report.

- Debt Management Action Plan: This is the score card that you use to keep track of your debt repayment progress (see Chapter 5).

✔ **Education:**

- Enrollment Records

- Diplomas, Certificates

- Grade Cards or Transcripts

- Progress Reports

✔ **Employment:**

- Employee Handbook (current)

- Employee Benefits Handbook (current)

- Paycheck Stub (most current only, if cumulative)

- Employee Evaluations (all)

- Resume (current)

- Continuing Education Units (CEU) (all required documentation of CEU requirements, if applicable)

✔ **Healthcare (for informational purposes only):**

- Medical Records

- Vaccination Information

- Receipts

✔ **Home Repairs and Maintenance:** Retain records for any home services or repairs — plumbing, electric, lawn maintenance, carpentry, and so on — as well as any receipts for equipment you may have purchased for as long as you own the item.

✔ **Insurance:** Retain copies of personally owned insurance policies, such as auto, home, boat, life, disability, long-term care, or any other type of insurance you may have.

✔ **Investments:**

- Bank Investment Account Statements

- Brokerage Accounts: Although you aren't required by law to keep your account application, I suggest that you go ahead and put it in this file. I recently testified in a lawsuit where the new account application was used as evidence to help win the case for the victim. Hopefully, you'll never need it. You should also keep any notes or correspondence from the broker (for as long as you own the asset) and prospectuses (the one issued when the investment was originally made and the most current for each investment position held), as well as annual reports (keep most current for each investment position held) and monthly or annual, if cumulative, account statements (retain indefinitely). Also file any transaction confirmations for at least three years after the investment is sold.

- Mutual Fund Statements: The documents you need to file include the following: account applications (no requirement to keep); notes or correspondence from your advisor; prospectus (initial and most current); annual report (most recent only); monthly account statement (if cumulative, retain current monthly statement as well as each year-end cumulative statement); and transaction confirmations (for at least three years after you sell the investment).

- Retirement Plans: Be sure to retain your summary plan description, investment options, current account statement (no need to keep it, though, when the next one comes), and annual account summary statement (leave it in the file indefinitely).

- IRAs: You need to save your current account statement, any annual account summary statements (retain indefinitely), and any records of contributions, both from traditional (deductible and nondeductible) and Roth accounts.

- Other Investments: This category includes rental property, limited partnerships, dividend reinvestment plans, and investment club accounts.

✔ **Loans:** You need to keep all documents for each loan — whether a mortgage, home equity line of credit, or a signature, auto, or school loan — for as long as the loan is outstanding. This documentation includes proof of payment, as well as amortization schedules.

✔ **Read:** Use this folder as a parking place for important financial reading material that you'll get to at a more convenient time, such as an investment account newsletter that came in the mail. (Retain until completed, dropped, or moved to a more appropriate file.)

✔ **Tax Records:** Be sure to hang on to all receipts, 1099s, paycheck stubs, charitable contributions, and other items pertaining to the current year. In most cases, you need to keep tax returns and supporting records only for three years; however, I keep them indefinitely.

✔ **To Do (Pending Projects):** This category includes to-do items, such as an estimate for work you may have done on your home, or an investment prospectus that you haven't read yet. (Retain until completed or dropped.)

✔ **Utilities:** Retain current monthly statements for the following: water, gas, electric, phone (both landline and mobile), as well as cable or satellite TV.

✔ **Warranties:** Until the item is no longer under warranty, keep any whole house warranty as well as any warranty for an appliance or electronic.

✔ **Wills, Trusts, and Estate Planning:** File all current, executed estate-planning documents, as well as a list of beneficiary designations.

Worksheet 2-2 provides you with a master record of all the most important people in your financial and daily life, including their contact information and your account numbers, if applicable. It's really helpful to keep all this information in one place. And be sure to let your spouse or partner know where to find this list in case anything happens to you.

Worksheet 2-2 List of Advisors and Important Information

Category	Name/Title	Phone Number(s)	Address	Account Numbers
Business/ Employment				
Human Resources Officer				
Financial				
Banker				
Loan Officer				
Financial Advisor				
Broker				
Brokerage Accounts				
Brokerage Accounts				
Retirement Plan				
Other Investment Accounts				
Health				
Primary Care Physician				
Nurse				
Chiropractor				
Dentist				

Category	Name/Title	Phone Number(s)	Address	Account Numbers
Health				
Eye Doctor				
Specialist				
Insurance				
Home				
Auto				
Liability				
Boat, Motorcycle, etc.				
Life				
Health				
Disability				
Long-Term Care				
Medigap				
Legal				
Generalist				
Estate Planning Specialist				
Family Law				
Personal				
Employer				
Spouse's Employer				
Social Security Numbers				

(continued)

Worksheet 2-2 (continued)

Category	Name/Title	Phone Number(s)	Address	Account Numbers
Personal				
Children's Teachers				
Babysitter				
Guardian (as stated in will)				
Pet sitter				
Taxes				
Tax Preparer				

Determining Your Net Worth (And What It Reveals about You)

Your *net worth statement* is simply a listing of all that you own and all that you owe, and the difference between the two is your *net worth*. Your net worth is like a financial report card because it reveals a lot about you. In fact, people tend to be more comfortable talking about their sex lives than their financial lives. No one can *prove* whether someone has been a fantastic lover. However, one glance at a net worth statement, and you have a pretty good idea whether a person has made a lot of financial mistakes, had terrible misfortune, has been a fantastic money manager, or is just darn lucky.

I suggest that you go ahead and figure out your net worth now (using Worksheet 2-3), and update it each and every year, shortly after year-end, because that is when you receive the previous year's year-end statements on your mortgage, retirement accounts, pension, investments, bank accounts, and a slew of tax-related documents. This is an excellent time to update your net worth statement.

Don't beat yourself up over your current financial situation. It does no good; in fact, it actually is very harmful. Consider this the beginning of your quest for financial freedom. The only things that matter are the decisions you make in the present and the future regarding your financial life. You can't change the past. However, you can learn from your successes and failures of the past. Focus on what you can gain from the exercise in Worksheet 2-3 and then use it to help stay on track going forward.

Your net worth becomes a benchmark that you can use to measure your current financial status relative to others, relative to where you want to be, and year to year. You can use Worksheet 2-4 to measure your progress year after year.

Your result from Worksheet 2-3 becomes your first entry in your net worth tracking log in Worksheet 2-4.

Worksheet 2-3   **Statement of Financial Net Worth**

Assets	Value	Liabilities	Balance
Cash Accounts Checking Savings Money Market Cash on Hand	$ _____ _____ _____ _____ _____	**Home Mortgage**	$ _____
Personal Use Assets Residence Personal Property Auto(s) Boat(s) Vacation Home Other	$ _____ _____ _____ _____ _____ _____	**Home Equity Loan/Line of Credit** **Auto Loans**	$ _____ _____
Investment Assets Brokerage Accounts Mutual Funds IRAs 401(k), 403(b) Other retirement plans	$ _____ _____ _____ _____ _____	**Investment Loans** **Margin Account** **Loans Against 401(k), 403(b)**	$ _____ _____ _____
Cash Value of Life Insurance Policies	$ _____	**Loans Against Life Insurance**	$ _____
Loans / Accounts Receivable	$ _____	**Loans / Accounts Payable**	$ _____
Deferred Compensation	$ _____	**Salary Advances**	$ _____
Total Assets	$	**Total Liabilities**	$
		Total Assets Minus Total Liabilities = Net Worth	$

Worksheet 2-4   **Financial Net Worth Tracking Log**

Date	Total Assets	+	Total Liabilities	=	Ending Net Worth
_____	$ _____		$ _____		$ _____
_____	$ _____		$ _____		$ _____
_____	$ _____		$ _____		$ _____
_____	$ _____		$ _____		$ _____
_____	$ _____		$ _____		$ _____
_____	$ _____		$ _____		$ _____

You're probably wondering how to interpret all those numbers from Worksheets 2-3 and 2-4. Well, here are a few general guidelines to keep in mind as you think about your net worth statements:

✔ Remember that Personal Use Assets aren't working assets like Investment Assets. However, they still add to your net worth, which can be very misleading. Investment Assets are much more valuable then Personal Use Assets. Investment Assets tend to appreciate over time, unlike Personal Use Assets, which tend to depreciate, or at best keep pace with inflation, after you account for the expense of ownership and maintenance.

✔ Make sure to maintain a Cash Reserve balance of three to six months required living expenses (see Chapter 3).

✔ Total housing expenses, including mortgage debt, shouldn't exceed more than 28 percent of total income.

✔ Total debt, including your mortgage, shouldn't exceed more than 36 percent of total income.

✔ Minimize your use of all debt, with the possible exceptions of home mortgage, business, investments, and school loans. Used wisely, this type of debt can leverage your ability to acquire a home, start or expand a business, or advance your education — and thereby enhance your ability to earn more money. (Refer to Chapter 5 for more information.)

Keeping an Eye on Your Credit

Establishing and maintaining good credit takes time, but it is definitely worth the effort you put into it. Your credit is used to determine the interest rate you will pay on a home mortgage, a car loan, your auto insurance premiums, and possibly even affects employment. Having a credit score of 750 or above can save you tens of thousands of dollars in interest costs versus someone with a credit score of 650.

You can find a plethora of services available today touting that they will monitor your credit report and score for you. Many also provide some degree of identity theft protection. However, monitoring your credit doesn't eliminate the risk of identity theft; it merely helps you learn about any fraudulent activity as soon as possible.

But be careful; many of these services cost $40 to $200 per year and often aren't as valuable as they first appear.

Consider the following questions when comparing credit-monitoring services:

- ✔ **Is the service checking with just one or all three of the major credit bureaus?** The three major credit bureaus are Experian, TransUnion, and Equifax. You want the service to check all three.

- ✔ **How often is the information updated?** The more frequent, the more valuable.

- ✔ **How and how often will you be notified if something raises a "red flag"?** You should only use services that alert you of key changes to your file within 24 hours.

- ✔ **What is the cost of the service?** Typically, you should expect to pay $40 a year for one bureau monitoring service to $200 a year for ongoing monitoring of all three credit bureaus.

- ✔ **Does the service provide identity theft insurance?** If so, how does it work, and how much does it cover? Be sure to ask potential services their policy on identity theft. (For more on this insurance, see Chapter 5.)

You can monitor your credit reports yourself and save a lot of money. You should request a copy from each credit bureau at least once per year. I suggest that you initially get a copy of your report and have your spouse or partner also request their reports immediately by calling (877) FACTACT or going online to www.AnnualCredit Report.com.

On an ongoing basis, I recommend requesting a copy of your credit report directly from Experian and then, about four months later, request your credit report from TransUnion. Four months later, request your credit report from Equifax.

The contact information for the three major credit bureaus is as follows:

- ✔ **Equifax:** P.O. Box 740241, Atlanta, GA 30374; phone 800-685-1111; Web site www.equifax.com.

- ✔ **Experian:** P.O. Box 2002, Allen, TX 75013; phone 888-322-5583; Web site www.experian.com.

- ✔ **TransUnion:** P.O. Box 1000, Chester, PA 19022; phone 800-888-4213; Web site www.transunion.com.

Although the information you find on each of these credit reports may differ quite a bit, most information is duplicated. (For additional information on credit and debt, refer to Chapter 5.)

If your credit score is below 750, here are the key factors to improving your credit:

- ✔ **Make sure that the information on your credit report is accurate.** Are there accounts that don't belong to you? Do balances appear even when an account has been paid in full? If you find that information isn't accurate, check out the section "Disputing Inaccuracies on Your Credit Report," later in this chapter.

- **Pay your bills on time — every time.** Send credit-card payments several days in advance of the billing cycle cutoff date instead of the due date listed on your statement.

- **Keep your outstanding balances at 30 percent or less of your total credit line per account.** This approach is just one of the many ways that help raise your credit score.

- **Avoid opening new accounts.** Transferring existing balances to a new lower rate card lowers your interest expense (often only temporarily), but it also lowers your credit score.

- **Keep the old accounts open, even if you don't use them.** But watch out that no one else is using them, either. The length of time you have maintained your accounts is key.

Not only is it important for you to monitor your credit report, you need to monitor your credit score. You can use Worksheet 2-5 to keep track of your credit score over time.

Worksheet 2-5   **Credit Score Monitoring Worksheet**

Example:

Date	Source	Score
4/15/07	www.myFico.com	738

Your turn:

Date	Source	Score
_____	_____	_____
_____	_____	_____
_____	_____	_____
_____	_____	_____
_____	_____	_____
_____	_____	_____

Use Worksheet 2-6 to plot your credit score over time. Remember, the higher the number, the better!

Worksheet 2-6   **Credit Score Monitoring Graph**

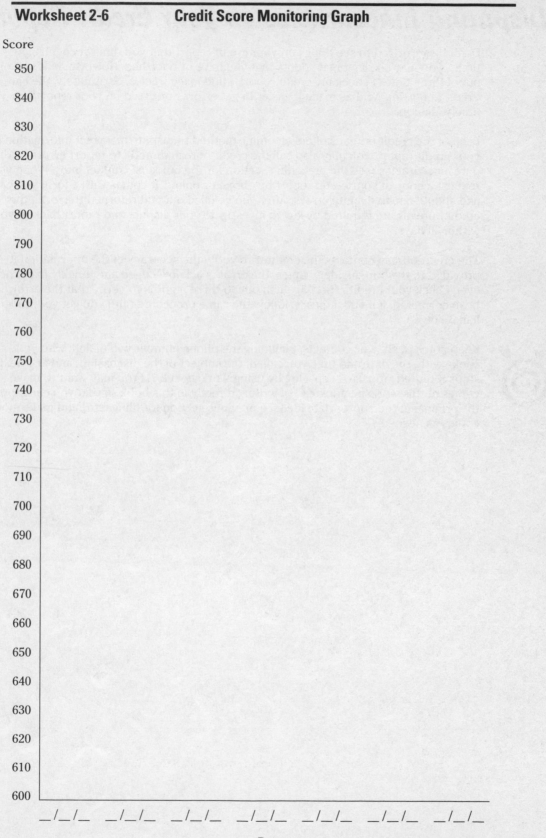

Date

Disputing Inaccuracies on Your Credit Report

Don't be surprised to see things on your credit report that you don't recognize. At times, you may see legitimate debts that you have or once had. However, in about one out of three times I check my credit report, I find inaccuracies. Fortunately, the Fair Credit Reporting Act has made it easier to get errors corrected on your report in a timely fashion.

Each of the credit bureaus offers an online method to dispute incorrect information on your credit report. You may also call the credit bureau directly to report errors or dispute inaccuracies (see the preceding section for the bureaus' contact info). When you request a copy of your credit report by phone or online, it comes with a form you can and should use to dispute errors. After you've filled out and returned the form, the credit bureaus are required by law to investigate your dispute and report back to you within 30 days.

The credit bureau contacts the creditor to verify the accuracy of the information it provided to the bureau. Many times, the error is acknowledged and quickly fixed; however, check your credit report again in one to three months to verify that the error has been corrected. If it still appears, follow the same procedure until you get your problem resolved.

Keep notes of all your contacts, including the phone number you dialed, who you spoke with, the date and time you called, the subject of the discussion, and any next steps required. You can keep a log by using Worksheet 2-7. (You may want to make copies of this worksheet instead of writing directly in this book so that you can store the original in the appropriate file [see previous section for filing info] and make more copies as needed.)

Worksheet 2-7   **Credit Report Dispute Resolution Log**

Concerning _____

Date	Time	Contact Name	Contact Number
__ / __ / __	_____	_____	_____

Notes

_____
_____
_____
_____
_____
_____
_____

Date	Time	Contact Name	Contact Number
__ / __ / __	_____	_____	_____

Notes

_____
_____
_____
_____
_____
_____
_____

Date	Time	Contact Name	Contact Number
__ / __ / __	_____	_____	_____

Notes

_____
_____
_____
_____
_____
_____
_____

Date	Time	Contact Name	Contact Number
__ / __ / __	_____	_____	_____

Notes

_____
_____
_____
_____
_____
_____
_____

Chapter 3

Analyzing Your Cash Flow

*B*udgeting is about as enjoyable as dieting, and neither works for most people. Budgets and diets are all about deprivation, which isn't a motivating concept. People may become motivated to stick to their diet to improve their health or appearance. But few people are motivated to follow a budget, mainly because it's not directly tied to an immediate positive outcome.

In this chapter, you discover a more logical, simplistic, yet powerful way to think about your income and expenses than you may have ever heard of before — all without a traditional budget. After you have the clarity and empowerment to direct your resources to most effectively accomplish your goals, you will have the motivation to stick to your cash flow spending plan (in other words, your budget).

Calculating Your Spendable Income

So you make $20,000, $40,000, or even $120,000 per year. However, don't be lured in to the common misunderstanding that you have $20,000, $40,000, or $120,000 per year to spend any way that you want. After you pay income, Social Security, and Medicare taxes on your gross earnings, you're likely down a third or more. Then you need to account for the costs related to earning these wages, such as commuting, dry cleaning, meals out, and child care — just to name a few. You may also take a vacation periodically or treat yourself to regular massage therapy to "decompress" from the stresses of your job.

What you have left after you take out all your must-pays — think taxes — is your *net income*. I like to call the amount that remains after you deduct your job-related expenses your *net, net income* or *spendable income*. To figure out your net income, gather together two to four (if paid weekly) copies of recent paycheck stubs and complete Worksheet 3-2 with the information taken directly from your paycheck stubs.

Some deductions occur monthly rather than per pay period, so two to four consecutive paychecks should reveal all deductions. For example, if you receive two paychecks per month and your medical insurance deduction only occurs with the first paycheck of each month, divide this amount by two when completing the worksheet.

In Worksheet 3-1, I also provide you with an example, which illustrates that an individual who earns $52,000 per year ($26 per hour) may actually have less than $7 per hour remaining to spend on the daily necessities of life. This remainder is the number you need to focus on.

Another important conclusion illustrated in this exercise is the fact that only $1,138 per month ($13,666 divided by 12) is available to cover all the expenditures not shown elsewhere on Worksheet 3-1. This $1,138 per month is all that remains after the wage earner has paid income and Social Security taxes, taken into account automatic deductions from his paycheck, and adjusted for job-related costs. Refer to Worksheet 3-3 for a listing of the potential required monthly expenses that must be covered with this net income.

Fortunately, in this example, the individual is also investing 10 percent of his gross income into his retirement plan. He is also saving taxes by taking advantage of his Flexible Spending Account and depositing the maximum allowable amount for child care. Because of this, he also pays less in income taxes than the ordinary person would.

Next time you consider making a purchase and you tell yourself, "Ah, it's only 20 bucks," calculate how long it will take to net $20 — for the person in this example, it takes nearly three hours of work. Stop and ask yourself whether the purchase is worth three hours of your work life and energy.

EXAMPLE

Worksheet 3-1   Calculating Your Spendable Income

1. Gross Income per pay period *$2,000*

   Minus:

   Taxes

Federal	*$225*
State	*$120*
Local/City	*$20*
Social Security (FICA)	*$128*
Medicare	*$25*

2. Total taxes withheld *$518*

   Automatic Payroll Deductions

Medical Insurance	*$54*
Life Insurance	*$6*
Disability Insurance	*$18*
Dental Insurance	*$16*
Charitable Contributions	*$10*
Retirement Plan 401(k), 403(b), and so on	*$200*
Retirement Plan Loan Repayment	*$*
Deferred Compensation Plan	*$*
Employee Stock Purchase Plan	*$*
Flexible Spending Acct FSA (Section 125)	*$192*
U.S. Savings Bonds	*$*
Other Automatic Drafts for Investments	*$*
Other Automatic Drafts for Expenses	*$*

3. Total payroll deductions (excluding taxes) *$496*

4. Net income per pay period (Line 1 – [Line 2 + Line 3]) ... *$986*

5. How many times are you paid per year? *26*

   a. Weekly = 52

   b. Every other week = 26

   c. Twice a month = 24

   d. Monthly = 12

6. Multiply Line 4 times Line 5 for annual net income *$25,636*

7. List traditional job-related expenses (annual)

    Expense

    Commuting costs   _$2,750_

    (Daily round trip 20 miles × $0.40 mile × number
    of workdays per year [approximately 250], plus
    parking at $3/day)

    Clothing and clothing maintenance   _$1,400_

    (Suits/uniforms, dry cleaning, shoes, accessories)

    Child care (included in FSA in Step 2)   _$_

    Unreimbursed business expenses   _$300_

    (Association dues, union dues, subscriptions, licenses,
    and so on)

8. List nontraditional job-related expenses (annual)

You may incur these expenses due to the stress of your job, long hours, or
working conditions. Examples include dining out frequently because you're
working long hours, going out for lunch instead of preparing them at home,
treating yourself to much-needed massage therapy or vacations to help
decompress from the stresses of your job, and so on.

    Expense

    Dinner out twice a week versus meals at home   _$2,000_

    (Family of 4, dining out costing approximately $20 per
    meal more than preparing at home × 100 meals per year)

    Lunch out versus preparing lunches at home   _$1,000_

    (Assuming lunches for worker only, not entire family,
    at an additional $4 per day)

    Purchasing coffee or soda at work   _$500_

    (Assuming two drinks per day at $1 more than bringing
    from home or drinking water)

    Monthly massage-therapy sessions   _$720_

    Lawn mowing service versus do-it-yourself   _$1,300_

    All-inclusive family vacation versus less expensive
    alternatives (half of actual additional cost, partner   _$2,000_
    covers other half)

9. Total annual expenses on Lines 7 and 8   _$11,970_

10. Subtract Line 9 from Line 6 for annual spendable income

11. Divide Line 10 by number of hours worked per year
    (traditional full-time work equals 2,000 hours)

    Equals your net hourly spendable income   _$6.83_
                                                                                 per hour

Worksheet 3-2   Calculating Your Spendable Income

1. Gross Income per pay period $ _____

    Minus:

    Taxes

             Federal $ _____

             State $ _____

             Local/City $ _____

             Social Security (FICA) $ _____

             Medicare $ _____

2. Total taxes withheld $ _____

    Automatic Payroll Deductions

             Medical Insurance $ _____

             Life Insurance $ _____

             Disability Insurance $ _____

             Dental Insurance $ _____

             Charitable Contributions $ _____

             Retirement Plan 401(k), 403(b), and so on $ _____

             Retirement Plan Loan Repayment $ _____

             Deferred Compensation Plan $ _____

             Employee Stock Purchase Plan $ _____

             Flexible Spending Acct FSA (Section 125) $ _____

             U.S. Savings Bonds $ _____

             Other Automatic Drafts for Investments $ _____

             Other Automatic Drafts for Expenses $ _____

3. Total payroll deductions (excluding taxes) $ _____

4. Net income per pay period (Line 1 – [Line 2 + Line 3]) $ _____

5. How many times are you paid per year?   _____

             a. Weekly = 52

             b. Every other week = 26

             c. Twice a month = 24

             d. Monthly = 12

6. Multiply Line 4 times Line 5 for annual net income $ _____

7. List traditional job-related expenses (annual)

Expense	Annual Cost
Commuting costs	$ _____
Clothing and clothing maintenance	$ _____
Child care	$ _____
Unreimbursed business expenses	$ _____

8. List nontraditional job-related expenses (annual)

    You may incur these expenses due to the stress of your job, long hours, or working conditions. Examples include dining out frequently because you're working long hours, going out for lunch instead of preparing them at home, treating yourself to much-needed massage therapy or vacations to help decompress from the stresses of your job, and so on.

Expense	Annual Cost
_____	$ _____
_____	$ _____
_____	$ _____
_____	$ _____
_____	$ _____
_____	$ _____
_____	$ _____
_____	$ _____
_____	$ _____
_____	$ _____
_____	$ _____

9. Total annual expenses on Lines 7 and 8 $ _____

10. Subtract Line 9 from Line 6 for annual spendable income $ _____

11. Divide Line 10 by number of hours worked per year (traditional full-time work equals 2,000 hours)

    Equals your net hourly spendable income $ _____

Figuring Out Where to Spend Your Money

After you determine your actual spendable income (see preceding section), you can focus on how that remaining money needs to be spent. I like to segregate expenses into three categories: needs, wants, and luxury items. But how do you distinguish between the three?

Imagine that you're a participant in the reality TV show *Survivor.* To survive in the game, what must you have? Fire for warmth, purified water, and cooked food; water and something to boil it in; and food and shelter — albeit crude. These items you must have for basic survival are *needs!*

On the other hand, what would you *like* to have if you were on *Survivor* — things that aren't required to survive, but that would definitely make life more comfortable? Possibly, you may wish you had a machete, a flint, a tarp, and fishing equipment. These items aren't required to survive, but they sure make survival more comfortable — a perfect example of *wants!*

The reward challenge winners on *Survivor* receive luxury items, such as a hammock, blankets, steak dinners, sodas, or a cruise to a posh resort with hot showers, massage, and a five-course meal. These items that go beyond basic needs or even wants — those cushy extras — are *luxuries!*

Now, taking a lesson from this reality TV show — what do you really *need* to spend your money on in life? And what do you do if you have some extra money each month after your needs are met? This section answers your questions and helps you figure out what you need and what you want. And because you will likely use up all your resources before you get through all your wants, just put the luxury category out of mind for now.

Adding up your required expenses

Your required expenses, or *needs,* must come first. To figure out what your required expenses (needs) are, you can begin to fill out Worksheet 3-3 by entering the total amount you're personally responsible for, or the total for the household, whichever is easier. (Sorry, no enhanced phone services, cell phones, cable TV, or high-speed Internet, unless required for employment, are included in needs.)

Worksheet 3-3   Required Monthly Expenses (Needs)

Shelter:

    Home Mortgage or rent $_____

    Utilities:

        Electric $_____

        Gas $_____

        Water, sewer, and trash pickup $_____

        Basic phone service $_____

Protection: Include the things you can't afford to be without.

    Life insurance $_____

    Disability insurance $_____

    Homeowners or renters insurance $_____

    Health insurance $_____

    Auto insurance $_____

    Healthcare/medical and dental care $_____

    Prescription drugs $_____

    Child care $_____

    Rainy-day fund (minimum of 10 percent of gross income) $_____

Food: This category doesn't include dining out.

    Groceries (basic essentials only) $_____

Clothing and clothing maintenance: Presuming that you have
some clothes now, ask yourself what else you really need. $_____

Basic Hygiene:

    Personal: Toothbrush, deodorant, soap (for example) $_____

    Household: Laundry detergent, toilet paper, and so on $_____

Transportation:

    Automobile loan or lease payments $_____

    Auto maintenance $_____

    Gasoline $_____

    Other: Tolls, parking, public transportation $_____

Legal Requirements:

Real estate and property taxes $_____

Child support $_____

Alimony $_____

Required debt payments not listed elsewhere

    School loans $_____

    Personal loans $_____

    Credit cards $_____

    Other debt $_____

Total required monthly expenses (Needs) $_____

After-tax income (from Worksheet 3-2, Line 1 – Line 2) $_____

Note: If you included all expenses for the household, add
the after-tax income of both spouses/partners together.

(After-Tax Income minus Total Needs) **Surplus or Shortfall** $_____

So where do you go after figuring out what you're spending on needs? If you have a
surplus after meeting your required living expenses, go ahead and check out the section on using your excess money for wants. However, if your income comes up short
(negative or close) after figuring out your needs, go ahead and skip to the section
"Solving for Shortfalls," later in this chapter.

If you aren't already doing so, I strongly encourage you to set up automatic monthly
withdrawals from your paycheck or your checking account to automatically pay for or
fund each of the required expenditures from Worksheet 3-3. That way, your requirements are met automatically each and every month, and whatever is left over is yours
to spend however you see fit.

Wading through your wants

Hopefully, you find yourself with some "extra" money after determining and paying for
your needs (see preceding section), and you can begin to use some of that money for
the items or services you want. You can use Worksheet 3-4 to figure out your wants
and how much you'd like to be spending on them.

When determining what to do with your surplus, just remember that magic number
(the amount of surplus from Worksheet 3-3) and don't exceed that amount when
addressing your wants.

Worksheet 3-4   Desired Monthly Expenditures (Wants)

Shelter:

Home renovations or remodeling $_____

Home furnishings $_____

Utilities

　　Cell phone(s) $_____

　　Long-distance phone charges $_____

　　Cable or satellite TV $_____

　　High-speed Internet $_____

Additional Savings:

Children's college $_____

Retirement $_____

Vehicle replacement fund $_____

Other financial goals $_____

Food:

Groceries (beyond basic essentials) $_____

Dining out $_____

Meals purchased at school or work $_____

Snacks and drinks purchased at school or work $_____

Clothing and clothing maintenance: (beyond basic essentials) $_____

Personal:

Haircuts, color, perms, manicures, massage $_____

Gifts: Birthday, anniversary, wedding, holiday $_____

Charitable donations $_____

Entertainment:

Health club or other club membership(s) $_____

Vacations $_____

Summer camp, sports, lessons, hobbies $_____

Books and magazine and newspaper subscriptions $_____

Parties: Holiday, birthday, social $_____

Household:

Home maintenance: Lawn care, exterminators, painters $_____

Domestic help: House cleaning, babysitters, pet sitters $_____

Transportation: (beyond basic essentials included in Needs)

Automobile loan or lease payments $_____

Vehicles and related expenses for children $_____

Auto maintenance $_____

Gasoline $_____

Other: Tolls, parking, public transportation $_____

Total desired additional monthly expenses (Wants) $_____

After-tax income (from Worksheet 3-2, Line 1 – Line 2) $_____

(After-Tax Income – [Total Needs + Total Wants])
Surplus or Shortfall $_____

After you add all your needs from Worksheet 3-3 together with the list of wants from Worksheet 3-4, you will likely discover that you have little or no surplus cash flow. If you determine that you have negative cash flow, you should revisit Worksheet 3-4 and prioritize your expenditures so that you don't plan to spend more than you bring in.

Solving for Shortfalls

If you have a shortfall after you calculate your required expenses (see Worksheet 3-3), something has got to give. Worksheet 3-3 should include only those items that are truly required. Yes, you really do have to pay taxes and your mortgage or rent and buy groceries, but you may need to re-evaluate the amount of money you're paying for these needs. Consider the following suggestions when you're faced with a shortfall:

- ✔ **Don't completely cut out any of your required expenditures.** You may be tempted to consider dropping insurance coverages and/or saving the amount of money you need to be saving for a "rainy day" if you don't have surplus cash flow or don't have as much as you might like. You aren't doing yourself any favors by skipping these items, and the decision will come back to haunt you sooner or later. Get used to thinking of these items as required expenditures; they really are necessities. Maybe not this month or even this year, but eventually you will be confronted head on with these expenses. Be prepared. (For more on insurance, see Part V.)

- ✔ **Review each of the needs categories and consider ways to cut down on necessary expenses.** For example, you may be able to obtain less expensive insurance and save money on groceries, clothing, and transportation by shopping around.

- ✔ **Consider your employment.** Often times, the only reasonable option you, your spouse, or partner may have is to increase your income by working overtime (if that is an option), taking on a part-time job, or possibly even changing jobs.

Tracking Expenses: Figuring Out Where Your Cash Is Going

Tracking your expenses is especially useful when your outgoing cash flow exceeds your income. Fortunately, you don't need to go back and tally up months' worth of checking account registers, credit- and debit-card statements, and cash withdrawals. I find that this is a very time-consuming and painful exercise. Just estimate!

Consider using Worksheet 3-5 to help you monitor your spending for the next couple of months. As you pay your bills, complete the worksheet.

Worksheet 3-5   **Tracking Expenses**

Cash Flow Monitoring

Item	Month 1	Month 2

Housing
- House payment
- Rent payment
- Lease payment (not mortgage)
- Property improvements
- Home association dues
- Household incidentals (supplies)
- Household furnishings
- Other: _____
- Other: _____
                                    Subtotal: _____

Food
- Groceries
- Dining out
- @ Work
- @ School
- Other: _____
- Other: _____
                                    Subtotal: _____

Clothing
- Clothing
- Dry cleaning
- Other: _____
- Other: _____
                                    Subtotal: _____

Personal Care
- (Hair styling and so on)
- Other: _____
                                    Subtotal: _____

Automobile
- Monthly payment
- Operating expenses (gas, oil, and so on)
- Maintenance
- Lease payment
- Other:
  _____   Subtotal: _____

Property Tax
- Automobile
- House
- Boat
- Trailer
- Other:
  _____   Subtotal: _____

Cash Flow Monitoring

Item	Month 1	Month 2
Utilities		
Telephone	_____	_____
Cellular phone	_____	_____
Water	_____	_____
Electric	_____	_____
Gas	_____	_____
Trash removal	_____	_____
Cable	_____	_____
Internet	_____	_____
Other: _____	_____	_____
Other: _____	_____	_____
Subtotal:	_____	_____
Entertainment		
Books, newspapers, magazines	_____	_____
Parties (attending or hosting)	_____	_____
Movies (theatre, video, plays, and so on)	_____	_____
Club dues (golf, music, and so on)	_____	_____
Other: _____	_____	_____
Other: _____	_____	_____
Subtotal:	_____	_____
Unreimbursed Business Expenses		
Travel	_____	_____
Vehicle rental	_____	_____
Parking	_____	_____
Lodging	_____	_____
Meals	_____	_____
Entertainment	_____	_____
Other: _____	_____	_____
Other: _____	_____	_____
Subtotal:	_____	_____
Alimony (paid)	_____	_____
Subtotal:	_____	_____
Child Support (paid)	_____	_____
Subtotal:	_____	_____
Childrenís Expenses		
Lessons, sports, camp, and so on	_____	_____
Daycare	_____	_____
Domestic help (babysitter)	_____	_____
Other: _____	_____	_____
Subtotal:	_____	_____
Gifts		
Birthdays	_____	_____
Christmas/other holiday	_____	_____
Anniversaries	_____	_____
Other: _____	_____	_____
Other: _____	_____	_____
Subtotal:	_____	_____

Cash Flow Monitoring

Item	Month 1	Month 2

Charitable Contributions
(Churches, schools, and so on)
Other: _____
Other: _____
Subtotal:

Medical Expenses
Doctor visit copay
Prescription copay
Dental care
Vision care
Other: _____
Subtotal:

Insurance
Health
Automobile
Homeowners
Renters
Life
Disability
Long-term care
Umbrella liability
Professional liability
Other: _____
Other: _____
Subtotal:

Credit Cards
Credit card #1: _____
Credit card #2: _____
Credit card #3: _____
Credit card #4: _____
Credit card #5: _____
Credit card #6: _____
Other: _____
Other: _____
Subtotal:

Other Liabilities
Student loans: _____
Personal loans: _____
Business loans: _____
Other debts: _____
Other debts: _____
Subtotal:

TOTAL _____   _____

If you're looking for a simpler method of tracking your expenses, you can use Worksheet 3-6 to track every cent of your surplus money that you have to spend. Begin with the total surplus shown at the bottom of worksheet 3-4.

Write down every occasion you spend your surplus money, whether you purchase a soda at work, buy gasoline on the way home, or go to the movies. Account for every cent. Also, track whether you paid by cash, check, or debit or credit card; who you paid; and whether the expenditure falls into the need or want category.

Use one log for each pay period. Note at the top of the worksheet how much your beginning surplus is (if you complete Worksheet 3-4, you can find this amount at the bottom of that worksheet) and subtract from that amount each expenditure.

Worksheet 3-6 **Expense Tracking Log**

EXPENSE TRACKING LOG

Beginning surplus $_____ Must cover all expenditures until __/__/__

Date	Amount	Method	To Whom	Need or Want	Notes

By keeping your eye on the "magic number" (your surplus cash flow after meeting your required expenses), you can simply spend your money any way that pleases you — so long as you don't exceed the "magic number." No more detailed budget keeping required.

Chapter 4

Changing Your Dreams into Goals

• •

• •

Sometime throughout your life, you may have had someone encourage you to "dream big" or "reach for the stars." But have you ever taken the time to really examine what your dreams are and how you can actually turn your aspirations into goals? Well, now is your chance to do more than just daydream about that island vacation or your child's college fund. The time has come to turn your dreams into realities.

It has been said that a goal is just a dream with a deadline. This chapter is designed to help you convert the dreams that matter most to you into measurable goals. After you can measure it, you can manage it, and you will achieve it.

In this chapter, I don't differentiate between personal goals and financial goals, because they're interrelated. Some of your dreams and goals may not cost any money. However, if they don't, they at least take time and energy. Your time and energy are likely the most valuable resources you have, and they can produce money; however, money can't easily produce time and energy.

Financial planning involves channeling your resources — all of them — to best accomplish *what matters most* in your life. You not only need to consider your financial assets and liabilities, but your personal assets and liabilities, dreams, goals, and fears as well. Financial instruments (investments, insurance, retirement plans, savings strategies, and so on) are just tools that you'll utilize along your financial journey through life, and you'll get to them later in this book. However, first things first: What matters most in your life?

Delving into Your Dreams

No matter what you want to call it — brainstorming or brain dumping — it is time to dream big without holding back and to get those dreams written in stone. (Well, I guess paper will have to do for now.) Think of all the things you want to do and see or who you want to become. Then, using Worksheet 4-2, list the dreams that are most important to you at this time. You can use Worksheet 4-1 as an example if you need help getting started or if you get stuck in the middle.

The following instructions walk you through how to use Worksheet 4-2:

1. **In the What column of Worksheet 4-2, quickly list the first 30 goals that come to mind when responding to the question, "What 30 things would you most like to see, do, accomplish, and experience in your life?"**

   Dig really deep and list 30 goals — no more, no less. The first five or ten may come to you easily. However, if you get stuck, consider all the possibilities, including:

   • What do you want to do? (activities, hobbies, routines, interests)

   • What or who do you want to see? (travel, cultural events, family, friends)

   • Who do you want to be? (personal development, career, volunteerism, community involvement, philanthropy)

   • What experiences do you want to have? (vacation with spouse, continue your education, make a charitable donation to your favorite cause, provide a legacy for your children)

2. **Review your list of goals and rank each by their priority. Indicate in the left column how important achieving each item is to you by selecting from the following Priority list:**

   A = Must achieve (no choice)

   B = Would love to achieve (but will live if you don't)

   C = Would really be nice to achieve, but not at the cost of A or B goals

3. **Indicate in the When column approximately when you want to, or when you must, achieve each of your stated goals.**

   Be as specific as possible. If an actual date or deadline is involved, use that date. If you have no deadline, provide yourself with as much guidance as possible.

4. **In the What's Required column, try to list the resources you need in order to accomplish the stated goal.**

   Do you need time, energy, labor, money, or help? Be as specific as possible. Say, for example, that you want to remodel your kitchen this year. You may need to do some research and gather specific details regarding what exactly will be involved in your remodeling project.

   • How much of the work can you complete yourself compared to how much of the work licensed professionals must perform?

   • Do you have friends or family members who are willing, able, and available to assist you?

   • How much time and energy do you anticipate needing to invest personally?

   • How much will purchasing the materials and supplies cost?

   • How much will the licensed professionals cost?

   • Will you need to finance any or all of these costs?

   • What are your financing options?

5. **In the What Are You Willing to Do column, write what you are willing to do to achieve this goal.**

   The achievement of goals often involves much more than just money. Some goals may be so important to you that you are willing to forego or postpone many of your other dreams to ensure that your most important goals are achieved. You must make the call.

   To help you determine how you plan to allocate your time, energy, and money to accomplish your goals, ask yourself the following questions:

   - What are you willing to sacrifice to achieve specific goals?

   - Is achieving a certain goal so important to you that you are willing and able to earn more money if that is what is needed?

   - Is the desired timeframe for achieving this goal something that you can adjust?

   - Are you willing and able to sell something to raise the money needed to achieve the goal?

   - Are you willing and able to do more of the work yourself to reduce your out-of-pocket costs?

   - Are you willing and able to dedicate the time and energy necessary to achieve this goal?

   - Do your spouse/partner and family support your efforts for the goals in which they are involved?

6. **For now, leave the Revised Priority ranking field blank; you can fill it in after going through the exercises in the section "Determining Your Most Important Goals," later in this chapter.**

Worksheet 4-1   Exploring Your Dreams (Example)

DATE COMPLETED _____   DATE REVISED _____

	Priority	What?	When?	What is Required?	What Are You Willing to Do?	Revised Priority
	A= Must do B= Love to C= Nice to	Just brainstorm... The order doesn't matter at this point	Be as specific as possible	From you, others, money?	What are you willing to do to achieve this?	After going through the following exercise, revisit your prioritizations
1	B	Learn conversational Chinese	12 Months	Time, commitment, money for tutor	1) Spend 10 minutes in the mornings and evenings practicing 2) Pay tutor $120/mon for lessons	
2	A	Remodel main bathroom	Within 2 years	Approximately $4,000 for supplies, We'll do the labor.	1) By skipping our annual vacation, we will have the time and money to accomplish this goal	
3	B	Travel to every destination in the national park system	By age 60	Our family vacations need to focus on achieving this goal	1) Spend each family vacation visiting at least 2 destinations 2) Purchase or borrow a camper	
4	A	Finish remodeling kitchen	In 5 months	$6,000	1) Spend bonus on kitchen	
5						
6						
7						
8						
9						
10						
11						
12						
13						

DATE COMPLETED _____   DATE REVISED _____

Priority	What?	When?	What's Required?	What Are You Willing to Do?	Revised Priority
A= Must do B= Love to C= Nice to	Just brainstorm... The order doesn't matter at this point	Be as specific as possible	From you, others, money?	What are you willing to do to achieve this?	After going through the following exercise, revisit your prioritizations

#						
14						
15						
16						
17						
18						
19						
20						
21						
22						
23						
24						
25						
26						
27						

Worksheet 4-2   **Exploring Your Dreams**

DATE COMPLETED _____   DATE REVISED _____

Priority	What?	When?	What's Required?	What Are You Willing to Do?	Revised Priority
A= Must do B= Love to C= Nice to	Just brainstorm... The order doesn't matter at this point	Be as specific as possible	From you, others, money?	What are you willing to do to achieve this?	After going through the following exercise, revisit your prioritizations
1					
2					
3					
4					
5					
6					
7					
8					
9					
10					
11					
12					
13					
14					

DATE COMPLETED _____   DATE REVISED _____

	Priority	What?	When?	What's Required?	What Are You Willing to Do?	Revised Priority
	A= Must do B= Love to C= Nice to	Just brainstorm... The order doesn't matter at this point	Be as specific as possible	From you, others, money?	What are you willing to do to achieve this?	After going through the following exercise, revisit your prioritizations
15						
16						
17						
18						
19						
20						
21						
22						
23						
24						
25						
26						
27						
28						

Have your spouse or partner complete this exercise in Worksheet 4-2, too. It's amazing just how much you can discover about yourself and your significant other when you really dig deep regarding your financial life goals. Plus, you want to make sure that you're both fully aware of each other's priorities. It's unlikely that you'll come up with most of the same goals. That's okay. You're an individual, and you may also be part of a couple. You'll have individual goals, and you'll also have goals you want to achieve with your spouse. And your goals will be different — frequently. There is nothing wrong with differences. The only thing that can go wrong is not exploring what matters most to you and sharing that with your spouse.

Determining Which Dreams Matter Most

So you may know what your dreams are, but do you know which ones are most important to you? How can you know which ones to focus on as you begin to shape your goals? (See the section "Developing an Action Plan" for more on establishing goals.) In this section, I'd like you to approach the same subject — what you want or dream of — from a markedly different perspective. Instead of a brainstorm of 30 goals that come to mind, look at your dreams as the things that matter most to you.

After reading George Kinder's book, *The Seven Stages of Money Maturity* (Dell), and participating in a workshop of the same name, I walked away with three very remarkable questions, which you can find in Worksheets 4-3 through 4-5. These questions can help you discover what truly matters most to you, so you can know which dreams to focus on and make into goals. (See the next section on this topic.)

Work through the questions in Worksheets 4-3, 4-4, and 4-5 and record your responses in the space provided. (If you haven't created your wish list, you may find it easier to do Worksheet 4-2 first.) Be sure to invest thoughtful time and energy as you ponder the questions. If you really devote yourself to this task, you may begin to develop a realization and level of clarity about your dreams that you may not have had before. You may discover that some things no longer have the importance they once had, while other ambitions have now become most important in your life.

After you finish answering the questions in Worksheets 4-3 through 4-5, go back to Worksheet 4-2 and revisit the Priority Rankings column with the three questions in mind. You may want to revise your priority ranking at this stage. Use the Revised Priority field on the right-hand side of Worksheet 4-2 to record any changes.

You can also have your spouse or partner answer these questions on his or her own, and then compare notes. What you discover may raise your level of commitment and motivation to certain dreams tremendously, and you're more likely to pursue and achieve the dreams to which you're most committed.

Worksheet 4-3 **Reframing Your Priorities Question #1**

I want you to imagine that you are financially secure, that you have enough money to take care of your needs, now and in the future. The question is . . . how would you live your life? Would you change anything? Let yourself go. Don't hold back on your dreams.

Describe a life that is complete, that is richly yours.

© George D. Kinder 1999

_____

_____

_____

_____

_____

_____

_____

_____

_____

_____

_____

Worksheet 4-4   Reframing Your Priorities Question #2

This time you visit your doctor who tells you that you have only 5 to 10 years left to live. The good part is that you won't ever feel sick. The bad news is that you will have no notice of the moment of your death. What will you do in the time you have remaining to live?

Will you change your life, and how will you do it?

© George D. Kinder 1999

_____

_____

_____

_____

_____

_____

_____

_____

_____

Worksheet 4-5   **Reframing Your Priorities Question #3**

This time your doctor shocks you with the news that you have only one day left to live. Notice what feelings arise as you confront your very real mortality. Ask yourself:

What did I miss? Who did I not get to be? What did I not get to do?

© *George D. Kinder 1999*

_____

_____

_____

_____

_____

_____

_____

_____

_____

Developing an Action Plan

After you've figured out your wish list and have prioritized what matters most (see previous sections), you can then put structure to and create an action plan for these dreams to become goals. And with that action plan, your dreams can become realities.

Each goal must be a top priority, something you have the desire and capacity to achieve, and be measurable. First, use Worksheet 4-6 to identify your primary goals based on their level of importance. Then, in Worksheet 4-8, sort them by time period and action items involved. (See Worksheet 4-7 for an example.)

Worksheet 4-6　　　　　　　　**Primary Goals**

Goal 1: What

_____

_____

_____

When

_____

_____

_____

Goal 2: What

_____

_____

_____

When

_____

_____

_____

Goal 3: What

_____

_____

_____

When

_____

_____

_____

Goal 4: What

_____

_____

_____

When

_____

_____

_____

Goal 5: What

_____

_____

_____

When

_____

_____

_____

Goal 6: What

_____

_____

_____

When

_____

_____

_____

Goal 7: What

_____

_____

_____

When

_____

_____

_____

Worksheet 4-7 **Action Plan (Example)**

Which, if any, of your goals could you meet right now?

#1
What: Getting my estate plan updated.

Why: To protect my family and make things as easy as possible upon my death.

When: As soon as possible. Okay, okay, I'll call the estate planning attorney tomorrow morning and make an appointment.

How: Hire the estate planning attorney. Provide him with my basic financial record and pay the bill.

#2
What: Pay down my home equity line of credit.

Why: I have extra money in my checking account. I could apply that money to my home equity line of credit and save myself over 5 percent per year in interest costs.

When: Now.

How: Write a check from the checking account with the excess cash reserves to my mortgage company. Mail check along with payment voucher to the mortgage company.

Which, if any, of your objectives could you achieve within the next 12 months?

#1
What: Tile the hallway.

Why: Because the current flooring is gross and outdated, and I've already purchased the tile.

When: During the second half of July. I don't really have the spare time or energy until then.

How: I'll need to rent a wet saw and buy some supplies. The total cost of these items should be under $200. I will also need to finagle assistance from one or two friends for the two-day project. I've got a couple of friends in mind. I'll need to return a similar favor to them someday.

Which, if any, of your objectives could you achieve within the next five years?

#1
What: Converting the workshop into a guest house.

Why: Have separate living quarters for long-term guests, possibly my parents in their later years, and to enhance the value of our home.

When: We don't have a looming deadline for this goal. However, we really appreciate extended visits from friends and family members. Without having a separate living area, we and our guests may grow tired of too much time together. Given these feelings and the costs involved with renovating the space, I want to begin construction within five years.

How: We can and want to do a lot of the remodeling work ourselves. However, we will need to hire professionals to plumb and wire the kitchen and bath. We want to have the option to hire a carpenter to do the rough-in of the walls and ceiling as well.

We have made a list of all the things that need to happen and obtained best guess estimates on the total cost of the project. We expect to spend up to $20,000 renovating this space, but don't currently have any money set aside for this goal. We don't want to borrow it either. Therefore, over the next 60 months, we will save $300 per month in a money market account earmarked for this goal.

Now it's your turn. Complete the following exercise addressing each of the items you listed as your Primary Goals on Worksheet 4-6. Don't worry if some of the "Hows" aren't known at this time. The remainder of this workbook will be indispensable in addressing the remaining "Hows."

Worksheet 4-8 **Action Plan**

Which, if any, of your goals could you meet right now?

#1

What:
_____

Why:
_____
_____
_____

When:
_____

How:
_____
_____
_____
_____

#2

What:
_____

Why:
_____
_____
_____

When:
_____

How:
_____
_____
_____
_____

Which, if any, of your objectives could you achieve within the next 12 months?

#1

What:
_____

Why:
_____
_____
_____

When:
_____

How:
_____
_____
_____
_____

#2

What:
_____

Why:
_____
_____
_____

When:
_____

How:
_____
_____
_____
_____

Which, if any, of your objectives could you achieve within the next 5 years?

#1

What:
_____

Why:
_____
_____
_____

When:
_____

How:
_____
_____
_____
_____

#2

What:
_____

Why:
_____
_____
_____

When:
_____

How:
_____
_____
_____
_____

What other goals would you like to achieve in the intermediate term?

#1

What:
_____

Why:
_____
_____
_____

When:
_____

How:
_____
_____
_____
_____

#2

What:
_____

Why:
_____
_____
_____

When:
_____

How:
_____
_____
_____
_____

What goals would you like to achieve in the long term?

#1

What: _____

Why: _____

_____

_____

When: _____

How: _____

_____

_____

_____

#2

What: _____

Why: _____

_____

_____

When: _____

How: _____

_____

_____

_____

#3

What:
_____

Why:
_____
_____
_____

When:
_____

How:
_____
_____
_____
_____

#4

What:
_____

Why:
_____
_____
_____

When:
_____

How:
_____
_____
_____
_____

Part II

Getting the Most
Out of Your Money

The 5th Wave   By Rich Tennant

"The funny thing is he's spent 9 hours
organizing his computer desktop."

In this part . . .

1 address the healthy use of credit and help you get the most out of your money by employing proven strategies that help you spend your money wisely. I also focus on ways to get your family involved in the money-management decisions and responsibilities. Working together families can achieve much more, with less strife, and your family members can gain skills that they won't learn anywhere else.

And when it comes to getting the most out of your money, taxes can't be ignored — no matter how much you may like to try. Understanding how to minimize your tax liabilities can help you get even more out of the money you bring in, which is why I also cover taxes in this part.

Chapter 5

Using Credit Wisely

Debt has skyrocketed over the last few years, although most incomes have remained fairly consistent. Part of this increase is due to the refinancing of home mortgages and the growth in home equity loan balances as a direct result of the housing boom, which took place in many parts of the United States over the last few years. To make matters worse, mortgage companies have been issuing home loans well in excess of healthy guidelines, and the result has been an unprecedented number of foreclosures and bankruptcy filings.

And unfortunately, *consumer debt* — credit cards, auto loans, and personal loans — has also skyrocketed. In fact, consumer debt, including credit cards and auto and personal loans, has more than doubled from 1990 to 2000, and the trend continues. Part of the reason may be because credit-card issuers are the most aggressive and predatory lenders — next to payday loan companies. Since 1990, personal credit-card debt alone has tripled. The slogan seems to be: Easy credit for everyone! Come and get it! Trade your financial freedom for instant gratification! But don't think for one minute that the credit issuers are here to do you any favors. This is their business, and they make a lot of money off you.

Knowing when and how to use credit can be tricky business. And if you find yourself deep in debt, you may feel strangled by the pressure of paying it off. In order for you to have the upper hand when it comes to your credit, you need to figure out how much debt you can really afford to have, how much debt you already have, and how to get rid of unhealthy debt for good. I provide hands-on tools for you to do just that in this chapter. (For info on figuring out your credit score, check out Chapter 2.)

Determining How Much Debt You Can Afford

No one is going to look out for your backside except you — especially when it comes to your credit. Just because a mortgage company or a credit-card issuer will give you money doesn't mean you should take it. According to your lender, you may qualify for more debt than you know you can afford in your current situation or for your long-term financial plans. And the guidelines that many companies use to determine whether you're in a good position (or financially "healthy" enough) to increase your indebtedness aren't always in your best interest.

Before you take on more debt, you need to determine the amount of money you can afford to borrow while still having money available to do other important things in your life — now and in the future.

When calculating your allowable amount of debt, you need to know two terms: front-end ratio and back-end ratio. Your *front-end ratio* is your total monthly housing cost divided by your gross monthly income. The *back-end ratio*, on the other hand, is the total of all of your debts and your housing costs divided by your gross monthly income. When adding up these expenses and debt, your front-end ratio should never exceed 28 percent, and your back-end ratio needs to stay at or below 36 percent.

For example, check out Worksheet 5-1. In this worksheet, you can see that the borrower passed the front-end ratio, but failed the back-end ratio. The combination of housing costs and other debts eat up 40 percent of this borrower's gross income.

Worksheet 5-1	Maximum Debt Ratios (Example)

Front-End Ratio = 28 percent Max

Total monthly housing expenses*	$ 1,143
Divided by	
Total monthly household income (gross)	$ 5,000
Equals	23%

Back-End Ratio = 36 percent Max

Total monthly housing expenses*	$ 1,143
Plus all other monthly debt payments**	$ 853
Divided by	
Total monthly household income (gross)	$ 5,000
Equals	40%

*Includes principal, interest, taxes, and insurance

**Includes student loans, auto loans, credit card, and all other personal debt.

Another 25 to 30 percent goes to income taxes and Social Security taxes, leaving this borrower with only about 30 to 35 percent of his gross income ($1,750) to spend on everything else he needs now and in the future — at least until those other debts are paid off. This borrower must cover all other expenses, both required and discretionary, with only $1,750 per month.

If he's single, the problem isn't nearly as grim; however, if the borrower in Worksheet 5-1 is young and hasn't saved much or anything towards retirement, he should be saving at least $500 per month for this goal. If he's older and hasn't saved much or anything toward retirement, the amount he needs to save each month goes up dramatically. See Chapter 11 for more information on saving for retirement.

For now, go ahead and presume that the borrower is young and begins saving 10 percent of his gross income for retirement. Now he's down to $1,250 per month, and that amount has to cover all insurance premiums (other than homeowners), all utilities, groceries, household and personal supplies, gasoline, auto maintenance, child care, dental care, gifts, dining out and entertainment, vacations, home repairs, and so on.

Bottom line: If you breach the front-end or back-end ratio, you'll find yourself struggling to make ends meet, let alone achieving any other financial objectives you may have. If you find that you're already breaching one or both of these ratios (like the borrower in Worksheet 5-1), you need to start getting rid of some debt (figure out how in the section "Developing a Plan of Attack to Wipe Out Debt" later in this chapter).

To figure out where you stand with your current debt, go ahead and complete Worksheet 5-2.

Worksheet 5-2   **Maximum Debt Ratios**

Front-End Ratio = 28 percent Max $ _____

Total monthly housing expenses*

     Divided by

Total monthly household income (gross) $ _____

     Equals   _____%

Back-End Ratio = 36 percent Max

Total monthly housing expenses* $ _____

Plus all other monthly debt payments** $ _____

     Divided by

Total monthly household income (gross) $ _____

     Equals   _____%

---

*Includes principal, interest, taxes, and insurance

**Includes student loans, auto loans, credit card, and all other personal debt.

If your current debt exceeds the ratios I mention, see the section "Developing a Plan of Attack to Wipe Out Debt," later in this chapter, to find out how you can reduce it.

Reviewing Your Monthly Statements with a Critical Eye

Look over each and every one of your credit-card statements each month. You may be surprised to find charges on your account that aren't yours, or you may not have realized just how much you're charging each month. Worksheet 5-3 provides a checklist of items you need to look for on your statements as well as why these items are important.

If you see anything you're unsure about or that's incorrect on any part of your credit-card statement, call the credit-card company immediately and resolve the issue.

Worksheet 5-3   Credit-Card Statement Review Checklist

❏ **All charges are mine and correct.** If you see charges that you aren't certain about, contact your credit-card company immediately. It should provide you with as much clarification as it has about the charge, and presuming you still don't recognize it, the company will begin an investigation with the merchant in question.

❏ **All payments I made during the reporting period have been posted correctly and timely to my account.** Credit-card companies often take seven to ten days or more to receive and process a payment that you made. Keep track of when you mail a payment or authorize a telephone or online payment. Having a credit-card company conveniently post payments one day past the due date and charge a late-payment fee isn't unheard of, so keep an eye out on that too.

❏ **No fees were charged during this billing cycle.** If you were charged a fee, review all fees charged. Do they appear correct? Other than the potential annual fee, you should have no other fees such as late fees, over-limit fees, or returned-payment fees.

❏ **The interest rate hasn't changed since my last statement.** If your interest rate has changed, find out why by calling the credit-card company. Interest rates can go up upon the expiration of some special short-term, extra low interest rate, also known as the *teaser rate,* period or sooner, if you fail to make payments by the due date and/or if you exceed your credit line at any time.

❏ **I have verified the payment due date.** This deadline is the "drop-dead" date for payments to be received. Many credit-card companies have the right to substantially increase your interest rate and assess a late-payment fee if you miss this deadline.

❏ **I have made note of the statement closing date.** Sending your payment in on time to be credited before the statement closing date can help your credit score.

Getting Rid of Solicitations

You may feel bombarded and worn down by lenders soliciting your business. Also, by limiting or eliminating credit-card and loan offers, you will be less apt to apply for this "easy" credit.

One way to minimize the number of solicitations you receive from would-be lenders is to get your name added to no-call or no-solicitation lists, which you can do by following the checklist in Worksheet 5-4. Eliminating these solicitations also reduces the number of opportunities identity thieves have to establish credit in your name — and saves a few trees.

Registering your name with no-call or no-solicit lists doesn't in any way affect your ability to borrow money.

Worksheet 5-4   **Do Not Call or Solicit**

❑ Call 888-5OP-TOUT (888-567-8688) to have your name removed from the marketing lists that are sold by credit bureaus to potential lenders.

❑ Write the Direct Marketing Association to be removed from its direct mail and phone lists. Be sure to write a letter to each of the following:

  • Mail Preference Service, P.O. Box 643, Carmel, NY 10512

  • Telephone Preference Service, P.O. Box 1559, Carmel, NY 10512

  You can also contact the Direct Marketing Association online and request that your information be removed from their mail, telephone, and e-mail marketing databases:

  www.dmaconsumers.org/cgi/offmailing

  www.dmaconsumers.org/cgi/offphone

  www.dmaconsumers.org/cgi/offemaillist.html

❑ Register for the National Do Not Call list at www.donotcall.gov or by calling 888-382-1222.

Unfortunately, you can't eliminate all unwanted solicitations by getting your names on these lists. Charities, politicians, survey-takers, and companies that you currently do business with are exempt from these rules. However, you can still ask companies individually to add your name to their internal do-not-call lists.

Assessing Your Current Debt Situation

The first step in assessing your current debt situation is to list all mortgage and consumer debt, including credit cards, auto loans, student loans, and any other personal debt.

To begin your assessment, you want to get all your debt listed in the same place so that you can see it all at once. (Okay, you may need to take a deep breath first.) You can use Worksheet 5-5 to list your current debt situation. If you have a copy of your current combined credit report in hand, Worksheet 5-5 is easy to complete. If you don't, you'll need to pull copies of all your credit-card and loan statements to obtain this information. You should get a copy of your credit report each year. It's easy. If you haven't obtained one this year, you can get a free copy at www.annualcreditreport.com.

Worksheet 5-5 **Current Debt Situation**

Creditor / Current Balance / Interest Rate / Monthly Payment / Notes

1 _____ _____ _____ _____ _____

2 _____ _____ _____ _____ _____

3 _____ _____ _____ _____ _____

4 _____ _____ _____ _____ _____

5 _____ _____ _____ _____ _____

6 _____ _____ _____ _____ _____

7 _____ _____ _____ _____ _____

8 _____ _____ _____ _____ _____

9 _____ _____ _____ _____ _____

10 _____ _____ _____ _____ _____

11 _____ _____ _____ _____ _____

12 _____ _____ _____ _____ _____

13 _____ _____ _____ _____ _____

14 _____ _____ _____ _____ _____

15 _____ _____ _____ _____ _____

Add up the total of your required monthly debt service payments and divide that amount by your monthly gross income. The result is your back-end ratio.

TOTAL = CURRENT BALANCE   TOTAL = MONTHLY PAYMENTS

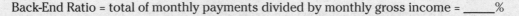

Back-End Ratio = total of monthly payments divided by monthly gross income = _____%

Back-end ratio should be no more than 36%.

After you've completed Worksheet 5-5, figure out which debts are *consumer debts*. One by one, I want you to review each of your consumer debts in detail and then complete Worksheet 5-6.

You can obtain some of the info you need to complete this worksheet from your credit report (if you have it handy); however, most of what you need is available only on your monthly account statement. Also, here are a few additional guidelines you need to know in order to complete Worksheet 5-6:

✔ To figure out the ratio of balance to available credit of an account, divide the current balance by the credit line. (For high credit scores, the ratio shouldn't exceed 30 percent.)

✔ If you currently have a teaser rate, expect that at some point in the near future the current interest rate will be adjusted drastically higher.

✔ When determining the term of your loan, you want to check whether you have a fixed or variable rate, a balloon payment, or loans amortized over a period of time (30 years, 5 years, and so on). Refer to Chapter 9 for explanations of this terminology.

Worksheet 5-6   **Consumer Debt Account Details**

Account #1

Credit issuer   _____

Current balance $_____

Credit line $_____

Ratio of balance to available credit   _____%

Current interest rate   _____%

Is this a teaser rate?   _____

Targeted monthly payment $_____

Minimum monthly payment $_____

Term of loan   _____

Date you opened the account   _____/_____/_____

Account #2

Credit issuer   _____

Current balance $_____

Credit line $_____

Ratio of balance to available credit   _____%

Current interest rate   _____%

Is this a teaser rate?   _____

Targeted monthly payment $_____

Minimum monthly payment $_____

Term of loan   _____

Date you opened the account   _____/_____/_____

Account #3

Credit issuer   _____

Current balance $_____

Credit line $_____

Ratio of balance to available credit   _____%

Current interest rate   _____%

Is this a teaser rate?   _____

Targeted monthly payment $_____

Minimum monthly payment $_____

Term of loan   _____

Date you opened the account   _____/_____/_____

Account #4

Credit issuer   _____

Current balance $_____

Credit line $_____

Ratio of balance to available credit   _____%

Current interest rate   _____%

Is this a teaser rate?   _____

Targeted monthly payment $_____

Minimum monthly payment $_____

Term of loan   _____

Date you opened the account   _____/_____/_____

Account #5

Credit issuer   _____

Current balance $_____

Credit line $_____

Ratio of balance to available credit   _____%

Current interest rate   _____%

Is this a teaser rate?   _____

Targeted monthly payment $_____

Minimum monthly payment $_____

Term of loan   _____

Date you opened the account   _____/_____/_____

Account #6

Credit issuer   _____

Current balance $_____

Credit line $_____

Ratio of balance to available credit   _____%

Current interest rate   _____%

Is this a teaser rate?   _____

Targeted monthly payment $_____

Minimum monthly payment $_____

Term of loan   _____

Date you opened the account   _____/_____/_____

Account #7

Credit issuer _____

Current balance $_____

Credit line $_____

Ratio of balance to available credit _____ %

Current interest rate _____ %

Is this a teaser rate? _____

Targeted monthly payment $_____

Minimum monthly payment $_____

Term of loan _____

Date you opened the account _____/_____/_____

Account #8

Credit issuer _____

Current balance $_____

Credit line $_____

Ratio of balance to available credit _____ %

Current interest rate _____ %

Is this a teaser rate? _____

Targeted monthly payment $_____

Minimum monthly payment $_____

Term of loan _____

Date you opened the account _____/_____/_____

Account #9

Credit issuer _____

Current balance $_____

Credit line $_____

Ratio of balance to available credit _____ %

Current interest rate _____ %

Is this a teaser rate? _____

Targeted monthly payment $_____

Minimum monthly payment $_____

Term of loan _____

Date you opened the account _____/_____/_____

Account #10

Credit issuer _____

Current balance $_____

Credit line $_____

Ratio of balance to available credit   _____%

Current interest rate   _____%

Is this a teaser rate?   _____

Targeted monthly payment $_____

Minimum monthly payment $_____

Term of loan   _____

Date you opened the account   _____/_____/_____

Developing a Plan of Attack to Wipe Out Debt

Are you losing sleep because of the amount of debt you're carrying? Are you wasting money on finance charges and feel like you will never get ahead? With an aggressive debt-reduction plan and your persistence, you can wipe out that debt — sooner than you might imagine.

A great, free tool that can help you quickly establish the most effective debt reduction plan for your unique situation is available online at www.quicken.com/planning/debt. The tool enables you to input all your current debts or just your consumer debt, if that is what's most troubling to you. You enter the current balances, interest rates, minimum monthly payments, and the actual monthly payments that you have been making. With this information, the online calculator tool reallocates your payments to help you first meet all minimum requirements and then applies any excess cash flow toward your highest interest rate cards so that these debts get paid off first, saving you substantial interest over time.

However, you don't need a computer or Internet access to develop and follow a debt-reduction plan. You can accomplish the same outcome by following the steps below, which takes focus and persistence, but no complicated math. For this exercise, focus only on your credit-card debt. Use Worksheet 5-7 to complete the following steps:

1. **List all your credit-card debtors in order of highest interest rate first.**

2. **List the current balances on each of these accounts.**

3. **List the minimum required monthly payment for each account.**

4. **Total the minimum required monthly payments.**

5. **Enter the total amount you have available each month (after paying your required expenses — see Chapter 3) to apply toward your debt-reduction plan.**

Generally, it's wise to apply only the required minimum payment to each credit card other than the one with the highest interest rate. However, you need to consider other factors as well. One of the most important factors is how the amount of debt on a card compares to the available credit on that card. A high debt balance to available credit ratio really hurts your credit score. Focus on maintaining no more than a 30 percent balance to available credit on any card. Pay down the high interest credit cards most aggressively and focus on reducing debt ratios if the interest rates are fairly similar.

6. **Record actual payments made and date of payment in the far right-hand column of Worksheet 5-7.**

Worksheet 5-7   **Debt Reduction Worksheet**

Credit Card	Interest Rate	Balance	Minimum Payment	Payment Applied ($ and date)
1.				
2.				
3.				
4.				
5.				
6.				
7.				
8.				
9.				
10.				
TOTALS		$	$	

Amount Available per Month $_____ to apply toward credit card debt balances in order of listing on this worksheet.

As you work through your debt-reduction plan in Worksheet 5-7, keep track of your progress on Worksheet 5-8.

Worksheet 5-8 **Debt Reduction Progress Log**

Months / Years

Chapter 6

Spending Thoughtfully

• •

In This Chapter

▶ Unearthing how you think and feel about spending money

▶ Determining whether you spend too much

▶ Discovering spending strategies to help you stay on course

▶ Exploring ways to reduce spending without cramping your style

• •

The average American is bombarded with thousands of advertisements every day. Trying to shelter yourself from those who want to part you from your money is nearly impossible. Between television, radio, billboards, Internet ads, junk mail, magazines, and the list goes on and on, you would have to become a hermit to avoid these solicitations — but that sounds a bit extreme.

No matter how much money you spend, you most likely won't look like a supermodel or perform like a world-class athlete simply by wearing the same clothes and makeup or buying the newest, most prestigious golf clubs or running shoes.

So, how do you block out these very motivating messages of Madison Avenue and stand strong against the onslaught? Well, I admit that not giving in to the spending frenzy isn't easy, but it can be done with a bit of self-discipline and perspective on what you really need. In other words, spending thoughtfully.

This chapter brings to light many tips and strategies that can help you make more thoughtful spending discussions on a regular basis. Only you can protect your financial future from the ever-present instant-gratification temptation.

Gauging How You Really Feel About Spending Money

To get onto the path of conscientious spending, it's helpful to step back and explore your current relationship with money: How does spending money make you feel? Why do you make the spending decisions that you do? Developing a better understanding of how your mind works when it comes to the subject of money can help you overcome challenges that you may face in saving and spending wisely.

Behavioral finance is a relatively new field of science that explores how people make decisions about money. One of the key principles is the concept of *mental accounting,* which is a game your mind plays on you.

I've provided you with Worksheet 6-1 to use to think through each scenario outlined and notate how you anticipate you would feel about each situation if it were to happen to you. If you feel that the money was a *windfall,* or in essence "found" money, check that box. Or if you feel that the money was "earned," something you deserved (similar to wages), check that box. Then indicate whether you would be more inclined to spend the money or save it based on how it came to you.

Worksheet 6-1   **Mental Accounting Quiz**

Windfall or Earned		Spend or Save		
☐	☐	☐	☐	1) You receive an unexpected refund on your income tax return of $2,000.
☐	☐	☐	☐	2) You receive an inheritance from your old, miserly Uncle Scrooge.
☐	☐	☐	☐	3) You cash in your company stock options for a nice profit.
☐	☐	☐	☐	4) Your employer gives you a profit sharing contribution or match on your retirement savings amount.
☐	☐	☐	☐	5) Your spouse or partner receives a ìsigning bonus" upon changing jobs.
☐	☐	☐	☐	6) You visit the casino and walk out with ten times more money than you started with.
☐	☐	☐	☐	7) One of your investment returns triples in value in just three years.

Reflect for a moment on your responses. Did you find yourself feeling more free or entitled to spend a windfall versus items that you considered earned? Because each of these scenarios illustrated a situation that may have been entirely unexpected, did you feel less guilty about spending the money? Did guilt even cross your mind? Did you view this newfound money as an opportunity to spend or save, or possibly both, depending on your own mental accounting? Think for a moment about these questions and then write your responses down in Worksheet 6-2.

Worksheet 6-2   **My Reflections**

_____

_____

_____

_____

_____

_____

_____

_____

_____

Do you feel more entitled to, or less guilty, spending money that comes to you as a *windfall*, compared to money that you earn? A dollar is a dollar. It shouldn't make a difference how the money came to you.

Your mind plays tricks on you — in Behavioral Finance, they call it *mental accounting*. You spend money less carefully when you feel you have received a windfall than if you earn it.

Remember: Focus on the fact that you have more money with which to accomplish the goals most important in your life. Don't waste a windfall. Use those dollars just as thoughtfully and appropriately as you would dollars that came in your paycheck.

Another fundamental principal of behavioral finance illustrates that people are naturally *loss averse*. In other words, they feel more *pain* from losing money than they feel *pleasure* in gaining the same amount of money. This aversion to losses helps explain why some people continue to hold on to a bad investment, because after they sell it, the loss becomes *real* to them. You may also see other symptoms of loss aversion in overly conservative investment portfolios.

Being averse to loss is a very normal and healthy human emotion. However, the most successful money managers are able to minimize their emotional urges and make rational decisions with regard to their money.

Figuring Out Whether You Overspend

Have you ever purchased things that you later regretted? Have you acquired "stuff" and now don't know why? Did you ever take yourself shopping or treat yourself to something that may have been impractical or inappropriate for you at the time?

Well, I have — plenty of times. But I'm not proud of it. Unhealthy spending can be compared to unhealthy eating. Money is something that touches most aspects of your life. You can't avoid money — just like you can't avoid food. Making bad decisions about your food intake can ruin your physical health, just as making poor money decisions can devastate your fiscal health. Fortunately, the human body has the ability to withstand a lot more abuse than your bank account or credit report. Maintaining good fiscal health takes an ongoing investment of energy, time, and persistence.

You probably don't like to think that you may be wasting your personal or family resources, and neither do I. However, remember that everyone is human and susceptible to making spending decisions based on irrational emotions rather than logical and practical facts — but that doesn't mean you have no influence or control over your urges to lay down your hard-earned cash.

Awareness and acknowledgment are the first steps to improvement. I've worked on becoming conscious of my own tendency to spend money without thinking and can now make better decisions with that awareness. And most likely, if you knew you were making reckless, thoughtless decisions that could negatively impact your future, you wouldn't do it either.

So take a minute to ask yourself: Do you overspend? Maybe the answer is a resounding "Yes!" Or maybe you feel that you don't overspend — or at least don't do it regularly. Care to find out? To figure out whether you're overspending, take the quiz in Worksheet 6-3. Circle Yes or No in response to each question.

Worksheet 6-3   **Are You Overspending?**

Yes   No   1) Are you saving at least 10 percent of your gross income for retirement?

Yes   No   2) Do you have a cash reserve equal to at least three to six months worth of your monthly expenses?

Yes   No   3) Do you wish you had more storage space in your home?

Yes   No   4) Do you ever feel that your spouse/partner or kids spend more than they need to?

Yes   No   5) Do you have items you purchased that you have not used or use very rarely?

Yes   No   6) Pretend you're a participant on the Newlywed Game, and your spouse/partner (or close friend) was asked how you would answer the following question:

Where is (your name) favorite place to shop?

_____ A)   Clothing Store

_____ B)   Jewelry Store

_____ C)   Sporting Goods Store

_____ D)   Hardware Store

_____ E)   Book / Music Store

_____ F)   Other Store

Would your spouse/partner or friend have any trouble making the selection? Would he or she have difficulty choosing only one? Do you think you would agree with the response?

Reflect on your responses to the questions in Worksheet 6-3. If you answered Yes to questions 1 and 2, you're probably doing really well. I find that with desire and dedication, we all can improve if need be.

However, if you answered Yes to questions 3, 4, and 5, you or someone in your household has spent a lot more than necessary, and this excess spending may be a chronic problem, which is keeping you from achieving your financial goals.

Regarding the final question, if your spouse or friends jokingly tell people that you have forwarded your mail to your favorite store, you may be an overspender! If they debate about two or more choices, you may be an overspender! (I'm hearing Jeff Foxworthy's voice.) However, if you and your spouse or friends can't quite figure out which store type would be your favorite, maybe you're not a shopaholic at all.

Note: Personally, I have a major weakness in bookstores — imagine that. With this awareness, I can moderate or completely eliminate my spending in this category. If I don't enter a bookstore or go online shopping, I can't overspend — at least in this area.

It can be difficult to change spending habits you may have had for years — although you may be aware that these habits cost you money or are irrational, unhealthy behaviors. But changing old habits takes time and persistence. It took a long time to get where you are now with your spending, and it is reasonable (and I argue healthy) to recognize that adapting behaviors to become a much healthier consumer does take time, so don't get discouraged if you discover that you are, in fact, overspending.

One of your greatest assets — if not *The* greatest asset you have — is your ability to earn money. Unfortunately, if you are anything like most people, your biggest liability is your penchant for spending it. Use this critical asset thoughtfully. Thoughtful, conscientious, deliberate spending actually reduces total outflow, while adding to your quality of life.

You likely can't afford to follow the herd, and it's not wise to try to keep up with the Joneses. In the modern classic, *The Millionaire Next Door,* the authors profiled dozens of self-made millionaires. These millionaires had several common characteristics. In my opinion, the most relevant characteristic or behavior trait they all shared is that they were and continue to be thoughtful spenders. Another word for it is *frugal.* They save a portion of every dollar they make. They make spending decisions very thoughtfully. Most don't "look" like what you might think a millionaire looks like. In fact, if they did "look" like a millionaire — fancy clothes, jewelry, cars, houses, and trips — they wouldn't have achieved their millionaire status.

Would you rather look like a millionaire or have the financial security of becoming one? Most people can't have both. Pick up a copy of *Cosmopolitan* for tips on looking like a millionaire. Continue with this workbook for guidance on becoming a millionaire.

You can't have your money *working* for you if you spend it all.

This concept is not living *within* your means, but rather living *beneath* your means. Living *within* means that you can make ends meet. Living *beneath* means that you have money remaining to save and invest for other things you need and want in your life.

Managing Your Spending

The American way is to spend everything you bring in. But just because most people in the United States are doing it doesn't mean that this way of managing your spending is healthy or smart. The best way I have found to manage spending is to have money automatically drawn from my checking account or paycheck to fund those things that are necessities (utilities, insurance, house payments, retirement savings, and so on) or are most important to me (to figure out your needs, check out Chapter 3). If I didn't put my savings on autopilot, it wouldn't get done, at least not as easily and consistently as it could be done. Consistency and simplicity are key when it comes to achieving financial success.

What do you currently have set up as an automatic payment or investment? For example, do you have money withdrawn from your paycheck going into your flexible spending account or 401(k) plan at work? What else could you set up to occur automatically out of your paycheck or checking account? Use Worksheet 6-4 to explore all the expenses, loan payments, insurance premiums, and investments that you can set up to occur automatically. By automating your payments and investments, your bills get paid on time, every time, saving you hassle and potential late fees, and by investing automatically, you don't have a chance to spend the money before it gets put to work for your other goals.

Worksheet 6-4   **Automatic Money Management**

Current (Expenses set up to be paid or made automatically)

_____

_____

_____

_____

_____

_____

_____

_____

_____

Optional (Additional expenses, loan payments, insurance premiums, savings, or investments that you may benefit from by setting them up automatically)

_____

_____

_____

_____

_____

_____

_____

_____

_____

See Chapter 3 for more on managing your spending.

Developing Good Shopping Habits

Shopping can often feel like a black hole on your finances. Every time you step into a grocery store or a shopping center, you may feel like you come out flat broke. In order to not allow your shopping trips to turn into a spending frenzy, take time to think about how you can spend more thoughtfully.

When shopping, always keep the following in mind: Reduce, reuse, and recycle. For example, don't buy overly processed, prepackaged foods. The more packaging and processing involved, the more it will cost you. Reduce packaged and processed items. Prepackaged groceries generally cost at least twice as much as whole foods, often multiple times more. For example, you can buy ready-to-heat twice-baked potatoes for approximately $1 per serving, or you can buy the ingredients to make twice-baked potatoes from scratch for less than 15¢ per serving. Make up a giant batch and freeze the leftovers, and now you have your very own homemade, ready-to-heat, twice-baked potatoes for a fraction of the cost.

Also try to buy whole foods, in their natural state, whenever possible: fresh fruit, vegetables, meat, and dairy products. If you're limiting your fat intake, buy fresh eggs and discard half, or even all, of the yokes (the fat is in the yoke). This approach costs you about half as much as the reduced-fat egg substitute in a carton and is much fresher, with no additives, preservatives, or food coloring.

You can reduce trash by minimizing your use of paper towels, disposable plates and cups, and plastic shopping bags. Instead, reuse cloth towels and durable plates and cups and take your shopping bags with you to the grocery store. Many stores credit you 5¢ per bag for bringing your own. Not only are you saving money, but you're also saving landfills. Over the course of a year, simply reusing these items can save you tens of dollars. Just think of how many other items this concept could apply to.

You can reduce the number of items that you purchase by sharing with, or renting from, others. For example, say that you like to garden. A rototiller comes in handy once or twice a year, so instead of buying a rototiller, consider borrowing one from a neighbor or renting one.

The following are some other key ways to keep your shopping expenses at a minimum:

- **Use a shopping list and purchase only the items on your list.** By following this guideline, you can begin to better plan your expenditures. And if you stick to your list, you can eliminate those nasty impulse purchases. However, if you discover something that you truly do need while shopping *and* the item's on sale for a limited time, you may purchase that item, but recognize that it's an impulse purchase, not a thoughtful expenditure. You can use Worksheet 6-5 to begin your own shopping list.

- **Don't go grocery shopping when you're hungry.** It's common that people spend more and buy more processed — and, therefore, more expensive — food when they're hungry.

- **Buy dry goods in bulk.** Often (but not always), the more you buy, the cheaper the price.

- **Buy merchandise when it is going out of season.** Buy next year's winter coat or swimsuit when the prices are dirt cheap instead of at the beginning of the season when it's not on sale. And when you're shopping for clothes, buy wash-and-wear clothes rather than dry-clean only.

- **Shop at discount stores.** Deep-discount grocery stores, such as Aldi's, can save you a lot of money.

- **Avoid brand names when a generic equivalent is available.** Often times, the generic form is made by brand-name companies and is of the same quality. Buying generic items can definitely help a lot. You can save 50 percent on average over the leading competitor.

- **Use "old-fashioned" household cleaning products instead of expensive cleaners.** This approach nets even more savings than buying generic. Boric acid, ammonia, and vinegar can replace almost all traditional household cleaners. A substantial supply of these effective cleaning products will run you about $3. You can easily spend two to three times that amount per month on modern household cleaning products that work no better. Peroxide and baking soda are effective and inexpensive alternatives to toothpaste, tooth-whitening products, and mouthwash. One year's supply of baking soda and peroxide sets you back almost $2. However, the equivalent store-bought products can easily cost more than $100 for a family of four.

- **Don't buy items that you won't use often.** Sure, an item may be on sale, but if you don't use it, don't spend the money on it, no matter how great a deal it is.

- **Don't buy impulsively.** If the item you want to purchase isn't on sale, I recommend a 30-day "cooling off" period. After 30 days, if you still feel you must buy the item, you may return to the store and purchase it. Now the purchase is a planned expenditure and not an impulse decision. However, what tends to happen is that after a few days, the item no longer has the attraction it originally had, and the hassle of returning to the store for that one item may be enough to deter you.

Worksheet 6-5   **Creating a Shopping List**

Groceries

_____

_____

_____

_____

_____

Personal Supplies

_____

_____

_____

_____

_____

Household Supplies

_____

_____

_____

_____

Other

_____

_____

_____

_____

Perhaps these ideas have given you some food for thought on how you can adjust your own habits to shop a little wiser. Go ahead and jot down some ways that you can begin to adjust your own shopping habits in Worksheet 6-6, perhaps borrowing from this list or coming up with some ideas of your own.

Worksheet 6-6 **Money-Wise Shopping**

What are some ways you can adjust your shopping habits?

_____

_____

_____

_____

_____

_____

_____

_____

_____

_____

It takes about 12 weeks to develop a habit, and developing good spending habits requires focus, dedication, and persistence. Try to make the money-wise shopping strategies you list in Worksheet 6-6 a priority for the next 12 weeks so that they have time to take hold in your life.

Entertaining on a Shoestring

Do you want to socialize with friends and family while spending as little money as possible? Here are a few ideas that are proven winners:

- **Covered-dish dinners:** Hosts provide the main course, and guests bring side dishes and desserts. The benefits of this type of gathering are that no one has too much work or cost to absorb and everyone gets to try lots of new and varied dishes. Bring the kids, hire one babysitter or older child to sit or entertain the children in the basement (or a separate part of the house), and the adults can visit or play cards upstairs or in the living room.

- **Wine-tasting party:** This type of get together can be a very educational and fun experience (and not to mention thrifty). Here's how it works: The host's responsibilities are to invite friends or family, lay out the rules, and provide glasses, crackers, fruit, and cheese for all. Then guests each bring a bottle of wine. The host predetermines the rules, such as the following: Bring red wine, $10/bottle maximum, with bottles disguised in paper bags. After all the guests have arrived, randomly number the bags, open the wine bottles, and begin the tasting. Discuss the characteristics and qualities of each wine and vote on your favorite while enjoying your cheese, fruit, and crackers and the company of your friends. At the end, unveil the winning selection.

✔ **Football party:** Hosts provide the theme entrée, which has something to do with the opposing team. For example, if your team is playing the Miami Dolphins, you may want to serve fish tacos. Rotate hosts with each game.

✔ **Game night:** Invite two to four people over after dinner to play Farkel (dice game of skill and luck; all you need is six dice and the instructions, which you can find on the Internet) or another game of your choice.

Using Worksheet 6-7, brainstorm ideas on how you can bring people together, have a lot of fun, yet spend very little money. I'm sure your friends and family will appreciate the quality time together as well as the frugality of these events.

Worksheet 6-7   **Entertaining Ideas**

_____

_____

_____

_____

_____

_____

_____

Chapter 7

Involving Your Family in Personal Finance

In This Chapter

▶ Getting the family on board

▶ Making everyone accountable for money management

▶ Discovering ways to involve your children

*Y*our financial plan should involve the dreams, goals, resources, and responsibilities of the entire family. If your family is made up of just you, you're the Chief Financial Officer or CFO of You, Inc.; achieving unanimous support of your financial mission should be pretty doable. However, if you have a spouse, partner, or children, you may have the responsibility of performing the functions of CFO, cheerleader, and coach. You may need to provide the guidance, encouragement, and support your family needs to develop a financial plan and follow it through. The success of any financial plan is dependent on the support, persistence, and dedication of all people involved.

Without the participation of the entire household, you'll face a continual uphill battle when it comes to your finances. In this chapter, I focus on communicating big-picture objectives as well as day-to-day and ongoing roles and responsibilities with all family members. I also share examples of how you can involve your children in your daily interactions with money and help empower them to make money-wise decisions for themselves while supporting the family's financial planning efforts.

Making Financial Planning a Family Affair

Remember the little yellow road-sign shaped signs often seen in the back window of so many cars and minivans — Baby on Board? Hey, you may even have one of those signs yourself. Although some people post this sign because they're proud parents, most people do it to alert fellow drivers that they have very precious cargo on board.

This slogan can be carried over to your personal financial life: Family on Board! You have very precious cargo that is sharing this financial life journey with you; they are depending on you. Good!

Your family also needs to be "on board" conceptually. Your spouse, partner, or children can be a help or a hindrance. As a family, you will face many challenges along your financial journey. But if family members are truly on board, they will work to help find solutions and not create additional challenges for you.

How do you get your family on board with your financial goals? You must inspire them, just like a coach might. A coach needs the cooperation and coordination of each player on his team. In order to get teams to pull together, great coaches lead by example and command the utmost respect from each and every team member. Their team members strive to perform at their very best each and every game, not only for themselves, but also for their coach and their team. Great coaches inspire greatness.

So how can you inspire your family when it comes to your personal finances? Share your vision, in living color, with your family members — your team. When you present your vision, make sure that you include the vivid details of why a goal is important to you and your family, and what accomplishing this goal will enable you all to enjoy. Elaborate on the payoff for putting in the hard work, compromise, or sacrifices that may be required to achieve these goals. The example in Worksheet 7-1 not only points out the objective but also provides a few suggestions to help engage family members into designing creative solutions instead of just focusing on problems. The example also highlights the fact that choices must be made and concludes with the critical *What's in it for me?* element.

Worksheet 7-1 **Involving Your Family (Example)**

We can have most of the things that really matter to each of us and our family. However, we can't have everything that each of us may want. Heck, no one can. Even rich people can't. If we come together to make wise decisions about our money, we will be able to do more of the things we would really love to do and less of the stuff that none of us wants to do — even though these things still must get done.

For instance, let's talk about yard work.

Option #1: We could hire a company to care for our lawn and pay them for their service, but then we don't have that money to do something we would rather do.

Option #2: We could share the lawn work and use the money we save to do something fun, like go to the water park after we're done doing yard work. If all of us chip in, we could get the lawn work done in a couple of hours and spend the rest of the day at the water park. It wouldn't cost any more than Option #1, but doesn't that sound like more fun?

Option #3: I could do all the yard by myself. Because I'll be busy with yard work, I won't be available to accompany you to the swimming pool. Plus, I'll be tired and dirty and not really up for doing much of anything the rest of the day. So, you'll just have to find something around the house to do. And I'd like to add that taking care of "our" yard by myself all the time isn't really how I want to spend my time either.

We all have decisions to make. We only have so much money to work with and lots of things that we need and want to do. We can't have everything we need and want, so we have to make choices. Let's talk about other family responsibilities and the choices we have.

Now you must figure out how to inspire your own family. I provide you with some space in Worksheet 7-2 to write down what you'd like to say to your family as you seek to bring them on board with your financial future. What subjects are near and dear to your spouse's or children's hearts? Start there — they'll be highly motivated to help you help them get what they want.

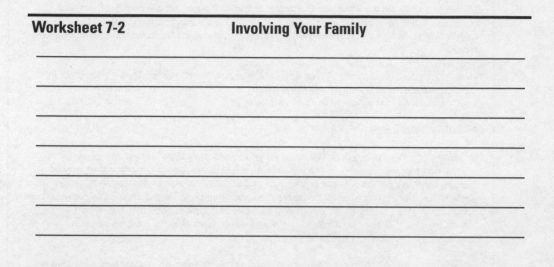

Worksheet 7-2   **Involving Your Family**

Sharing Money-Management Responsibilities

Allowing and encouraging your family members to participate in the family's financial decisions and money-management responsibilities is beneficial in many ways. But mainly, the more informed everyone is, the more you can work together for your shared goals.

I don't know how many times I've heard the line, "We never learned about money at school, and my parents definitely never talked about it — at least while we were around." Where are your children going to learn to make informed decisions about money if you don't teach them? What happens to the spouse or partner who was never interested or involved in the family finances if something happens to you? Are you really doing them any favors by taking on this responsibility single-handedly?

The answer is no. You must make managing money a shared responsibility within your family. No one learns this stuff in school; it's an on-the-job learning experience. Allow your family some on-the-job experience while you're around for guidance. For example, Worksheet 7-3 explores some ways that one individual shares money-management responsibilities with his family members — for his benefit and theirs. After reading through Worksheet 7-3, write down in your own words your desires and thoughts about involving your family in the big picture financial goals and decisions, as well as your periodic and daily responsibilities, in Worksheet 7-4.

Worksheet 7-3   **Sharing Responsibilities (Example)**

Big Picture/Decisions

My spouse and I will work together to design a financial plan that will help our family accomplish our most cherished financial objectives. We will use this workbook as the foundation to design our financial plan and to serve as a guide for our discussions about money.

I will take on the lead role as the family's CFO. However, I want my spouse to be involved in all major decisions affecting our future. If anything ever happens to me, I want to make certain that my surviving family will be okay.

Monthly Meetings

Once a month, my spouse and I will sit down and invest an hour reflecting on how we progressed toward our goals in the previous month, what issues or opportunities may be facing us in the near future, and how we can and should deal with these issues together. We pledge to set aside one hour at the same time each month to have a productive conversation about our family's finances. We pledge not to focus our conversation on what we did wrong, but rather use this time to reinforce the positive behaviors that we want to instill in ourselves, each other, and our children.

My spouse is really not interested in personal finance. However, she recognizes that this is very important to me and for our family. I don't want her to feel that I hold the purse strings. I don't want to be the bad guy or the one who is always telling our children no. We are a partnership. I need her input, cooperation, and support.

Daily Responsibilities

Although my spouse isn't nearly as interested in financial planning as I am, she's the primary day-to-day financial manager and decision maker for our household. She is also more likely to interact with our children regarding the constant decisions that we have to make about money. Both of us are very motivated to raise money-wise kids. We feel that the more we involve our children and allow them to participate in these discussions and decisions, the more they will learn, and the more supportive they will be of our family's financial plan.

Worksheet 7-4   **Sharing Responsibilities**

Big Picture/Decisions

_____

_____

_____

_____

_____

_____

_____

_____

Monthly Meetings

_____

_____

_____

_____

_____

_____

_____

_____

Daily Responsibilities

_____

_____

_____

_____

_____

_____

_____

_____

_____

Raising Money-Wise Kids

Involving your children in money management discussions and decisions is extremely valuable. (See the section "Making Financial Planning a Family Affair" earlier in this chapter for more details.) Children can be helpful or very challenging when it comes to effectively managing your money.

I'd like to share ways you can interact with your children to help instill healthy money-management behaviors in them:

✔ **Give children specific roles with regard to daily money management activities.** Ideas include opening and sorting the mail or depositing everyone's change (coins) into the families "vacation fund" jar each day.

Involve children in periodic responsibilities, such as helping to pay bills by writing checks and stuffing envelopes, clipping coupons from the Sunday paper, going into the bank and interacting with the teller, or making decisions and purchases for the family when grocery shopping.

✔ **Help children discover that compromises are normal.** No one can have everything they could ever want or dream about. The smarter you are about each and every money management decision, the more you'll have to work with for the things that matter most.

✔ **Allow your children the opportunity to earn their own money and make their own decisions about what to do with it** — with minimal influence on your part. If it isn't dangerous or illegal — regardless of how practical you think it is — allow them to proceed. This is the best time and place for your children to practice managing their money. Having this kind of responsibility and autonomy — while living under your roof — gives them opportunity to feel the pain of making bad decisions, but they'll learn invaluable lessons about money management while you're nearby to provide guidance when necessary.

Here's a great example of these principles: Not long ago I was at a Walgreen's and witnessed a young mother interacting with her three children, all under age seven, in the most amazing way I've ever seen.

The woman was unloading a small grocery cart at the checkout counter with the help of her sons. Her daughter was carrying a fistful of coupons. I overheard the woman enthusiastically tell her children that because of a special on tuna fish, they were able to buy six cans for the price of three. They also took advantage of many other two-for-one specials, and the mother was very alert to share this fact with her children. The children picked up on the mother's enthusiasm and were excited with their accomplishments.

After all the purchases were rung up by the cashier, the woman asked her daughter to hand their coupons to the cashier. When the receipt was produced, all the kids huddled around their mother to see the results of their shopping adventure. They discussed the receipt together, and once again, the mother enthusiastically stressed exactly how much money they saved with their coupons. The daughter yelled, "Yeah, Mommy!" with the same kind of joy and excitement that you would expect when winning a Little League baseball game. And this was just a trip to Walgreen's.

This young mother had successfully engaged her children in the joys of being involved in day-to-day money management decisions. They each had a role and responsibilities. They worked as a team. They didn't buy candy or toys. They didn't whine or pout. They had fun and were learning extremely valuable lessons.

Imagine having that kind of fun with your kids at a drugstore or a grocery store. Take a moment now and consider ways that you can involve your children in daily activities and responsibilities that affect the family's finances.

In Worksheet 7-5, consider ways to involve your children in the family's finances. Think of ways your children are, or could become more, involved from earning their own money doing chores around the house or making decisions about spending money.

For example, say that your daughter is turning 10 in a couple of months. This is an occasion for a big birthday bash. Explore all the different, fun things that she'd like to do, while staying within a set budget. You pick the budget amount and let her propose the possibilities she has explored.

Or say that your son wants a car when he turns 16. What options are available to help him to acquire a car and pay for insurance, gasoline, and upkeep? Are you willing and able to contribute financially? If so, to what extent can you transfer some or all of the very *grownup* responsibility to your son?

Worksheet 7-5	Getting Kids Involved

_____

_____

_____

_____

_____

_____

_____

_____

_____

_____

_____

_____

_____

I'm not a fan of anyone giving money to their children in the form of an allowance without certain responsibilities attached. No one receives a paycheck just for being a member of the family. Everyone has duties and responsibilities. If you elect to provide your children with an allowance, it should be directly tied to the adequate and complete fulfillment of their contributions to the family.

For example, a 4-year-old has very little need for money, but it's a great age to begin learning about how to make smart money decisions, and the direct correlation between work and reward: I'll pay you $1 per week if you pick up your toys, help set the dinner table, and make sure that the cat has food and water.

I strongly encourage you to allow your children to make as many decisions as possible about how they spend their money — given some minimal guidelines for safety. Without the opportunity to practice making wise financial decisions, children won't learn these valuable lessons until much later in life, when they're likely dealing with much more significant issues. Allow them to make little mistakes and grow from those mistakes while you're around to guide and direct them.

For example, I once worked with a family who had a wonderful, simple way of handling the subject of allowances with their children. This couple's policy was that every member of the family had jobs to do, and no one got paid to do these jobs.

To give you an idea, their two children, ages 4 and 6, had the responsibility of making their beds every morning. They also were expected to pick up their dirty clothes, toys, and homework and return those items to their respective places when finished. The children also helped prepare the dinner meal and load the dishwasher. They could earn allowances for any jobs performed above and beyond the required family responsibilities. And all money earned from any source, including allowances, and gifts, would be divided into three categories; one-third must be saved, one-third must be shared, and the remaining one-third could be spent (see Worksheet 7-6), which played itself out in the following ways:

✔ **Saved:** The children had savings accounts at their local bank, and every time they received any money, the first thing they would do is trot down to the bank and deposit one-third of the money in the bank account. The children would carry their own money, instruct the teller as to what they wanted to do, and did this all with little or no intervention from their parents.

✔ **Shared:** The second portion of the children's money could be shared in any way that the child deemed appropriate, as long as the money was being shared with people in need. The children generally contributed the money to their church.

When the couple's son was a little older, he learned of a boy named Byron in a remote village in Africa. The boy was the same age as the couple's son. Byron truly needed the basic essentials of life — clean water, food, and healthcare. The couple's young son was so deeply moved by the story of Byron that he decided that he wanted to become Byron's sponsor. One-third of his income would not be enough money to provide the monthly sponsorship fee. However, that didn't stop this motivated young man. He knew that he was genuinely blessed. He had the opportunity to raise more money by doing chores around his house, for his extended family and for neighbors. He made the choice himself. He wanted to sponsor Byron and that is exactly what he did. They became pen pals, and to this day, both boys' lives have been changed for the better — and it all started with the parents' policy that their children must share one-third of their income with someone else in need.

✔ **Spent:** The final third of any income earned or received could be spent. These parents allowed their children a considerable amount of freedom with regard to how they elected to spend their money. They could spend their money immediately, but when it was gone, it was gone. No loans or advances came from Mom and Dad. If the children spent their money each and every week, nothing would be left for a bigger purchase later. Over time, the children learned to budget their money and plan their expenditures to get the best "bang-for-their-bucks."

Suffice it to say that these parents knew how to raise money-wise kids, and you would be wise to follow in their footsteps.

Explore your current policies toward awarding allowances in Worksheet 7-6 and then consider how you can improve on those policies, noting any changes you'd like to happen in Worksheet 7-7.

Worksheet 7-6   **Current Allowance Policies**

Expectations:

_____

_____

_____

_____

_____

_____

_____

Amount of Allowance and Payment Frequency:

_____

_____

_____

_____

_____

_____

_____

_____

_____

Rules/Guidelines for Usage:

_____

_____

_____

_____

_____

_____

_____

_____

Worksheet 7-7   **Improved Allowance Policies**

Expectations:

_____

_____

_____

_____

_____

_____

_____

Amount of Allowance and Payment Frequency:

_____

_____

_____

_____

_____

_____

_____

Rules/Guidelines for Usage:

_____

_____

_____

_____

_____

_____

_____

Chapter 8

Minimizing Taxes

In This Chapter

▶ Paying just as much tax as you're required

▶ Itemizing or taking the standard deduction

▶ Reducing your burden at tax time

The easiest way to minimize the taxes you pay is to not make any money. However, that's not a smart financial-planning strategy. My objective is to make as much money as I can, while paying as little tax as possible.

You may be like me — the subject of taxes isn't something I enjoy studying or even thinking much about. But neither you nor I can ignore the subject — it won't go away. Knowing some important, yet often misunderstood basics, like those that I cover in this chapter, can help make sure that you're not missing out.

For a more in-depth and lengthy discussion on your taxes, check out the latest version of *Taxes For Dummies* by Eric Tyson, also brought to you by Wiley Publishing.

Paying No More Taxes Than You Have to Pay

You may shortchange yourself and not take the deductions for which you're entitled because you're worried about being audited. Or possibly you may be paying too much tax by not understanding the benefits of itemizing deductions. Another common misunderstanding is the real value of tax deductions. For most people, just getting your stuff together to prepare your returns each year is burdensome, but it doesn't have to be this way. In this chapter, I address each of these issues simply and directly.

Discovering AGI and your effective tax rate

Your *AGI* is your adjusted gross income, a number you need to know if you're planning on pursuing deductions (and for exercises in this chapter). The quickest way for you to determine your AGI is to refer back to your last tax return. You can find your AGI for the previous year on the first page of your 1040 return on line 37. If your income and deductible expenses aren't expected to change much this year as compared to last year, use last year's AGI for your planning purposes throughout this chapter.

Another important bit of information you should calculate while you have your tax return out is your *effective tax rate,* which is the actual percentage of your gross income that you pay in income taxes Here's how you do it:

1. **On the first page of your 1040, find your Total Income on line 22.**

2. **Move on to the second page of your 1040 and locate your Total Tax on line 63.**

3. **Divide line 63 by line 22 to determine your federal effective tax rate.**

4. **To approximate your total tax rate, including state and local income taxes, refer to those tax returns, identify your Total Tax, and divide that amount by your Total Income.**

5. **Add your federal tax rate to your state and local tax rates to arrive at your total effective tax rate.**

By knowing how much of every dollar you earn goes out in taxes, you're better able to make informed decisions about the real cost of any money decision. For example, if you have an effective tax rate of 30 percent, you'd have to *earn* about $1.43 to net one dollar, after-tax to spend.

You'll also want to know your effective tax rate to be able to more accurately determine the value of tax-deductible expenses. This knowledge helps keep things in perspective.

Figuring out your allowable deductions

So how do you know what you can safely deduct on your taxes? If you don't own a home or aren't making large charitable contributions, you may likely be best served by taking the standard deduction. The *standard deduction* is every taxpayer's minimum "gift" from the IRS. You're entitled to the larger of the standard deduction or your itemized deduction. However, if you don't qualify for the standard deduction, generally because someone else — like your parent — claims you as a dependent on his or her tax return, but you have significant medical or dental expenses, pay interest or real estate taxes on your home, or make large charitable contributions, you can save a substantial amount of money by itemizing your deductions.

Quickly review Worksheet 8-1 to determine whether itemizing may benefit you. Indicate with a checkmark the items that apply to your personal situation. If you mark home mortgage interest alone, that may be enough to warrant itemizing. Go ahead and mark all items that may apply to you.

Worksheet 8-1   **Tax Deduction Opportunities**

Mortgage Interest (Use Form 1098 received from lender in January of each year):

- ❑ Mortgage on primary residence
- ❑ Second mortgage on primary residence
- ❑ Home equity line of credit
- ❑ Mortgage on second home/vacation home
- ❑ Other mortgages
- ❑ Discount points paid on mortgage

Note: Points that you pay when you initially buy your primary residence are deductible in that year. However, if you refinance or the property isn't your primary residence, points are deducted gradually over the life of the loan.

Real Estate and Property Taxes (Keep receipt of taxes paid):

- ❑ Real estate taxes paid on primary residence
- ❑ Real estate taxes paid on secondary residence
- ❑ Property taxes paid on personal property

State and Local Income Taxes:

- ❑ Boxes 17 and 19 Form W-2 received from employer in late January
- ❑ Estimated state and local tax payments made
- ❑ State and local tax refunds from prior tax year applied to current year's liability

Charitable Donations:

- ❑ Cash donations
- ❑ Donations of property

Medical Expenses (must exceed 7.5 percent of adjusted gross income [AGI] to be deductible):

- ❑ Deductible medical expenses include medical insurance premiums you pay, doctors' fees, hospital and lab fees, prescription drugs, medical supplies, dental and vision care costs, and supplies.

Note: Although medical expenses are deductible, you likely won't get to deduct these expenses because they must exceed 7.5 percent of your AGI to apply.

Miscellaneous Tax Deductions (must exceed 2 percent of AGI to be deductible):

- ❑ Union or professional dues paid
- ❑ Subscriptions for work-related publications
- ❑ Cost of uniforms or equipment required for employment
- ❑ Cost of continuing education required for employment
- ❑ IRA custodial fees if you pay these fees directly
- ❑ Safe deposit box rental
- ❑ Investment advisory and tax preparation fees and expenses
- ❑ Cost of books and periodicals used in managing your investments
- ❑ Legal fees if they involve your job, taxes, or investments

Remember that Worksheet 8-1 isn't an exhaustive list, but it covers the majority of items that likely apply to you. For more information, or if you're just having trouble getting to sleep, read IRS Publication 529. Go to `www.irs.gov/publications/p529/index.html` to read this publication online.

As the documents listed in Worksheet 8-1 come to you throughout the year, place them in a file labeled *Tax Info*, and you'll be one giant step closer to having your paperwork together to complete your tax return. For more on this topic, check out the section "Maintaining Good Records" later in this chapter.

Itemized deductions are limited or phased out if your AGI exceeds $156,400 for single, married filing jointly, and head of household taxpayers ($78,200 for married filing separately). Unfortunately, you can do little if you find that your itemized deductions are limited or phased out because of your income being too high unless you anticipate your earnings dropping significantly next year. If that is highly likely, you'd be best served by postponing any payment of tax-deductible items until next year, if possible, when your deductions won't be limited.

Other than that, just keep this fact in mind: The value of your itemized deductions may not be as great as they appear, due to the phase out for people with higher incomes. So if you're one of the lucky ones who makes too much money, Uncle Sam has found another way to get a bit more.

Getting specific with charitable deductions

Knowing how to claim charitable contributions can get a bit sticky, but don't worry. The process is easier than you might think. The IRS states that you're entitled to deduct the *fair market value* (meaning what a willing buyer would pay) of items, in good condition, that you donate to qualifying charities. However, the vast majority of people miss out on tax savings to which they're legally entitled because they don't know how to determine the fair market value for their donations.

For the simplest method of figuring out the fair market value of particular items you donate, I suggest using the TurboTax ItsDeductible program if you make regular donations of personal property. The software costs about $20 and can easily save you many times that amount in taxes. The ItsDeductible program has compiled pricing data based on extensive research of resale outlets as well as recent market data from eBay and provides you with the fair market value of an item as well as a detailed report for your tax filing purposes. And you shouldn't need to buy the software each year because values tend to remain fairly steady or inflate slightly over time.

The rules changed in 2006 regarding charitable contributions. Now you must get a receipt from the charity substantiating *all* your contributions or donations. Also, items must now be in "*good*" or better condition to qualify for a deduction.

Determining Whether the Itemized or Standard Deduction Is Best for You

You should itemize your deductions if your total deductions are more than the standard deduction (see Worksheet 8-2). For each dollar that exceeds the standard deduction, you will reduce your taxable income by that amount.

Example: Your itemized deduction exceeds the standard deduction by $5,000. If you have an effective tax rate of 30 percent, you will save yourself an additional $1,500 in taxes by itemizing ($5,000 x 0.30 = $1,500).

Worksheet 8-2 — Standard Deductions for Taxpayers in 2007

Filing Status	Standard Deduction
Individual taxpayer	$5,350
Married filing jointly	$10,700
Head of household	$7,850

Note: If you're 65 or older and/or blind, your standard deduction will be even higher than what you see in Worksheet 8-2.

Use Worksheet 8-1 to guesstimate whether the sum of your itemized deductions will exceed the standard deduction that you're entitled to take. (If you haven't yet completed this worksheet, I suggest you do so now.) If you own a home, make substantial charitable contributions, or pay substantial state and/or local real estate or property taxes, you will be best served by itemizing. Worksheet 8-2 provides you the opportunity to tally up the total of your anticipated deductions if you itemize. Worksheet 8-3 illustrates whether you'd save more money by itemizing your deductions or by taking the standard deduction.

Worksheet 8-3 — Tallying Up Your Deductions

Itemized Deduction	Amount
Mortgage and investment interest	$
Real estate and property taxes	$
State and local income taxes	$
Charitable contributions	$
Medical expenses (in excess of 7.5 percent of AGI)	$
Miscellaneous deductions (in excess of 2 percent of AGI)	$
Total	$

Using Worksheet 8-4, compare the total of your itemized deductions in Worksheet 8-3 to the standard deduction to which you're entitled based on Worksheet 8-2 to determine which alternative is most advantageous to you.

Worksheet 8-4 — Choosing between Itemized or Standard Deduction

To determine whether you should itemize or choose the standard deduction, complete these steps:

1. Enter the total of Itemized Deductions $ _____
   from Worksheet 8-3.

2. Subtract the applicable Standard Deduction $ _____
   listed in Worksheet 8-2.

3. Calculate your net result. $ _____

After completing Worksheet 8-4, you know that you should itemize your deductions if the net result is a positive number; however, if the net result is negative, you should take the standard deduction.

If you aren't married but co-own a home with someone, you can actually save a lot of money with proper tax planning. Arrange your expenditures so that one person, preferably the person in the highest tax bracket, pays all the tax-deductible expenses for the household, such as the mortgage payment and charitable contributions. The other co-owner then pays for nondeductible household expenses, such as groceries, utilities, and so on. This way, one of you is able to take the full itemized deduction, while the other one takes the standard deduction. This strategy could save you up to $2,000 per year. However, married couples filing jointly or separately can't do this.

Overestimating the value of the tax breaks available with home ownership is a common misunderstanding. The after-tax cost of a home mortgage is more expensive than most people are led to believe. For example, you have $13,000 in mortgage interest, real estate taxes, and few other deductions. Your total itemized deductions are $13,000. However, you were entitled to a standard deduction of $10,300 regardless of your expenses merely by being married and filing jointly. So the real tax deductible benefit of your home mortgage and property taxes is less than $2,700, not $13,000. Generally, you receive a very small incremental tax break by having a mortgage.

Real estate agents, mortgage brokers, financial advisors, and possibly you frequently adjust your gross mortgage interest rate by your marginal tax bracket and conclude that your mortgage is only costing you X amount after adjusting for the tax savings. For example, say that your home mortgage rate is 6.25 percent. If you were to adjust for tax savings by multiplying your mortgage rate times your tax bracket (for example, $0.0625 \times [1-0.33] \times 100 = 4.19$ percent), you would say that your net after-tax cost of the mortgage is 4.19 percent. Wrong! You were entitled to the standard deduction, so the *difference* between the two numbers is the real benefit. Your net cost of the mortgage rate is closer to 5.84 percent.

Maintaining Good Records

Throughout the year, you likely receive a significant amount of paperwork, some of which needs to be retained to prepare your tax return. Other documents may need to be retained to substantiate prior-year tax reporting. Maintaining your documents in an organized fashion will not only help you avoid missing valuable deductions to which you may be entitled, but will also help ensure that your income tax return is complete and accurate. If not, you can be out a lot of money in penalties and interest when errors are discovered.

If you haven't already segregated this paperwork into its appropriate files, I recommend that you flip over to Chapter 2, where I give you a detailed description about how to get your paperwork in order. As you wade through this stack of paperwork, you will likely find the necessary documentation needed to prepare your income taxes.

Worksheet 8-5 lists the files I recommend to keep your tax-related documents organized. These files should be incorporated into your general household filing or record-keeping system, which you can find in Chapter 2. And when tax time rolls around, all you have to do is pull out these files, and you're ready to prepare your tax return.

Worksheet 8-5   Tax Organization Files

File Name	File Contents	Retain How Long?
Bank accounts	Monthly account statements	Until year-end reconciliation
Brokerage accounts	Year-end statements	Indefinitely
Canceled checks	Related to home improvements	As long as you own the property
	Tax-deductible items	Indefinitely
	Non-deductible IRA contributions	Indefinitely
Credit-card statements	All monthly statements	At least one year
Income	Paycheck stubs, royalty statements	Until W-2 or 1099 is received
Investments	Monthly statements, buy/sell confirmations	Indefinitely
Receipts	Major purchases, anything related to your home or investments	Until you no longer own
Retirement plans	Year-end account statements	Indefinitely
Tax return 20___	Return and supporting documentation for that year	For at least seven years from filing date. (You'll need at least seven files for your prior years' tax returns.)
Tax info	Documentation for current year — anything you checked on Worksheet 8-1	Until tax return is filed, tax then move into Tax Return 20___ file

If you pay bills online, print a confirmation statement and retain it in lieu of a canceled check.

Maintaining efficiently organized and complete records related to your personal finances helps you in so many ways. Not only can you avoid wasting time or stressing out when you can't find important documents, but you can also avoid wasting money in late payment fees and additional interest charges, not to mention how much better you will feel should you get one of those wonderful audit notices in the mail from the IRS.

I once read a quote in the *Wall Street Journal* that said the average white-collar worker spends six weeks every year looking for stuff. I'm sure you can find a lot better way to spend your precious time. Invest a few hours to set up a logical filing system for yourself and implement that system. You'll be glad you did!

Part III
Thinking about the Future

The 5th Wave   By Rich Tennant

"When we bought it 5 years ago, the mortgage payments seemed huge. But we got used to it. Please, pull up an orange crate and make yourself comfortable."

In this part . . .

Regardless of your personal situation, age, or income, owning a home, providing a college education for your children, achieving financial security (retiring), and making sure that your wishes are carried out when you're gone are very likely primary goals in your financial life. In this part, I help you achieve these goals.

Chapter 9

Planning for Big-Ticket Purchases

....

In This Chapter

▶ Prioritizing big-ticket purchases

▶ Owning a home: Financial factors to consider

▶ Determining how much you can afford

▶ Knowing your mortgage payment options

▶ Refinancing your mortgage

....

*B*efore making any impulse purchases or signing contracts to make a big purchase, invest time to explore the rationale for these decisions and how they may impact your other financial objectives. All your choices matter, especially the larger ones involving your money, so take a moment to think them through and do a little number-crunching before you buy.

After you've determined that the expenditure is worth making, proceed wisely. In this chapter, I explain key issues involved in making common big-ticket purchase decisions and help you become a more financially savvy consumer.

Evaluating a Big-Ticket Purchase

When confronted with a decision about making a big-ticket purchase ask yourself, "Is this [*fill in the blank*] one of my most important financial objectives?" If your answer is no, step back and ask yourself the following:

✔ What am I willing to give up in order to have *this item?*

✔ Is spending money on this big-ticket purchase really worth it?

If you answer yes, substitute one of your primary financial objectives and do as a savvy shopper would do. Spend away — carefully, that is.

Here's an example: Would you choose to trade your car in on a newer model now, even though it's running perfectly fine? Ask yourself what sacrifices you'd be willing to make:

✔ Are you willing to work 20 hours of overtime per week for six months?

✔ Are you willing to sell your motorcycle?

✔ Are you willing to charge the cost of your plane tickets to Florida next winter (which ends up costing you twice as much as paying cash)?

Too many times you may take the easiest short-term option and say, "Charge it." Financing provides immediate gratification and postpones the pain of having to pay for a while. If you aren't willing to raise or earn what you need to make this purchase immediately, you need to ask yourself: Is this thing so important that you're willing to give up twice as much for it over time? These decisions can make or break your financial plans.

You will have times when financing a big-ticket item is the only way to purchase what you need. The primary big-ticket items, other than retirement and college funding, are homes and vehicles, which you likely need or choose to finance. But before you finance anything, make sure that you have all the relevant facts, enabling you to make an informed, thoughtful decision. (Read more about financing in the section "Exploring Your Home Financing Options.")

Owning Your Own Home: The Pros and Cons

Before getting into financing strategies, start with a thorough examination of the pros and cons of your decision to buy a home. If the advantages outweigh the disadvantages, proceed to the financing discussion. If they don't, you haven't wasted much time, and you've avoided making a costly financial mistake.

If you're considering buying a house or selling the one you currently own, use Worksheet 9-1 to guide your decision as to whether home ownership is right for you. Put a checkmark in each box that applies to your situation.

Worksheet 9-1	The Pros & Cons of Home Ownership
PROS	**CONS**
❏ Pride of ownership	❏ Responsibilities of ownership
❏ Appreciation potential	❏ Risk of having to sell at the wrong time
❏ Tax deduction	❏ Coming up with the down payment
❏ Hedge against inflation	❏ Inflexibility: You can't just pack up and move when the lease is up
❏ Helps to build good credit	❏ If you have a poor or no credit history, this loan is going to really cost
❏ You can remodel or change your home as you see fit	❏ Paying for and dealing with required maintenance and repairs
❏ Flexibility to have pets, a garden, make noise, and so on	❏ Making long-term commitments to a location
❏ Storage space or garage	❏ No amenities, such as a park, swimming pool, gym, and so on
❏ Location	❏ Location

In Worksheet 9-1, you identify the major advantages and disadvantages of owning a home. This decision involves considering all reasonable options before you come to a final conclusion. Can you lease an apartment or home and better fulfill your personal needs and objectives? Are there any other options to consider?

Another important consideration is how long you plan to stay in the home. As a general rule, to cover just the costs of buying and selling the home (which includes obtaining a mortgage and an appraisal, application fees, inspections, movers, title insurance, legal fees, and real estate commissions), a property has to appreciate at least 15 to 20 percent for you to break even. In addition to knowing how long you plan on staying in the home, you also need to be able to guesstimate how your new home will appreciate over that time. In most real estate markets, this rate of appreciation typically takes three to seven years.

Buying a home makes little or no sense if you don't plan to stay there at least three years. Nolo, the nation's oldest and most respected provider of legal information for consumers, has a series of great calculators you can access at no charge through their Web site at www.nolo.com. One is entitled, "Should I rent or buy?" You plug in all the facts and assumptions, such as inflation rate on rental prices, your tax rate, average maintenance costs when owning your own home, appreciation expectations, and how long you plan to stay, and the calculator does the math for you.

If you determine that purchasing a home has overwhelmingly more advantages than disadvantages, and you're confident of your willingness and ability to stay in the home for a number of years, you can begin to explore how much home you can afford.

Figuring Out How Much Home You Can Afford

Worksheet 9-2 allows you to compute the maximum amount you likely can afford to spend on your monthly mortgage payment. You can then use this monthly mortgage cost to compute how much house you can afford to buy in Worksheet 9-4. (Worksheet 9-3 walks you through those calculations.)

If you have a positive number on the last two lines of Worksheet 9-2, you have met the healthy borrowing guidelines. Even if you have a negative number in either the front ratio or back ratio columns, you may be fine carrying this much debt. However, exceeding both ratios for any length of time is unwise.

Your real estate agent and mortgage lender are there to help you buy as much house as you can *qualify* to buy. That doesn't mean that you can *afford* it. Real estate agents and some lenders couldn't care less about these "old-fashioned" guidelines. Real estate prices have skyrocketed in recent years, and some lenders will lend money to people without credit or much income. Watch out! They aren't doing you any favors.

Worksheet 9-2 **Housing Cost Guidelines**

	Front-end ratio = 28%	Back-end ratio = 36%
Gross monthly income	$ _____	$ _____
Multiplied by	0.72	0.64
(1–0.28) = 0.72		(1–0.36) = 0.64
Equals Subtotal A	$ _____	$ _____
Mortgage payment	$ _____	$ _____
Real estate taxes	+ $ _____	+ $ _____
Homeowners insurance	+ $ _____	+ $ _____
Auto loan(s)		+ $ _____
Student loan(s)		+ $ _____
Home equity line of credit		+ $ _____
Credit-card debt		+ $ _____
Other debt		+ $ _____
Equals Subtotal B	$ _____	= $ _____
Net difference A minus B	$ _____	= $ _____

Keep your total housing costs to less than 28 percent of your household gross income, and total debt (including housing costs) under 36 percent of gross income.

Following these borrowing guidelines will help you avoid spending more than you can afford, thereby causing you to forsake your other financial goals in life. You can have a home and a life, too!

Another guideline for determining how much house you can afford — one you may have heard about — is that you can qualify for a mortgage equal to 2½ to 3 times your gross annual wages (see Worksheet 9-3). These results are remarkably similar to those produced using the front- and back-end ratios, but they're not as precise. However, this simple calculation will get you in the ballpark.

Worksheet 9-3   Mortgage Qualification Quick Test Example

1. Enter your household gross annual income. $ _____ $75,000

2. Multiply that amount times 2.5. $ _____ $187,500

3. Multiply your gross annual income by 3. $ _____ $225,000

4. How much do you have for the down payment? $ _____ $10,000

5. To get your target purchase price, add line 4 to line 2. $ _____ $197,500

6. Add line 4 to line 3 to calculate your maximum purchase price. $ _____ $235,000

Worksheet 9-4   Mortgage Qualification Quick Test

1. Enter your household gross annual income. $ _____

2. Multiply that amount times 2.5. $ _____

3. Multiply your gross annual income by 3. $ _____

4. How much do you have for the down payment? $ _____

5. To get your target purchase price, add line 4 to line 2. $ _____

6. Add line 4 to line 3 to calculate your maximum purchase price. $ _____

Exploring Your Home Financing Options

You've determined that you want to buy a house. The worksheets from the preceding section helped you gather essential information so you can now determine what financing options you have available and how best to maximize those options.

Here are some key questions you need to consider to determine the most appropriate type of mortgage for you and your circumstances:

- How long do you plan to live in the home?
- Would you prefer a stable monthly payment, or can you handle the uncertainty of an adjustable mortgage payment?
- How much money do you have to use as a down payment?
- Are you a veteran?
- Are you a first-time homebuyer?
- How is your credit?

Also consider the following key issues:

- Current fixed interest rates on conventional, FHA, and VA loans
- Current interest rates on adjustable-rate mortgages
    - 3-year fixed, then annually adjustable-rate mortgage (3/1 ARM)
    - 5-year fixed, then annually adjustable-rate mortgage (5/1 ARM)

Choosing between a fixed-rate mortgage and an ARM

In the last few years, Americans have experienced historically low mortgage loan rates. Conventional wisdom has been that if you can obtain a fixed-rate mortgage at about 6 percent or less, you should lock in that rate for as long as possible. However, conventional wisdom may not apply to your circumstances.

For example, I once bought a house and had the following mortgage options: a 30-year fixed-rate mortgage for about 6 percent or a 3/1 ARM at 4.625 percent. I expected to stay in the home for three to five years and definitely not more than seven. My initial rate of 4.625 percent for the ARM was locked in for three years. At the end of the three-year period, if interest rates increased, my rate could go up a maximum of 1 percent each and every year. Given the substantial difference at the time between a 30-year fixed and a 3/1 ARM, I calculated that in the worst-case scenario, I would reach the point where I would break even in year seven. (For more on the break-even point, check out the section "Determining your break-even point" later in this chapter.)

If you're in a similar position (not planning on staying in a property for more than five to eight years), you likely would be best served considering an adjustable-rate mortgage (ARM). However, the decision depends on the differential between the 30-year fixed mortgage rates and interest rates available on 3/1 and 5/1 ARMs.

For up-to-date rates on all types of mortgages in your area, visit www.bankrate.com. Bankrate provides information, quotes, and calculators to assist you in making informed decisions about your home-financing options based on rates available in your market at that very moment. Your local newspaper likely also publishes current mortgage rates available in your market.

Currently, you can't find much benefit in taking an adjustable-rate mortgage compared to a fixed-rate mortgage. However, when the difference between a fixed rate and an ARM is 0.5 percent or more, and you have a high likelihood that you won't be in the property much longer than the fixed term of your adjustable-rate mortgage, you can save money by selecting the ARM.

To determine the monthly principal and interest due on a mortgage balance at a specific interest rate, visit www.bankrate.com or www.nolo.com and use the mortgage calculators. If you don't have access to the Internet or a financial calculator, you can estimate your annual mortgage payment with Worksheet 9-6. (See the example in Worksheet 9-5.)

Worksheet 9-5   Estimating Your Mortgage Payment (Example)

1. Mortgage balance $ ___$200,000___

2. Divided by 1,000   = ___200___

3. Take this result and multiply it times the factor provided in the amortization table below, corresponding to your mortgage term and interest rate.

Years	5%	6%	7%	8%	9%	10%
15	96.34	102.97	109.80	116.83	124.06	131.48
20	80.24	87.19	94.40	101.86	109.55	117.46
30	65.05	**72.65**	80.59	88.83	97.34	106.08
40	58.28	66.47	75.01	83.87	92.96	102.26

Rate

4. Enter the result of Step 2 times the amortization factor from the table above to arrive at your annual principal and interest payment on your mortgage.

Annual mortgage payment $ ___$14,530.00___

5. Divide by 12 to arrive at an estimate $ ___$1,210.83*___
of your monthly mortgage payment

* Excluding homeowners insurance and real estate taxes.

Worksheet 9-6   **Estimating Your Mortgage Payment**

1. Mortgage balance $ _____

2. Divided by 1,000   = _____

3. Take this result and multiply it times the factor provided in the amortization
   table below, corresponding to your mortgage term and interest rate.

Rate

Years	5%	6%	7%	8%	9%	10%
15	96.34	102.97	109.80	116.83	124.06	131.48
20	80.24	87.19	94.40	101.86	109.55	117.46
30	65.05	72.65	80.59	88.83	97.34	106.08
40	58.28	66.47	75.01	83.87	92.96	102.26

4. Enter the result of Step 2 times the amortization factor from the table above
   to arrive at your annual principal and interest payment on your mortgage.

   Annual mortgage payment $ _____

5. Divide by 12 to arrive at an estimate $ _____
   of your monthly mortgage payment

* Excluding homeowners insurance and real estate taxes.

After you know the current interest rates available in the marketplace and the approximate amount of your monthly mortgage payment (from Worksheet 9-6), you can decide, based on the numbers, whether a fixed-rate or adjustable-rate mortgage is better for you and, if so, for how long.

Determining your break-even point

Your *break-even point* is the point in the future where the financial impact of your decision to go with one type of mortgage over another meets. Earlier in this chapter, I shared a scenario about a time when I chose an ARM and didn't reach my breakeven until the seven-year mark. If I happened to sell the property or refinance the mortgage before the seven-year mark time, I made a smart gamble by taking the adjustable rate mortgage.

For example (as you can see in Worksheet 9-7), in year four, my effective mortgage rate was 5.625 percent, which was still below the initial fixed rate of 6 percent. So in this scenario, for the first four years, I was clearly ahead by having the ARM. However, where is the break-even point? Worksheet 9-7 illustrates how that break-even point was computed. If I sold the property anytime before year seven, I would be ahead substantially by selecting the 3/1 ARM, even if interest rates went straight up over those years.

Worksheet 9-7 Breakeven ARM versus Fixed Mortgage (Example)

$ ___$150,000___ **Mortgage**	**30-year**	**3/1 ARM***	Cumulative **ARM Advantage**
Years 1, 2 and 3			
Interest rate	6.00 %	4.625 %	
Monthly payment	$ 899.33	$ 771.66	+$4,596.12
Year 4			
Interest rate	6.00 %	5.625 %	
Monthly payment	$ 899.33	$ 863.96	+$5,020.56
Year 5			
Interest rate	6.00 %	6.625 %	
Monthly payment	$ 899.33	$ 960.96	+$4,281.00
Year 6			
Interest rate	6.00 %	7.625 %	
Monthly payment	$ 899.33	$ 1,062.21	+$2,326.44
Year 7			
Interest rate	6.00 %	8.625 %	
Monthly payment	$ 899.33	$ 1,167.22	-$888.24

* Assume maximum interest rate increases

To determine your breakeven point when considering an ARM versus a fixed-rate mortgage, use Worksheet 9-8.

Worksheet 9-8   Breakeven ARM versus Fixed Mortgage

$ _____ Mortgage   <u>30-year</u>   _____ ARM*   **Cumulative**
<u>**ARM Advantage**</u>

Year 1

    Interest rate   _____ %   _____ %

    Monthly payment $_____ $_____   +/−$_____

Year 2

    Interest rate   _____ %   _____ %

    Monthly payment $_____ $_____   +/−$_____

Year 3

    Interest rate   _____ %   _____ %

    Monthly payment $_____ $_____   +/−$_____

Year 4

    Interest rate   _____ %   _____ %

    Monthly payment $_____ $_____   +/−$_____

Year 5

    Interest rate   _____ %   _____ %

    Monthly payment $_____ $_____   +/−$_____

Year 6

    Interest rate   _____ %   _____ %

    Monthly payment $_____ $_____   +/−$_____

Year 7

    Interest rate   _____ %   _____ %

    Monthly payment $_____ $_____   +/−$_____

* Assume maximum interest rate increases

Choosing your fixed-rate term

Assume that you plan to stay in your new home indefinitely and are most comfortable selecting a fixed-term mortgage. You may be wondering whether you should take out a 15-, 20-, 30-, or one of those new 40-year fixed-rate mortgages.

Using Worksheet 9-9, consider the ramification of this decision. As you can see in this worksheet, the buyer agrees to a purchase price of $235,000 and makes a down payment of 20 percent, which means the amount he is financing is $188,000. If he had chosen a 30-year fixed rate, his payment would be $1,158 per month, excluding homeowners insurance and real estate taxes. However, by choosing a 15-year fixed rate, he obtains a lower interest rate but a much higher payment.

Worksheet 9-9	30-year versus 15-year Fixed-Rate Mortgage Comparison (Example)	
Home price	$235,000	
Less down payment 20 percent	$ 47,000	
Amount financed	$188,000	
	30-year fixed	15-year fixed
Interest rates	6.25%	5.75%
Monthly payment	$1,158	$1,561

If you have ample and stable cash flow, plenty of cash reserves, and don't like the idea of having long-term mortgage debt, go with the 15-year mortgage. However, this is not the case for most people. The difference in payment — approximately a third more for the 15-year mortgage than for the 30-year mortgage — isn't a commitment that many people should take on.

By going with a 30-year fixed rate, the monthly payments are much more manageable for most people. However, should you choose to accelerate the repayment of your mortgage, which I'm not at all opposed to, you can retain the utmost flexibility while still knocking years off your mortgage payments by simply adding an additional $100 per month to your mortgage payment. Of course, the more you can afford to pay, the better, because you'll pay off your mortgage faster and save a lot on interest.

If you pay more than your monthly payment, be sure to clearly specify to your mortgage company that the additional dollars are to be applied against the principal balance of your mortgage; otherwise, they won't be.

You may have heard of *biweekly mortgages*. This concept has a lot of merit. However, you shouldn't have to pay extra for this service. You can create your own biweekly mortgage by submitting one half of your monthly mortgage payment every other week in advance of when it's due. At the end of the year, you'll have made 26 biweekly payments — the equivalent of 13 monthly payments in a year. This simple strategy knocks about six years off the term of the 30-year mortgage and saves you tens of thousands of dollars in interest over the life of your mortgage.

Comparing Mortgage Options

Shopping online for mortgages can be a very efficient way to research your mortgage options, and it provides 24-hour convenience from the comfort of your own home or office. I encourage you to visit www.fanniemae.com, www.freddiemac.com, www.hud.gov, and www.mbaa.org. These Web sites offer information on mortgage programs that may be available to first-time homebuyers, veterans, or other special-interest groups.

When shopping online for a mortgage, you can also go directly to a specific lender's Web site, such as www.wellsfargo.com, or to an auction site, such as www.lending tree.com. *Auction sites* allow you to complete a loan application, which is sent to a number of lenders for their review. Those providers interested in providing you a loan send you offers. The convenience of using the auction sites is that you only have to complete one loan application, you generally don't have an application fee (at least at this point in the process), and you now have several mortgage options to compare.

Before obtaining a mortgage online with a company you've never heard of, be sure to check with your state's regulatory agency to verify whether they're licensed and regulated to do business in your state. You can check out the lender online with the Federal Deposit Insurance Corporation at www.fdic.gov.

Even if you elect to get quotes from various mortgage providers online, I also suggest that you check local mortgage providers. Your local newspaper most likely provides quotes, at least on a weekly basis, for some of the most competitive mortgage lenders in your community. You may find that working with a local mortgage provider is most convenient. As you see later on in this section, the amount of paperwork that you're required to pull together and provide to the lender is substantial. When working with a local lender, the loan-acquisition process may be easier than working with an online lender.

Be sure to ask the following questions of potential mortgage lenders:

- **What is the current interest rate of the mortgage being considered?** (News flash . . . the lower, the better!)

- **Are *discount points* (money you spend to buy down the interest rate) or *origination points* (fees that some lenders charge) included?** Generally, you'll want a loan with the lowest interest rate without discount points. However, if you have lots of extra cash on hand and plan to stay in the home for a very long time, you may benefit from paying discount points. You should be able to completely avoid origination points.

- **Will you please provide me with a good-faith estimate illustrating all my fees and closing costs?** If the lender refuses, then don't do business with it!

- **Can I lock in the interest rate, and if so, what will it cost me to do so?** Lenders will allow you to secure an interest rate in advance of closing on your mortgage. You may want to lock in the current rate if you suspect rates will go up before closing. Lenders will charge a fee to provide you with a guaranteed rate. The lower the fee, the better!

- **What is the minimum down payment required for this loan?** Many loans require a 20 percent down payment. The lender will need to know how much of a down payment you plan on making to determine the right loan options for you.

✔ **What is required for me to obtain a prequalification or preapproval letter?** (For more on preapproval, check out the "Getting Preapproved" section, later in this chapter.)

✔ **Is there a prepayment penalty on this loan?** I can think of absolutely no reason to obtain a mortgage that has a prepayment penalty. If the lender is offering a loan with a penalty for paying it off early, walk away. The chances of your staying in that home and not refinancing your mortgage at some point over the next 30 years are highly unlikely.

Use Worksheet 9-10 when gathering quotes and feedback on the preceding questions from a variety of lenders.

Worksheet 9-10	Mortgage Comparision Worksheet		
Loan	1	2	3
Interest rate	%	%	%
Points			
Total fees*	$	$	$
Rate lock	Y/N	Y/N	Y/N
Cost of lock	$	$	$
Minimum down payment	%	%	%
Monthly payment	$	$	$

You may find that you're actually comparing two or more loans from the same mortgage company, which is fine. The attempt is to get you the most appropriate loan for the best price.

You must remember that the cost of your mortgage includes not only the interest rate, but also the closing costs, which can be substantial. Typically, you should anticipate closing costs to be in the neighborhood of $1,200 to $1,500, but the closing costs do vary greatly between lenders. Generally, these costs must be paid out of pocket, along with any discount points at closing. However, closing costs and discount points are negotiable items, and you may be able to negotiate with the seller to pay these costs for you. If the seller isn't paying these costs for you, don't forget these additional costs must be paid along with your down payment when you close on the mortgage and obtain the deed to your new home.

Getting Preapproved

I strongly recommend that before you get serious about making an offer on a new home, you obtain from your mortgage lender a prequalification letter at minimum, or better yet, a preapproval letter.

A preapproval letter from a lender is much more significant than a prequalification letter. Prequalification often takes just a few minutes, and many lenders provide this service at no cost to you. However, a prequalification letter is a nonbinding offer by the lender to provide you a loan for a certain amount of money. The problem with a prequalification letter is that the lender hasn't verified your financial information.

Rather, they're indicating that if everything you stated can be verified and your credit rating is solid, they will provide you with this loan.

Preapproval, on the other hand, involves your lender actually verifying the financial information you provide. The lender will contact anyone they need to receive verification of your income, assets, debts, and credit history. After it verifies this information, it issues a letter stating that you are approved for a certain amount of mortgage for a certain period of time. Some lenders charge a small fee to provide a preapproval letter; however, this fee is generally refunded to you at closing.

You have several very good reasons for obtaining a preapproval letter prior to entering into any negotiations regarding the house purchase, including the following:

- Your mortgage company has done a thorough review of your financial information and has provided you with the letter stating that they will give you a loan for a certain amount of money. It's obligating itself to provide you with this loan. A potential buyer who already has a preapproval letter from a lender stands a much better chance of having his purchase offer accepted than someone who is making their offer contingent upon obtaining financing.

- The preapproval letter provides you with confirmation of how much money (loan plus your down payment) you have available to spend on your new home.

Preapproved borrowers are attractive to potential sellers. Sellers don't need to worry that if they accept your offer, you could be turned down for a loan. Also, you may be able to close more quickly than another competing buyer, because you have already completed the time-consuming process of being approved for your mortgage.

If your financial circumstances change significantly from preapproval to closing, your preapproval letter may no longer be valid. Contact your lender immediately if your circumstances change.

Hopefully, I've convinced you that obtaining a preapproval letter is another important step in making that big-ticket purchase decision of buying a home. To obtain a prequalification letter or a preapproval letter and, subsequently, a mortgage, lenders are going to ask you a series of questions. The following is a list of the information and documents that you need to pull together to obtain your prequalification or preapproval letter, and eventually your mortgage:

- **Employment and income:** Be able to answer these questions about your employment: Where do you work? How long have you worked there? How long have you worked in the industry? What is your annual income? How is your compensation derived? How stable is your income?

- **Liabilities:** Lenders will want you to answer these questions: What current debts do you have? What is your minimum monthly payment required to satisfy these debts? What is the actual monthly payment that you've been applying toward these debts? Of your total debts, how much is directly applicable to credit cards and auto loans?

- **Assets:** Be sure to know the answer to these questions: What is your current bank balance? Where will the money come from to make your down payment and pay any closing costs and discount points, if applicable?

- **Credit:** The lender won't typically ask you any questions about your credit history and instead pulls a copy of your credit report.

I strongly encourage you to review your credit report personally to make certain that you have done everything possible to improve its accuracy prior to making loan application. Refer to Chapter 5 for more information.

Documents that you need to provide to your lender or prospective lender are listed in Worksheet 9-11. As you prepare to apply for your loan, you can use this checklist to make sure that you have all the necessary information.

Worksheet 9-11   Documents Needed for a Mortgage Application

❏ Copies of your federal income tax returns and W-2s for the last two years (However, if you are self-employed, additional income verification will most likely be requested.)

❏ Copies of the recent paycheck stubs showing your name and Social Security number, name and address of your employer, and cumulative year-to-date information on earnings and withholding

❏ Proof of any other income, such as interest and dividends, Social Security, Veterans benefits, disability or retirement benefits, alimony, or child support

❏ List of all creditors, balances owed, and minimum monthly payments required

❏ Verification of all assets including retirement account statements, brokerage account statements, mutual fund statements, and any other investment assets or savings

❏ Verification of your current mortgage or rent payments

❏ Eventually, a sales contract for the house that you'd like to buy (Of course, a sales contract doesn't apply during the preapproval stage.)

Finding the Right Home

Now that you have invested time determining the amount of money you can afford to spend on a new home, the type of mortgage that may be most appropriate for you, and a preapproval letter from the lender of your choice, it's time to go house hunting.

I encourage you to begin in your home search by driving around prospective neighborhoods, visiting open houses, and utilizing the Web to do a lot of your preliminary legwork.

Many Web sites draw from a central database, also known as the Multiple Listing Service (MLS). The National Association of Realtors has one of these Web sites at www.realtor.com. Another resource is www.homes.com. In many locales, major real estate companies dominate the marketplace. I encourage you to also visit their Web sites.

Pinpointing the key features

Before you get too attached to a certain property, make sure that you have thought through the issues that are most important to you and what you want out of this new home. Consider using Worksheet 9-12 as a guideline and brainstorm on the issues that are most critical when comparing properties. Complete one worksheet per property you are considering.

Worksheet 9-12   **Key Features Wanted in New Home**

Location:

Distance to employment _____

Proximity to family _____

Proximity to child care _____

School district _____

Access to public transportation _____

Proximity to airport, train station, and so on _____

Desired amenities nearby (parks, walking or
bike trails, and so on) _____

How does this property compare to others in
the neighborhood? _____

Are home values in the neighborhood stable? _____

Is the neighborhood undergoing revitalization? _____

Are there any special assessments or taxes for
this neighborhood? _____

What other issues involving location are
important to you? _____

Features of property:

Number of bedrooms _____

Number of bathrooms _____

Garage capacity _____

Style of home _____

Master bedroom on first floor _____

Master bathroom _____

Laundry facilities on first floor _____

Handicap accessible _____

Washer and dryer _____

Formal dining room _____

Dine-in kitchen _____

Built-in dishwasher _____

Formal living room _____

Separate space for home office _____

Basement _____

Ample storage space _____

Fireplace _____

Deck or patio _____

Fenced in yard _____

Shade trees _____

Level driveway _____

Ample space for gardening or
outdoor activities _____

Homes association dues _____

Amount of initial repairs or
remodeling required _____

Other critical features you'd
like in your new home _____

Hiring a real estate agent

As a home buyer, consider hiring a real estate professional as your buyer's agent. It costs you nothing and can save you thousands of dollars.

I suggest that you save your additional time and energy and allow a real estate agent, empowered with the information in Worksheet 9-12, to locate the properties best meeting your needs. If you have little or no experience buying a home — this is a must! If you are too busy doing what you do for a living and taking care of your family, let a real estate agent work for you.

Find a real estate professional that has extensive experience buying and selling properties in the neighborhoods in which you are most interested. Cruise the neighborhood and jot down the names, phone numbers, and companies of the realtors listing properties — also, notate the properties' addresses. Then, when you return home, visit the real estate agents' companies' Web sites, read about the real estate agents, and check out the properties listed. Soon you will discover who the "movers and shakers" are in your target real estate market.

Knowing When to Refinance

When you're considering refinancing a loan, you look at many of the same issues that you initially looked at when checking out your loan options, including the following:

- How long do you plan to stay in the home?
- What is your current interest rate?
- What interest rate could you obtain on a new mortgage?

✔ Will you be refinancing your mortgage and pulling out additional cash to use for other purposes such as paying off credit-card debt?

If you have significant equity in your home, and you need to tap that equity to pay off high interest, nondeductible debt, finance a child's college education, pay for necessary home renovations, or any other purpose you deem worthwhile, refinancing may be your best option. However, refinancing isn't the only option for tapping into home equity.

Be careful not to use any money that you obtain through refinancing as a quick fix for a systemic problem. If you are going to put your home at risk to pay off your credit cards, do yourself a big favor and don't let it happen again.

With the refinancing, you need to keep in mind that closing costs will be levied against you. I feel it is safe to assume that somewhere between $1,200 and $1,500 is the typical cost to refinance.

Worksheet 9-13 helps you determine whether refinancing is a good idea.

Worksheet 9-13   **Should I Refinance?**

Current mortgage balance $ _____

Current interest rate   _____ %   New interest rate   _____ %

Current monthly payment $ _____   New monthly payment $ _____

Net difference per month (monthly savings $ _____
between new payment and current payment)

Cost to refinance $ _____

Divide your cost to refinance by your monthly $ _____
net difference to determine how many months it
will take you to break even

Divide the above number by 12 to determine the $ _____
number of years it will take to you to break even

Planned stay in this house   _____

If you plan to stay in the house for at least a few years beyond your break-even point (for more on this topic, see the previous section "Determining Your Break-even Point" in this chapter), you should probably refinance at this time. The process of shopping for a new home mortgage to refinance an existing mortgage is exactly the same as the process you went through to obtain your first mortgage. Please refer to earlier segments of this chapter for additional information regarding obtaining a mortgage.

Saving in advance

When you have young children, and/or significant surplus cash flow, saving for college costs in advance may be your best option. For purposes of illustration, assume that you want to have enough money available to pay for your newborn child to attend community college for two years and then an in-state public university for two more years (and after that she's on her own). Also, for this example, don't assume any financial aid — at least not yet.

The College Board (www.collegeboard.com) is a not-for-profit membership association whose mission is to connect students to college success and opportunity. The College Board is a very robust Web site where you can obtain the current costs for the two institutions you're considering: Johnson County Community College (JCCC) and the University of Kansas (KU). While at JCCC, your student will live at home, so the only expenses incurred are tuition, fees, books, and supplies. While attending KU, the student will live on campus, and you must add the room-and-board expenses to the tuition, fees, and so on. After doing the math, you can see in Worksheet 10-2 how much you must now save on a monthly basis in order to have the money for your child to go to college.

Worksheet 10-2   College Savings Calculation (Example)

1. Year 1 cost you plan to cover $ _____2,730_____

2. Year 2 cost you plan to cover $ _____2,730_____

3. Year 3 cost you plan to cover $ _____12,650_____

4. Year 4 cost you plan to cover $ _____12,650_____

5. Additional funding you plan to cover $ _____

6. Add up the totals from lines 1 through 5   = _____30,760_____ total

7. In how many years will your child enter college   _____18_____

8. Divide line 6 by line 7 to arrive at savings per year   = $ _____1,709_____ /year

    or

    Divide line 8 by 12 to arrive at monthly savings   = $ _____142_____ /month

Okay, so Worksheet 10-2 makes calculating how much you need to save for your one newborn child a cinch. But what if you have three children, ages 11, 9, and 5? You can work through this same calculation for each of your children and then add the amounts together. Your monthly savings requirement in this example becomes $848.16; go ahead and make it an even $900 a month. (A little cushion never hurt anyone.)

Now it's your turn. Use Worksheet 10-3 to calculate how much you need to save over what period of time to have the money available to fund college expenses for each child. You can go to www.collegeboard.com to find the most recent cost information for colleges and universities across the United States.

No financial aid has been factored into the calculations in Worksheet 10-3. You can use this worksheet to determine how much you need to save if you want to send your child to college and not take into consideration financial aid. Heck, your child may not qualify because you make so darn much money!

Worksheet 10-3   College Savings Calculation

1.   Year 1 cost you plan to cover $ _____

2.   Year 2 cost you plan to cover $ _____

3.   Year 3 cost you plan to cover $ _____

4.   Year 4 cost you plan to cover $ _____

5.   Additional funding you plan to cover $ _____

6.   Add up the totals from lines 1 through 5   = _____ total

7.   In how many years will your child enter college   _____

8.   Divide line 6 by line 7 to arrive at savings per year   = $ _____ /year

     or

     Divide line 8 by 12 to arrive at monthly savings   = $ _____ /month

You may have heard a lot about the costs of a college education inflating 4 to 8 percent per year over the last 20 or 30 years. I haven't included a separate adjustment to offset the effects of inflation, nor have I accounted for any returns on your savings or investments for college. Based on historic inflation of college costs, I feel that it is appropriate to presume that, at best, you achieve an after-tax return on your education funds equal to the inflation rate. In other words, whatever earnings your college savings accumulate after-tax will equal the increase in college costs.

Paying as you go

Do you think you'll have enough income to cover your child's college costs as she incurs them? If so, you may consider paying as you go. Or you may find a combination of savings and support from your current cash flow while your child is in college to be your best strategy.

For example, say that you want to earmark $200 a month to go toward offsetting any costs for your son's college education. Your son Danny is currently 15 and plans to start college in three years. So, your computation would go as follows: $200 times 36 months equals $7,200. When your teenager gets ready to attend college three years from now, you will have accumulated enough money to pay for two years of tuition, fees, books, and supplies at a community college or possibly one year of the same type of expenses at an in-state public university.

Then, over the next four years while Danny is in college, you will accumulate, or possibly write checks directly to your student or the college, another $9,600, which you pay out of your current income. This strategy goes a long way toward paying for a big portion of your child's tuition and fees. Should you desire and find it financially appropriate to more fully fund your child's college education expenses, your next option is borrowing (see later sections in this chapter on borrowing).

You can use Worksheet 10-4 to calculate how much savings you will be able to come up with in advance and how much will be available from your cash flow while your kids are in college. You may be able to make up for any remaining balance through grants and loans in your child's name. Refer to the "Checking into Financial Aid" section later in this chapter for more information.

Worksheet 10-4   **Save Some and Pay Some**

1. How much money do you want to save $ _____ /month?
   for college funding?

2. How many months until your child begins college?   _____

3. Multiply line 1 by line 2 for total savings accumulated. $ _____

4. In addition to this monthly savings amount, how $ _____
   much additional money do you feel you can access
   each month to provide to your college student?

5. Multiply line 4 times the number of months $ _____
   your child will attend college.

6. Add lines 3 and 5 together for your total $ _____
   funding provided.

Borrowing options for students and parents

After you've tapped out all other options, borrowing money to pay for college is your last resort. Your student should exhaust her borrowing options before you consider taking on any debt to pay for her college education.

The best way to fund college costs, if borrowing is necessary, is to have your child borrow the money herself. Through federal student loan programs and financing programs available through various institutions, students have a number of attractive options available to them to finance college costs.

Your child has many options as to how to go about obtaining a college education, such as participating in work-study programs; doing part-time work; acquiring student loans, grants and scholarships; attending college part-time while working full-time; or joining AmeriCorps, the Peace Corps, or the military. In the section entitled "Checking into Financial Aid," I go into detail about each of the traditional financial aid options that may be available to your student.

There is no such thing as financial aid for retirement! Putting yourself into debt to pay for your child's college education may have disastrous effects on your financial future. I strongly recommend that your student apply for financial aid and exhaust all other resources and options prior to your going into debt to pay for her college education.

With that said, if you borrow money for your child's college education, I suggest you consider the list of primary resources:

✔ **Federal PLUS loan:** This loan is the best of all these options. The *Parent Loan for Undergraduate Students* (PLUS) is a popular, accessible, and reasonably priced loan that parents (with decent credit) can access to borrow up to the full cost of a dependent student's education minus any other financial aid for which the student qualifies. Repayment must begin within 60 days of receipt, and you may have up to ten years to repay the loan plus interest. For additional information visit www.collegeboard.com or call the College Board toll-free at 800-891-1253.

✔ **Home equity line of credit:** A home equity line of credit isn't necessarily a bad option, but it comes in a distant second to the Federal PLUS Loan. The interest rate on the loan will be a lot higher, and borrowing against your home equity can put your home at risk of foreclosure if you can't pay the loan.

✔ **401(k) plan loan:** If your 401(k) plan has a loan feature, the maximum amount you can borrow is the lesser of $50,000 or 50 percent of your vested account balance. Contact your 401(k) administrator for details.

Borrowing from your 401(k) plan can be hazardous to your wealth! By borrowing money out of your 401(k) plan, that money is no longer invested, and although you will repay yourself interest on this loan, the money is still coming out of your other pocket. You aren't getting the full benefit of your 401(k) plan investments working for you. Also, the money you pull out of the 401(k) plan as a loan is pre-tax dollars, but the money you repay the loan with is after-tax. So you actually face a significant hidden cost in this borrowing strategy. Wham!

Another major negative to borrowing from your 401(k) plan is the possibility that you may not continue with that employer while the loan is still outstanding. In that event, you must repay the loan in full, or it will be considered a premature distribution, subject to a 10-percent early-withdrawal penalty and taxation. Double wham!

✔ **Unsecured loan from your bank:** Also known as a *signature loan,* this loan is often the most expensive. The bank charges a much higher interest rate because no asset, such as a house, is securing this loan. These loans are often difficult to qualify for unless you have impeccable credit or are willing to pay an expensive interest rate.

Using Worksheet 10-5, check the box in the left column if a particular source may be an option to pay for your child's college education, and if so, complete the available funds in the column on the right.

Worksheet 10-5	**Borrowing Options for Parents**	
Possibility	*Potential Sources*	*Available Funds*
❏	Federal PLUS loan	$
❏	Home equity line of credit	$
❏	401(k) plan loan	$
❏	Unsecured loan from bank	$

Setting Payment Expectations

One of the most beneficial things you can do for your child is communicate the expectations you have regarding paying for college and help your student set reasonable expectations. You may feel very strongly that your child participate in the financial responsibilities involved in obtaining this education. The cost of a college education may come as a shock to your child, so the sooner you help establish appropriate expectations, the better. Communicate expectations early and often.

One strategy that I think has a ton of merit is the collaborative agreement between parent and child, shown in Worksheet 10-6.

Worksheet 10-6   **College Promissory Note (Example)**

As your parent, this is my pledge to you: If you attend college, apply for financial aid in your own name, and raise any additional funds that may be necessary to pay for the tuition, books, fees, and supplies, I will repay any and all student loans that were required to fund your college education, under the following schedule:

Grade Point Average (4.0 scale)	Debt Repayment Promise
If you graduate with a 4.0	100%
If you graduate with a 3.0-3.99	80%
If you graduate with a 2.00-2.99	50%
If you fail to average C's or better or drop out	0%

Signature of Student

_____

Signature of Parent(s)

_____

_____

Benefits of the kind of collaborative arrangement you see in Worksheet 10-6 include the following:

✔ Your child must apply himself and show a good faith effort, or you won't pay anything toward his college education.

✔ If your student drops out of school, he's on his own.

✔ If your child applies himself and achieves a B average or better, you will repay 80 to 100 percent of the college costs.

✔ You don't have to start repaying these loans until six months after your student graduates, which allows you additional time to accumulate funds to repay the debt or to adjust your monthly cash flow in order to be able to more comfortably pay the debts.

Use Worksheet 10-7 to create your own promissory note.

Worksheet 10-7 **College Promissory Note**

As your parent, this is my pledge to you: If you attend college, apply for financial aid in your own name, and raise any additional funds that may be necessary to pay for the tuition, books, fees, and supplies, I will repay any and all student loans that were required to fund your college education, under the following schedule:

Grade Point Average (4.0 scale)	Debt Repayment Promise
If you graduate with a 4.0	%
If you graduate with a 3.0-3.99	%
If you graduate with a 2.00-2.99	%
If you fail to average C's or better or drop out	%

Signature of Student

_____

Signature of Parent(s)

_____

_____

Thinking about Education Savings Vehicles

If you've not yet started a family, your children are young, or you have substantial surplus cash flow, you should consider how best to save money to fund your children's college education fund. And I'm taking for granted that if you're reading this section, you want to have money available to pay for part of or all your child's college costs, or at least have funds available to lend to your child if needed.

Worksheet 10-3, earlier in this chapter, provided you the opportunity to calculate the annual and monthly savings needed to fund a specific level of college costs. If you haven't already done this exercise, you want to do so before implementing any of these college-savings strategies.

Accumulating assets in your name has very little negative impact on your child's ability to qualify for federal financial aid. However, should you decide to accumulate money in your child's name, approximately 35 percent of those assets will be deemed available to pay for college costs, and financial aid will be reduced accordingly. So keep most or all the money you save for your child's college education in your own name if you expect your scholar to qualify for financial aid.

Education Savings Accounts

If you're within the income limits, you can contribute up to $2,000 per year to a Coverdell Education Savings Account (ESA) for each child under the age of 18. Anyone with income of less than $95,000 ($190,000 if married filing jointly) may contribute. If you make too much money to contribute yourself, maybe that would be a great incentive for Grandma to contribute. You can even gift the money to Grandma to contribute on behalf of your child, if you are so inclined. Contributions aren't tax-deductible; however, the earnings grow tax-free and remain tax-free as long as they're used to pay for qualified education expenses.

You can open an ESA with a bank, mutual fund company, or any other financial institution that offers traditional IRA accounts. My first choice is investing with a low-cost, no-load (no commission) mutual fund company, such as the following:

- ✔ **Vanguard:** The initial minimum investment to open an account is $2,000. However, subsequent investments of as little as $100 can be made at any time, and from anyone — hint, hint, Grandma! A very simple, maintenance-free investment option is the Vanguard Target Retirement portfolio. You can select a Target portfolio designed for the year your child is to start college. For more information about Vanguard's education savings account, visit www.vanguard.com.

- ✔ **T. Rowe Price:** Like Vanguard, T. Rowe Price also offers target date retirement portfolios that can be excellent, low-cost, maintenance-free investment options for your ESA account. Their initial minimum investment is $1,000. However, that amount is reduced to $50 if you establish an automatic monthly savings program and add at least $50 a month to the ESA account. Find out more about your options at www.troweprice.com.

Education Savings Accounts *are* considered assets of the parent when determining financial aid eligibility. However, there are a lot of benefits, such as tax-free earnings, that should far outweigh the negative impact on financial aid qualification.

529 plans

Section 529 qualified tuition savings plans have evolved into one of the most attractive college savings programs available today. Just like ESAs (see preceding section), 529 plan assets accumulate tax-free, and if your child uses them for qualified education expenses, the withdrawals are tax-free, too.

The biggest difference between the ESA and 529 plans is the contribution limit. You can invest up to $100,000 or more into a 529 plan, and you have no limitation based on your income.

Another key difference is that 529 plans are state-sponsored programs. If your state offers good 529 plans, and you invest in one, you may be able to deduct all or a portion of your contributions on your state income tax return. Visit www.savingforcollege.com for outstanding information and resources about all 529 plans, and pay particular attention to the plans offered through your state.

Savingforcollege.com has a proprietary *5-Cap Rating* system it uses to evaluate and rate all 529 plans offered. The site also allows you to perform side-by-side comparisons of any 529 plans that you may be interested in, based on criteria that are important to you.

529 Plans are considered assets of the parent when determining financial aid eligibility.

UTMA/UGMA (Uniform Transfer to Minors / Uniform Gifts to Minors)

With the other education savings plans available today, I find no use for UTMA/UGMA accounts. With the 1986 tax law changes, the advantages of these accounts became extremely minimal — too minimal, in my opinion, for parents to give up the control of the assets — they have "gifted" the money to the child when opening the account. These accounts are not tax-deferred or tax-free education savings plans, and they pale in comparison to the Section 529 or Education Savings Accounts now available.

Series EE and I Savings Bonds

You can purchase up to $30,000 (face amount) of either Series EE or Series I Savings Bonds per year. You can purchase savings bonds, which are issued by the U.S. government, through local banks or through Treasury Direct (www.savingsbonds.gov) for as little as $25. Savings bonds may appeal to you if you're looking for a very low-risk investment. The current yield on savings bonds is 3.4 percent per year.

You receive no tax deduction for making this investment; however, the interest on these bonds is tax-free if the bonds are redeemed to pay for qualified education expenses and your income doesn't exceed the federal limitations in the year of redemption.

Checking into Financial Aid

Before you decide to skip this section — say you're presuming that your child won't qualify for financial aid — I encourage you to reconsider. Federal financial aid programs are intended to make up the difference between what your family can afford to pay and what college costs, and is available to virtually everyone. However, you may feel that your income or assets level is too high, and your child isn't eligible for financial aid, but most Americans do qualify for financial aid in some way, shape, or form.

Who decides how much your family is able to pay? The amount you're expected to be able to pay is referred to as the *expected family contribution,* or *EFC.* The federal government and college financial aid officers use needs-based formulas that analyze your family's financial circumstances.

The federal guidelines not only take into account your income and assets, but also consider the size of your family and the number of your family members in college. Although your child may not qualify for *grants* (money that doesn't have to be repaid) or the most attractive financial aid possible, she likely will need to go through the financial aid application process (submitting the Free Application for Federal Student Aid [FAFSA] application) and be turned down before she can apply for other financing. And you definitely will qualify for the Federal PLUS loan mentioned earlier in this chapter, presuming your credit is okay.

To obtain an estimate of what your expected family contribution would be, visit www.collegeboard.com and use its EFC calculator. Working through the College Board's EFC calculator only takes a few minutes, and it gives you valuable feedback regarding what to anticipate as your EFC. You can then plan how to best cover that amount by using one of the many funding options described in the section "Thinking about Education Savings Vehicles," earlier in this chapter. In order to complete this calculation, you need all the documents in Worksheet 10-8.

Worksheet 10-8   Data You Need to Calculate EFC

❏ Prior year tax returns for parents and student

❏ Recent paycheck stubs for parents and student

❏ Confirmation of any Social Security benefits received by parents or student

❏ Statement illustrating balance in Medical Spending Account of parents

❏ Statement illustrating any child support paid by parents

❏ Amount of any work-study earnings or financial aid received by student

❏ List of medical and dental expenses for the preceding year

❏ Bank account statements for both parents and student

❏ Listing of assets owned (in the name of) student's siblings

❏ Fair market value of parent's residence less outstanding mortgage(s)

❏ Listing of other real estate and investments owned by parents or student (excluding assets in qualified retirement plans, annuities, and life insurance)

❏ Fair market value of equity in any business owned by parents or student

❏ Fair market value of equity in farm owned by parents or student

❏ Value of any assets held in trust for student

After calculating your EFC, you may want to take a look at your options regarding federal student loans. With all loans, one of the primary issues you need to consider is the cost of the loan — specifically the interest and any loan acquisition fees. The least expensive loan is generally the one with the lowest interest rate. With the federal student aid programs, the cheapest loans are as follows:

✔ **Perkins loans** have the strictest needs-based requirements. A student may borrow up to $4,000 per year. The current interest rate is 5 percent, and payments don't commence until the student graduates.

✔ **Subsidized Stafford loans** are also needs-based loans. A student may borrow up to $2,625 in the first year of undergraduate studies, $3,500 in year two, and $5,500 in years three through five. As of the writing of this book, the interest rate is 6.8 percent per year. However, the federal government actually pays the interest due on the loan until the student is required to begin making payments six months after graduation. The loan must be repaid over ten years.

✔ **Unsubsidized Stafford loans** are *not* needs-based loans. The amount that may be borrowed is identical to the Subsidized Stafford loan program if the student is your dependent. However, if your student is independent, he may borrow up to $4,000 in each of the first two years of his undergraduate program and up to $5,000 in years three through five. The interest rate on this type of loan is also 6.8 percent per year, as of the writing of this book. However, the federal government doesn't pay any of this interest on behalf of the student. Repayment begins six months after graduation, and the loan must be repaid over ten years.

TIP

To get the most recent interest rates on student loans and detailed instructions about how to obtain these loans, visit the College Board's Web site at www.CollegeBoard.com.

Chapter 11

Saving for Retirement

- -

In This Chapter

▶ Determining what matters most in retirement

▶ Estimating how much money you'll need

▶ Maximizing your retirement savings strategies

- -

*P*icturing yourself in retirement may be difficult at this time in your life. Retirement may feel so many years away that you can't even fathom the idea of ever being able to retire. Or possibly you're middle-aged and feel that retiring someday is completely impossible. However, I doubt you'd be investing the time reading this chapter if you'd given up all hope.

I've also met a lot of people who don't resonate with the concept or word *retirement*. So, for the sake of our conversation on this subject, I would like you to think of *financial freedom* or *financial independence* as synonymous with the word *retirement*. Many people have absolutely no desire to stop working. However, those same people are looking for financial freedom and financial independence. They want to be able to choose what they do, when they do it, and for how long. You may be one of these people.

Every financial situation that I've encountered can be improved with proper planning. I'm confident that by working through this chapter, your sense of what you need to do to achieve financial independence will become an empowering force in your life. Unfortunately, you can't find any financial aid for retirement. However, that doesn't mean that you don't have substantial options. And fortunately, those options aren't nearly as complex as federal financial aid programs (see Chapter 10).

When it comes to retirement planning, you have the following four options:

✔ Spend less now and save more.

✔ Get better net, after-tax returns on your investments.

✔ Work longer.

✔ Die earlier (but that's not really a planning strategy I can recommend!)

To some degree or another, you have influence over the first three variables. In this chapter, I illustrate how these options impact your retirement objectives. For many people, the most palatable retirement solution involves a combination of all three of the variables mentioned.

Figuring Out What Matters Most in Your Retirement

The first step in retirement planning is to determine what matters most to you and your spouse or partner, if applicable. In Chapter 4, you may have already done a great deal of exploration and prioritization of your financial goals. However, in this section, I focus exclusively on the subject of your retirement.

Spend a moment now, reflect on your lifestyle in retirement, and think about how it will change from the lifestyle you enjoy today. Worksheet 11-1 is an example. As you ponder the subject of retirement, ask yourself these questions and use Worksheet 11-2 to notate your reflections:

- ✔ What are you doing?
- ✔ Where are you living?
- ✔ What activities are you enjoying?
- ✔ How do you spend your time?

Worksheet 11-1   What Retirement Looks Like to Me (Example)

My house will be paid off. I'll have much more time to pursue my hobbies and interests, which are traveling, seeing the world, and participating in the causes about which I feel strongly. I want to make sure that I have adequate healthcare and insurance. I need security. I want to spend a lot of time and money exploring the world for the first few years of my retirement. And I want to learn — about everything. I want people to know me by name at the library. I want to be involved and productive for as long as I can. I plan to garden, ride my bike to the market, spend time with friends, and possibly take up yoga and/or the piano. I want to be able to travel to see my grandkids frequently.

Worksheet 11-2   What Retirement Looks Like to Me

_____

_____

_____

_____

As you reflected on your lifestyle in retirement, you likely listed a lot of issues that involve money — maybe earning money and definitely spending money to support your desired lifestyle in retirement. This information is necessary to determine how much money you'll need in retirement and how much you'll need to save to achieve financial independence.

Calculating How Much You'll Need to Retire

If you're wondering how much money you need to retire, the quick answer that most financial advisors would tell you is 60 to 80 percent of your final working years' income to maintain your standard of living after retirement. That may or may not be representative of how you'd like to enjoy your retirement, but it's a starting place.

Take a closer look at how your monthly budget will change in retirement. You need to determine for yourself, based on what matters most to you (see preceding section), just how much money you'll need each month to have the retirement that you've dreamed of.

Take a look at an example monthly retirement budget in Worksheet 11-3. This example illustrates a monthly cash flow need in retirement of about 74 percent of this person's current budget.

Worksheet 11-3   Your Monthly Retirement Budget (Example)

Fixed Expenses	Currently	At Retirement
Mortgage or rent	$900	$0
Second mortgage or HELOC	225	0
Homeowners association dues	20	20
Homeowners insurance	85	85
Real estate taxes	200	200
Property taxes	60	60
Auto payment or escrow*	500	500
Auto insurance	140	140
Health insurance	0	600
Disability insurance	100	0
Utilities:		
Electric	100	100
Gas	50	50
Water	30	30
Trash	0	0
Cable	0	80
Phone	0	50
Other debts	0	0
Variable Expenses		
Personal maintenance		
Healthcare or prescriptions	400	600
Personal supplies or care	100	100
Home and auto maintenance	500	500
Gasoline, parking, and tolls	140	40
Groceries	280	280
Dining out	100	50
School or work lunches	40	0

Entertainment	50	500
Vacations or travel	250	833
Holidays or gifts	183	183
Books, magazines, or music	25	15
Sports, hobbies, or clubs	167	83
Child or pet care	100	20
Dry cleaning and clothing	250	20
Domestic help or lawn service	200	0
Charitable contributions	200	500
Retirement savings	2000	0
College savings	250	0

Totals

$ _____ 5,639 _____ $ _____ 7,645 _____

*As long as youíre driving, you're going to have this expense. You either need to be making car payments or saving up for the next car for as long as you drive.

What does this budget in Worksheet 11-3 tell you about this person's lifestyle in retirement? Consider the following observations:

✔ This person's home is paid for at retirement, but the insurance and taxes don't go away.

✔ Health insurance that was once provided by the employer is now the retiree's responsibility. Ouch!

✔ The retiree has no need to pay for disability insurance after retiring because the income she was insuring is gone.

✔ Cable and phone bills paid by the employer transfer to the retiree.

✔ Healthcare and prescription drug costs go up substantially; however gasoline, commuting expenses, clothing, and dry cleaning costs drop significantly after retirement.

✔ Dining out and school lunches go down, but vacations, traveling, entertainment, and charitable contributions are up drastically.

✔ The retiree in this example does his own lawn and home care.

✔ By the time of retirement, no additional retirement savings are necessary, and college savings are also funded.

Not only will the retiree in Worksheet 11-3 be able to sustain his standard of living in retirement, but he will also have money to do the things that matter most to him. However, be sure to note that this person currently has a mortgage payment and a home equity line of credit (HELOC) and is saving $2,000 per month for retirement, which is the primary reason for the reduced need in retirement.

Check out your retirement income needs as a percentage of your current cost of living by using Worksheet 11-4.

Worksheet 11-4   **Your Monthly Retirement Budget**

Fixed Expenses	Currently	At Retirement
Mortgage or rent	_____	_____
Second mortgage or HELOC	_____	_____
Homeowners association dues	_____	_____
Homeowners insurance	_____	_____
Real estate taxes	_____	_____
Property taxes	_____	_____
Auto payment or escrow*	_____	_____
Auto insurance	_____	_____
Health insurance	_____	_____
Disability insurance	_____	_____
Utilities:		
Electric	_____	_____
Gas	_____	_____
Water	_____	_____
Trash	_____	_____
Cable	_____	_____
Phone	_____	_____
Other debts	_____	_____

Variable Expenses

Personal maintenance

    Healthcare or prescriptions   _____   _____

    Personal supplies or care   _____   _____

Home and auto maintenance   _____   _____

Gasoline, parking, and tolls   _____   _____

Groceries   _____   _____

Dining out   _____   _____

School or work lunches   _____   _____

Entertainment   _____   _____

Vacations or travel   _____   _____

Holidays or gifts   _____   _____

Books, magazines, or music   _____   _____

Sports, hobbies, or clubs   _____   _____

Child or pet care   _____   _____

Dry cleaning and clothing   _____   _____

Domestic help or lawn service   _____   _____

Charitable contributions   _____   _____

Retirement savings   _____   _____

College savings   _____   _____

Totals

$ _____ $ _____

*As long as you're driving, you're going to have this expense. You either need to be making car payments or saving up for the next car for as long as you drive.

Divide total expenses in the At Retirement column by the total expenses in the Currently column to determine the percentage of current income you need in retirement to maintain you standard of living. Write your percentage here:

_____ %

What does this budget tell you about your lifestyle in retirement? Does it jive with what matters most to you, which you explore in the first section in this chapter? Using Worksheet 11-5, share your observations about what matters most in your life based on what the numbers in Worksheet 11-4 tell you. If you don't feel that what matters most for your retirement is reflected in your monthly retirement budget from Worksheet 11-4, can you adjust or rearrange any of the expenses to better reflect your priorities and values?

Worksheet 11-5   My Reflections about My Retirement Lifestyle

Thinking about Other Retirement Income

All your retirement income may not have to come from your savings alone, which I discuss in the next section. Do you have a company pension, did someone leave a bunch of money in a trust fund for you, or are you eligible for and planning to receive Social Security? If so, you need to factor in this additional income as well as the income that can be produced off of your current retirement savings.

Social Security represents only about 40 percent of the average retiree's income needs. And most observers feel that something drastic must occur now, or the Social Security system will be broke in 20 to 40 years. Tack on 20 to 40 years to your current age. Are you still going to be around and depending on Social Security when you're least able to be without it? Also, very few people now have old-fashioned defined-benefit pension plans. The responsibility of providing for your retirement is mostly or entirely up to you.

For my planning purposes, I assume that people under age 40 won't receive any Social Security retirement benefits. For people between the ages of 40 and 60, I feel that it is appropriate to discount the amount of Social Security benefits that they're expecting to receive by 50 percent. I also project life expectancy to age 100 minimum. Hopefully, I'm being extremely prudent with my estimates, but the last thing I want is for you to wake up broke.

Worksheet 11-6 helps you estimate the Social Security retirement benefit you're projected to receive. Find your current annual earnings in the left column and then the monthly projected benefit based on your year of birth. Keep in mind that you likely should reduce the estimated amount or completely ignore Social Security in your retirement planning.

Worksheet 11-6   Estimated Social Security Retirement Benefits

Social Security Retirement Benefits

Monthly Projected Benefit - Based Upon 2007 Calculations

Current Annual Earnings	Year Of Birth			
	1945	1946-50	1951-55	1956-60
7,000-13,000	567	588	615	631
14,000-20,000	737	749	770	797
21,000-27,000	879	896	925	964
28,000-34,000	1,020	1,042	1,080	1,130
35,000-42,000	1,172	1,199	1,246	1,308
43,000-50,000	1,333	1,366	1,423	1,497
51,000-58,000	1,495	1,534	1,600	1,687
59,000-66,000	1,656	1,701	1,739	1,786
67,000-74,000	1,755	1,779	1,822	1,875
75,000-82,000	1,824	1,855	1,905	1,964
83,000-90,000	1,895	1,932	1,988	2,053
91,000-97,500	1,965	2,005	2,068	2,139

	Year Of Birth			
	1961-65	1966-70	1971-75	1976-80
7,000-13,000	643	652	659	660
14,000-20,000	818	834	845	847
21,000-27,000	992	1,015	1,031	1,034
28,000-34,000	1,167	1,196	1,217	1,220
35,000-42,000	1,354	1,390	1,416	1,420
43,000-50,000	1,553	1,597	1,628	1,634
51,000-58,000	1,728	1,752	1,769	1,772
59,000-66,000	1,821	1,849	1,869	1,872
67,000-74,000	1,915	1,946	1,968	1,972
75,000-82,000	2,008	1,043	2,068	2,072
83,000-90,000	2,102	2,140	2,167	2,172
91,000-97,500	2,192	2,234	2,263	2,269

Explanation: The indicated retirement benefits are at the worker's normal retirement age (gradually increasing to age 67 by 2022).

Calculations reflect the midpoint of the indicated range. For example, the $1,497 monthly retirement benefit (right column under 1956-60 heading) is based upon $46,500 of Current Annual Earnings (midpoint of 43,000 - $50,000) and a 1958 Year Of Birth (midpoint of 1956-60). The underlying AIME assumptions used to calculate these retirement benefits (the PIAs) are based upon the AIMEs set forth in the 2007 National Underwriter Social Security Slide-O-Scope & Planner. These AIME amounts are approximate and are based upon the assumption that the worker has had 6% pay raises each year through 2007.

Determining Your Savings Requirements

After you determine how much income you need on a monthly basis in retirement, you can determine how much money you need to save to pull this off. Like it or not, you're responsible for accumulating all or the majority of the money needed to support yourself in retirement. Most people aren't saving nearly enough — and you may be one of these people. Nearly 50 percent of all workers saving for retirement have accumulated less than $25,000. Something has got to give. Either you need to increase your saving substantially or work longer (maybe both!). You can have the most impact on your retirement finances by adjusting these two variables.

Worksheet 11-7 provides the computation to help you determine how much money you need to accumulate to provide for your living expenses in retirement. Refer to Worksheet 11-8 for factors needed in this computation.

Worksheet 11-7   How Much Money Do I Need to Retire?

1. **Estimate your final salary by multiplying your current salary by the inflation factor in Worksheet 11-8 based on the number of years you have until retirement.** For example, if you're currently making $50,000 per year and plan to retire in 20 years, your formula is $50,000 × 1.81 = $90,500. In other words, by the time you retire, it will take over $90,000 to buy what $50,000 does today because of inflation.

   Current Salary $_____ × (inflation factor) _____ = _____
   Final Annual Salary

2. **Multiply this Final Annual Salary number times the percentage of your current income you determined in Worksheet 11-4 that you will need in retirement.**

   If, for example, your final salary computed to be $90,500, and the current income percentage you determined in Worksheet 11-4 was 74 percent ($90,500 × 0.74), you need $66,970. You can go ahead and round that number out to $67,000 per year needed in retirement.

   Final Annual Salary $_____ × (percentage) _____ = _____
   Annual Income Needed in Retirement

3. **Reduce the Annual Retirement Income number you determined in Step 2 by the amount you will receive from guaranteed sources, such as company pension, Veteran's pension, Social Security, an immediate annuity, and so on.**

   Refer to Figure 11-6 for an estimate of your Social Security benefit if you don't happen to have a recent Benefit Estimate Statement from the Social Security Administration. If you do, use those numbers instead.

   Presume for this example that you will receive $1,800 a month in guaranteed income. You need $67,000 per year in income. However, Social Security should provide $21,600 of the total income you need, leaving a balance of $45,400 per year to be covered by savings.

   Total Retirement Income Needed $_____ , less guaranteed income of $ _____ equals $ _____ per year.

4. **Calculate the amount that you'll need from your savings by multiplying your net retirement income need in Step 3 by 20.**

   Example: $45,400 net retirement income need × 20 = $908,000.

   Net retirement income need $_____ × 20 = $_____

5. **Take into account your current savings for retirement by multiplying the balance in your retirement account by the growth factor illustrated in Worksheet 11-8; this number is what your retirement nest egg should be worth at your target retirement date.**

   For example, if your current savings for retirement is $115,000 × growth factor of 3.87, $445,050 is available at retirement from growth on current savings.

   Current savings for retirement $_____ × (growth factor) _____ = $ _____ available at retirement

6. If your result in Step 5 is less than the result in Step 4, you need to save more to achieve your retirement income objective. Continue on to Step 7. Otherwise, you just keep on saving your current amount!

7. Subtract your result from Step 5 from your result in Step 4 to determine the remaining capital you need.

Example: $908,000 minus $445,050 = $462,950 additional retirement funds needed.

Result from Step 4 $_____ minus result from Step 5 $_____ equals $_____ , which is the additional amount you need to accumulate between now and your retirement date to achieve your objective.

8. Divide your required additional funds (from Step 7) by the multiplier in Worksheet 11-8 to determine the approximate amount of money you need to save each and every year to achieve your retirement objective.

Example: $462,950 divided by 41.00 = $11,291 required annual retirement savings

Additional funds needs $_____ divided by (multiplier factor) _____ = $_____ requirement annual retirement savings.

Worksheet 11-8	Factors in Saving for Retirement		
Years to Retirement	*Inflation Factor**	*Growth Factor**	*Multiplier*
5	1.16	1.40	5.75
10	1.34	1.97	13.82
15	1.56	2.76	25.13
20	1.81	3.87	41.00
25	2.10	5.43	63.25
30	2.43	7.61	94.46
35	2.81	10.68	138.24

* Assumes 3% annual inflation and a 7% annual return on investment.

Discovering the Best Ways for You to Save for Retirement

You can use many options to save for retirement. However, these vehicles aren't created equal. The following is a listing of my preferred retirement savings vehicles and the order in which I recommend you fund these options. Should you fulfill your savings requirement before you reach the end of the list, wonderful!

1. **Make use of your 401(k) or 403(b) plans.**

If you have a 401(k) or 403 (b) plan through your employer and your employer provides a matching contribution, I suggest that you first fund this account up to the limits of the matching contribution. For example, say that your employer matches 50 cents on every dollar that you contribute to your 401(k), up to 6 percent of your annual salary. Your salary of $50,000 x 0.06 (amount matched) equals an annual contribution of $3,000; plus, you'll receive another $1,500 from your employer matching contribution, giving you a total of $4,500 per year.

By participating in your qualified retirement plan at work and receiving a matching contribution from your employer, you're receiving a guaranteed rate of return of no less than 50 percent per year.

Based on the annual saving requirement of $7,687, which I calculate in the example in Worksheet 11-7, you still need to save an additional $3,187 per year for retirement.

2. **Check into a Roth IRA.**

   The Roth IRA is one of the most underappreciated and underused retirement vehicles available today. Everyone who qualifies to make a Roth IRA contribution and still needs to save for retirement should do so by utilizing a Roth.

   To qualify to make a Roth IRA contribution, individual taxpayers must have an adjusted gross income of less than $99,000 per year. That number increases to $156,000 per year for taxpayers filing jointly.

   You receive no tax deduction by contributing to a Roth IRA account; however, all earnings accumulate on a tax-deferred basis, and all withdrawals taken out during retirement are tax-free. You never have to pay tax on the earnings in this account.

   For example, if you currently make $50,000 per year, you are eligible to make a Roth IRA contribution. The maximum amount you can contribute to a Roth IRA account for 2007 is $4,000 if you're under 50 years of age and $5,000 if you're 50 or above. Regardless of your age, you should be able to fully fund your retirement savings requirement by contributing up to the matching amount in your 401(k) plan and making up the balance of your required contribution into a Roth IRA account.

3. **If you still need to save additional funds for your retirement, and you have money left over to save, consider the following options, depending on your individual circumstances:**

   - Option A: If you haven't yet built up a personal portfolio in your own name, invest in low-cost, tax-efficient vehicles such as *no-load index mutual funds* or *exchange-traded funds* (more on the specifics of these vehicles in Chapter 14). I strongly encourage you to consider accumulating money in your own name utilizing these tax-efficient options.

   - Option B: If you already have accumulated a fairly reasonable personal portfolio and feel comfortable that you have enough accessible funds in the case of an emergency, I suggest that you continue to fund your 401(k) or 403(b) plan beyond the matching contribution to fulfill the amount needed to fully fund your retirement savings.

 If you happen to be one of those extremely rare individuals who has already maxed out your contribution limits to your 401(k) plan and the Roth IRA, if eligible, the next best place for your money, in my opinion, is in your personal portfolio. You want to invest this money in the most low-cost and tax-efficient manner. I explain how to achieve these investment objectives in Chapter 14.

Utilize Worksheet 11-9 to help you allocate your annual required retirement savings contribution among the best retirement investment vehicles available to you today.

Worksheet 11-9   Retirement Savings Implementation Strategy

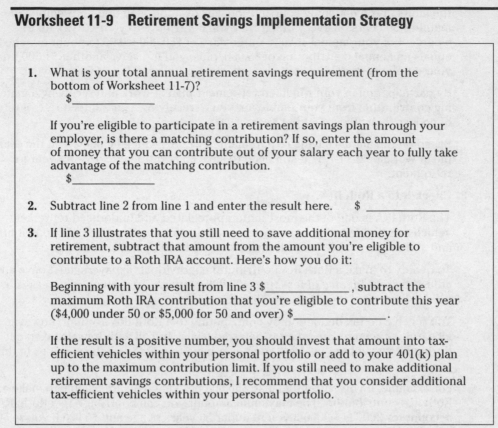

1. What is your total annual retirement savings requirement (from the bottom of Worksheet 11-7)?

   $_____

   If you're eligible to participate in a retirement savings plan through your employer, is there a matching contribution? If so, enter the amount of money that you can contribute out of your salary each year to fully take advantage of the matching contribution.

   $_____

2. Subtract line 2 from line 1 and enter the result here. $_____

3. If line 3 illustrates that you still need to save additional money for retirement, subtract that amount from the amount you're eligible to contribute to a Roth IRA account. Here's how you do it:

   Beginning with your result from line 3 $_____ , subtract the maximum Roth IRA contribution that you're eligible to contribute this year ($4,000 under 50 or $5,000 for 50 and over) $_____ .

   If the result is a positive number, you should invest that amount into tax-efficient vehicles within your personal portfolio or add to your 401(k) plan up to the maximum contribution limit. If you still need to make additional retirement savings contributions, I recommend that you consider additional tax-efficient vehicles within your personal portfolio.

Chapter 12

Thinking about When You're Gone: Estate Planning

In This Chapter

▶ Quantifying your gross estate

▶ Factoring in estate taxes

▶ Exploring your legacy and personal goals

▶ Determining the best estate-planning options

You may think that you don't care what happens after you're gone. But what about the family, friends, and stuff you leave behind? Do you care if the most important person in your life receives anything you may have of value, or are you okay with having the state decide how to divvy up your stuff? Who's going to go through your underwear drawer? Who will care for your beloved cat or, more importantly, your dependent children?

Estate planning is all about what you want to have happen to you, your dependents, and your stuff when you're gone. Estate planning also covers what happens if you're alive, but can't make decisions for yourself.

In this chapter, I show you why estate planning is so important and outline strategies you can implement to make certain that your needs are met and your wishes are carried out in the event of your death or incapacity.

 I'm not an estate-planning attorney. The information and suggestions provided in this chapter are for your education and empowerment. I encourage you to consult with a qualified estate-planning attorney to make certain that your wishes will be carried out in the manner that would be most efficient and effective for your goals.

For a more detailed discussion, check out *Estate Planning For Dummies* (Wiley) by N. Brian Caverly and Jordan S. Simon.

Calculating Your Gross Estate

The first thing you need to do when planning your estate is to calculate your gross estate. Then you can employ different estate planning strategies based on the size and composition of your estate. If you already completed Worksheet 2-3 in Chapter 2, enter your Net Worth total in Step 1. Otherwise, determine your gross estate by flipping over to Chapter 2 and completing Worksheet 2-3; then you can return to this chapter and finish the exercise in Worksheet 12-1.

Worksheet 12-1   **Calculating Your Gross Estate**

1. **If you haven't already, complete the Statement of Financial Net Worth Worksheet from Chapter 2 and input your Net Worth here $_____.**

2. **List all investments that you may own an interest in and their approximate values, if these assets aren't listed on Worksheet 2-3.**

   Asset   **Your Share**

   $ _____   _____

   $ _____   _____

   $ _____   _____

   $ _____   _____

   $ _____   _____

3. **List all the life insurance on your life:**

   Personally owned $_____

   Employer provided $_____

   Association / Credit Union $_____

   Military / Government $_____

   Social Security $_____255____

   Total of Life Insurance $_____

4. **Add your Net Worth from Step 1, plus the amounts from Steps 2 and 3 to calculate your Gross Estate and enter the total here.**

                              Total Gross Estate $_____

The number you came up with for your gross estate is probably a bigger number than you were expecting. That number represents, for most people, the *stuff* you need to figure out what to do with, and your estate plan tells the world what you want to happen to your *stuff* when you die.

Thinking about Estate Taxes

You may be one of the few people whose estate would have to pay federal *gift* or *estate taxes*, meaning that some of the "stuff" listed in the preceding section may end up going to Uncle Sam. How do you know if you're in that situation?

Worksheet 12-2 lists the amount of an estate that you can die with and not have to pay taxes. Remember that the figures listed in Worksheet 12-2 are accurate at the time this book is printed, but are subject to change. For the most up-to-date tax rates and exemption amounts, visit www.IRS.gov or contact an estate-planning attorney.

If your gross taxable estate happens to be less than the exemption amount for the current year or if you're married and plan to leave everything or all but the exemption amount to your spouse, no estate tax would be due. The same thing is true if you leave these assets to a qualifying charity.

Husbands and wives can transfer assets to each other during life and at death. You have no limits or taxes on this transfer. For example, if you marry or remarry a person who owns a home in his or her name individually, that home can be retitled into joint ownership. Your spouse would legally be giving you one half of the value of the home. No gift or estate transfer tax would be due because this transfer is made between a married couple.

If you transfer assets to anyone other than your spouse or if you don't have a spouse, those transfers are subject not only to estate taxation, but potentially state inheritance taxation as well. To avoid taxes on your estate, you could pass all or enough of your assets to a qualifying charity. (Enough would be any amount of assets over the exemption amount listed on the following worksheet.) If you find yourself in this situation, you have wonderful planning opportunities available to you, and I suggest that you consult with a qualified estate-planning attorney immediately if you don't have a current estate plan in place.

Worksheet 12-2	Exemption Amounts for Estate Tax	
Year	*Exemption Amount*	*Tax Rates on Amounts in Excess*
2007	$2,000,000	45%
2008	$2,000,000	45%
2009	$3,500,000	45%
2010	Unlimited	Not applicable

Identifying Your Legacy Goals and Personal Desires

If you worked through the previous sections, you likely discovered that you actually do have something of value that you would like to leave to people or causes that you feel strongly about. You have many different ways that you can go about making this happen (see the next section). In this section, I want you to focus on who or what causes you would like to provide some consideration for in the event of your death.

To get a better idea of what I'm talking about, take this example into consideration: Tom is currently not married and doesn't have any children. His parents are okay financially; however, his three siblings aren't as comfortable. Tom would like to leave some money to his siblings and also to one of his nieces. He doesn't have any desire to leave them a large windfall, but he would like to leave them something. Tom is thinking about giving $25,000 to each of his siblings and $10,000 to his niece to help her pay for college. He'd also like to leave $5,000 each to his two best friends. Whatever money is left over he'd like to go to the charitable organization, Operation Wildlife.

Worksheet 12-3 gives you the opportunity to think about and list who or what organizations you would like to leave your legacy. List names of people or organizations who you would like to receive a gift or inheritance upon your death. Also, include dollar amounts or percentages of your estate with the name of each recipient. In the event that you have any special requests or restrictions, also indicate those details. The information you provide in Worksheet 12-3 is essential to determining how best to implement your estate plan and fulfill your personal objectives.

| **Worksheet 12-3** | **Your Legacy Goals** |

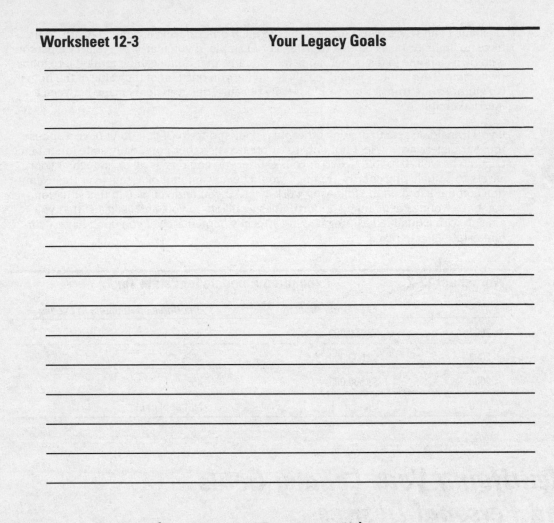

Figuring Out the Best Estate Planning Options for You

Estate planning provides not only for the efficient and effective transfer of assets at your death, but also for the instructions regarding the management of your financial affairs and the making of healthcare decisions if you're unable to do so for yourself.

The most common techniques employed by people to transfer assets upon their death are titling assets as

- ✔ **Joint tenants with right of survivorship:** Most average Americans own a home with their spouse, and the house is registered in joint tenancy with right of survivorship. They may also own personal investments, such as brokerage or mutual fund accounts titled with their spouse as joint tenants with rights of survivorship. This ownership type allows you to co-own assets with another person, and upon the first death, 100 percent of the asset transfers to the co-owner automatically, avoiding probate.

- ✔ **Beneficiary designations:** You may have a retirement plan at work, life insurance, and possibly an IRA account or two, all of which have beneficiary designations. A beneficiary designation instructs the retirement plan sponsor, investment account custodian, or the insurance company as to who is to receive the assets upon your death. Assets and insurance policies with beneficiary designations also avoid probate.

✔ **A will:** A *will* is a legal document that allows you to dictate in writing what you want to happen with your assets and who will care for your dependents upon your death. You can obtain a will from an attorney who specializes in estate planning, with off-the-shelf software programs, or from online resources like http://Nolo.com. A will becomes effective through the probate court process.

All assets that transfer by title or beneficiary designation upon death avoid probate. *Probate* is the legal process of settling an estate. However, it can be expensive and time-consuming. You can reduce probate fees and potentially save time by having as many assets as possible pass to your heirs through joint tenancy with rights of survivorship and by using beneficiary designations as much as possible. All other assets that don't transfer by title or beneficiary designation, such as personal property, vehicles, and your baseball card collection, need to be addressed in your will.

Worksheet 12-4 outlines the basic asset transfer techniques and options, including the most common ones.

Worksheet 12-4	Assets Transfer Strategies	
Subject	**Avoids Probate**	**Avoids Estate Tax**
Joint tenancy with right of survivorship	Yes	No
Tenants in common	No	No
Beneficiary designations	Yes	No
Transfer on death designations	Yes	No
Payable on death designations	Yes	No
Will	No	No
Revocable living trust	Yes	No
Irrevocable trust	Yes	Yes

In my opinion, the most critical (but not the only) reason why you need a will is to name the guardians for your minor children, presuming that you have minor children. Not only do you want to consider who should be the caretakers of your children while they are minors, but also, who should take care of the money for your children until they reach adulthood? You don't want to leave this issue for the state to determine.

Many people die without having executed a will. (*Executing* a will is the official term for having a written will properly signed, witnessed, and notarized.) In that case, your state of residence dictates how your assets will be distributed and who would be responsible for caring for your minor children. I think it's safe to assume that your desires will be different than what your state law would dictate. Don't take chances, especially with minor children. If you don't have a will, get one immediately!

I often find that the best caregivers aren't necessarily the best money managers, so I encourage you to consider who would be the best caregivers and who would be the best money managers for the assets you leave in trust to your children. The first part of Worksheet 12-5 provides you an opportunity to list the individuals that you would like to consider as primary caregivers for your children, if you (and your spouse, if applicable) are gone. The second part of Worksheet 12-5 asks you to consider who you would like to care for your children's money.

Worksheet 12-5   **Guardians of the Children and Their Money**

First Choice for Caregivers

_____

_____

_____

Second Choice for Caregivers

_____

_____

_____

Third Choice for Caregivers

_____

_____

_____

First Choice for Money Managers

_____

_____

_____

Second Choice for Money Managers

_____

_____

_____

Third Choice for Money Managers

_____

_____

_____

You may be wondering why I've provided three different choices for each caregiver and money manager. The reason is simple! Circumstances can change, and your first choice may no longer be qualified per your requests in your will, or they may be unwilling or unable to serve.

For example, imagine you die while your children are still in school. Your first choice of caregiver may be your sister; however, she lives halfway across the country. Upon your death, your children would not only be traumatized by the loss of their parent, but also be faced with having to re-establish themselves in a new home, with new friends and a new school. Maybe keeping your children in the same town or neighborhood where you currently live is very important to you, so you may choose to designate another family member or close friend as guardian.

Using beneficiary designations

You may be able to accomplish your asset-transfer objectives very simply through the proper use of beneficiary designations. You're likely familiar with beneficiary designations on life insurance policies, 401(k) plan assets, and IRA accounts, but you may not be aware that you can designate beneficiaries on other types of assets as well.

You may establish a *transfer on death* (TOD) or *payable on death* (POD) beneficiary designation on your bank accounts. This same type of beneficiary designation is also available with many brokerage accounts. Contact your brokerage company to establish a beneficiary designation on your personal account.

In a few states, you can have a beneficiary designation on your personal property and real estate. Contact your county's registrar of deeds office to find out whether this option is allowable and to figure out the process to register your beneficiary designation on personal property and real estate.

If you own assets titled joint tenants with right of survivorship, that account already has the equivalent of a beneficiary designation. Your joint owner will inherit 100 percent of the asset balance upon your death automatically.

Assets that transfer to your heirs automatically upon your death aren't subject to the terms of your will. The ownership of the account (joint tenants with right of survivorship) or the beneficiary designation takes precedence over your will. Those assets will be transferred directly to recipients without going through a long, tedious, and expensive probate process. Your will actually doesn't become effective until it has been entered into probate. The probate process typically takes 9 to 24 months to complete. By structuring your assets to minimize the number of items and total dollar value of assets that have to go through probate, you will save your *executor* (the one who you assign in your will to do this time-consuming, thankless job) a lot of time and your estate a lot of money.

Titling property joint tenants with right of survivorship and establishing beneficiary designations are the two most common probate-avoidance techniques. The third is a revocable living trust.

Considering a living trust

A *living trust* is a legal document created by you (the grantor) during your lifetime. Just as a will does, it spells out exactly what your desires are with regard to your assets, your dependents, and your heirs. The big difference is that a will only becomes effective after you die and your will has been entered into probate. A living trust bypasses the costly and time-consuming process of probate enabling your *successor trustee* (who fills basically the same role as an executor of a will) to carry out your instructions as documented in your living trust at your death, and also if you're unable to manage your financial, healthcare, and legal affairs due to incapacity.

Living trusts are available from estate planning attorneys, off-the-shelf software programs, and online resources, such as my suggestion for the do-it-yourselfer, `http://Nolo.com`.

A living trust is most appropriate for individuals who have complex financial or personal circumstances, such as substantial assets, a blended family, closely held business interests, or property in other states. If you have a complex situation or are uncomfortable trusting your personal knowledge and judgment with such important issues, I strongly recommend that you hire a qualified estate-planning attorney to draft this document. Yes, you'll spend more money, but you can rest assured knowing that your wishes will be carried out exactly as you desire.

A living trust can also be a very effective tool for an unmarried individual, regardless of financial situation, presuming that the individual's desires can't be fulfilled by utilizing beneficiary designations and the joint with rights of survivorship titling option and powers of attorney.

The two types of living trusts are as follows:

- ✔ **Revocable living trust:** With a revocable living trust, you transfer your assets into the ownership of the trust. You retain control of those assets as the trustee of your revocable living trust. You can change or revoke the trust at any time you want. The assets in the trust pass directly to your beneficiaries without going through probate upon your death. However, neither wills nor revocable living trusts avoid or minimize estate taxes. (For ways on how to avoid or minimize estate taxes, see the next item and section "Thinking about Estate Taxes," earlier in this chapter.)

- ✔ **Irrevocable living trust:** An irrevocable trust allows you to permanently and irrevocably give away your assets during your lifetime. After you give away these assets, you have relinquished all control and interest in these assets. Due to that fact, these assets are no longer considered part of your estate and aren't subject to estate taxes. As you likely imagine, an irrevocable trust is appropriate in only extremely rare circumstances, such as when you have more money than you or your spouse could ever use. Your beneficiaries would benefit at Uncle Sam's expense if you utilized an irrevocable trust to reduce your taxable estate before your death.

Living trusts (revocable or irrevocable) typically cost $1,000 to $3,000 per person.

Getting other important documents in order

Even with all your assets properly titled, your beneficiary designations in order, and a will or revocable living trust in place (see previous sections), you still have a few very important issues to take care of and documents to execute. For most people, the odds of becoming incapacitated are actually much higher than those of dying prematurely. You need some ancillary documents that address incapacity with regard to financial and medical decisions:

✔ **Financial power of attorney:** A financial power of attorney is a legal document that you need to complete your estate planning. This document generally should be drafted for you by a licensed attorney who specializes in estate planning. However, software programs are available, and you can find online providers of these documents as well. My preferred resource, if you don't use a qualified estate planning attorney, is the nation's premier legal resource for the do-it-yourselfer, http://Nolo.com.

This document enables you to appoint someone to make financial decisions and manage your financial affairs in the event that you can't make these decisions for yourself. I encourage you to not only select one individual as your financial power of attorney, but also select at least one successor, should your initial selection be unwilling or unable to perform these services.

✔ **Living will:** *A living will* spells out under what circumstances, if any, you want your life prolonged if you have no reasonable chance for recovery. This document is also available through estate-planning attorneys, Web sites such as http://Nolo.com, and from your local hospital. Keep in mind the forms available through the hospital are going to be very generic and likely not address some specific details that you may feel strongly about. At least with the forms from Nolo, you can tailor this document to your circumstances as best as you know how.

✔ **Durable power of attorney for healthcare:** This document is also part of a comprehensive estate planning package provided by any qualified estate planning attorney. You can able obtain this document from http://Nolo.com, or use the Five Wishes Brochure available through www.AgingWithDignity.org.

This document enables you to name a person, or possibly a couple of people, to make healthcare decisions if you're unable to make them for yourself.

✔ **Funeral instructions:** On a final note (no pun intended), I encourage you to write a letter spelling out your desires regarding your funeral arrangements. Rather than having your grieving loved ones wonder what you would have wanted, give them the gift of knowing your wishes in advance. Also be sure to tell them whether you have any prearranged or prepaid funeral plans and, if so, with whom. It'll help them out and likely save your estate a lot of money.

Unfortunately, funeral directors and their sales staff have been known to be very skillful in taking advantage of grieving people for their own financial gain. For example, if you don't specifically tell your family that you want them to keep your funeral service and burial services very modest, your heirs may follow the guidance of a skillful salesperson and spend thousands of dollars on stuff you never would have wanted.

Part IV
Building and Managing Wealth

The 5th Wave   By Rich Tennant

"I was so into my charts that one day she came in and told me she was running away with the pool boy. Now there's a trend I didn't see coming."

In this part . . .

1 help you determine how much risk you're willing to take by evaluating your current portfolio and needs. I also help you develop appropriate strategies for investing your hard-earned money to get the biggest bang for your buck without spending a lot of time researching, managing, and monitoring your investment portfolio.

Chapter 13

Evaluating Your Current Portfolio

. . . .

. . . .

*W*hether you have a substantial investment portfolio or haven't started investing yet, this chapter is for you. I cover the fundamental building blocks of an investment portfolio, addressing characteristics of primary asset classes, and help you explore in depth your tolerance for risk. Some asset classes, as well as a portfolio allocation, may be appropriate for you, but not for another investor, due to your personal objectives, your time horizon, and your tolerance for risk.

Evaluating Needs and Options for Cash Reserves

The concept of having money that you can get your hands on in a very short period of time so that you can cover several months' worth of your living expenses, if necessary, is a smart risk management and financial planning concept.

You never know when a catastrophe may strike. A catastrophe affects many aspects of our lives, both personally and financially. In nearly every event, money is part of the solution — sometimes the only solution. Imagine how losing your job or having a new job fall through, not being able to sell your house, having a major medical bill, or having a sick child or pet would impact your financial life. The purpose of having access to money at very short notice is to protect you as best as reasonably possible from risks that you can't afford to bear. (I talk more about managing risk in Chapter 15.)

Worksheet 13-1 provides a listing of the common and not-so-common sources of cash reserves that you could consider in the event of an emergency. Check the box at the left if that resource applies to you and then enter the approximate dollar amount accessible. Also note in the right-hand column how quickly those funds could be available to you.

Worksheet 13-1	Cash Reserve Options	
Resource	*Amount Accessible*	*When?*
❑ Cash on hand	$	Immediate
❑ Checking account	$	Immediate
❑ Savings account	$	Immediate
❑ Money market account	$	Immediate
❑ Home equity line of credit	$	Immediate*
❑ Credit-card cash advance	$	Immediate**
❑ Certificate of deposit	$	1 business day**
❑ Mutual fund investments	$	3 to 5 business days**
❑ Brokerage account	$	3 to 5 business days**
❑ Liquidating other investments	$	
❑ Borrowing from bank**	$	10 to 15 business days**
❑ Borrowing from family/friend	$	
❑ Borrowing from 401(k)	$	5 to 10 business days**
Total from all reliable sources	$	

*If you already have a home equity line of credit. However, if you're applying now, it may take three weeks. If you don't have any income and you try to obtain a home equity line of credit, you likely won't qualify.

**Significant fee, penalty, or potentially very inopportune time to borrow or sell.

The exercise in Worksheet 13-1 helps you explore all traditional avenues for raising cash. The total sum represents how much money would be accessible to you in the event of an emergency.

Now, refer to Worksheet 3-3. If you haven't had the opportunity to go through this worksheet, either do so now or give it your best guestimate. If you have already completed this exercise, list your actual total monthly expenses. Then divide that amount by the total cash you could raise, from all reliable sources at the same time, to reveal approximately how many months' worth of living expenses you can cover in the event of a catastrophe. How many months can you go without an income?

If you don't have six months or more coverage, you need to build up cash reserves in the types of accounts that are accessible within a short period of time, with little or no cost to access the funds.

You may also discover that most of the money you can get your hands on would cost you substantially more than you're comfortable paying or would potentially be very risky, and therefore, you decide that you need more money in safe, immediately available accounts.

You can't find one "right" answer for everybody. If you've worked for the federal government for 20 years, your income is considerably more predictable than a real estate agent's or a carpenter's income. The stability of your job, your income, your health, as well as your tolerance for risk, must all be taken into account to determine the "right" amount you should have in cash reserves. If in doubt, play it safe!

Discovering Your Tolerance for Risk

Determining risk tolerance is much more of an art than a science. When you think of risk in your investment portfolio, you may think of *volatility* (how much your investments go up and down). Most people do. However, *risk* is more accurately defined as the probability that you won't achieve your personal or financial objectives (which I discuss in Chapter 4).

Worksheet 13-2 contains a series of questions designed to help you identify just how much risk you're willing and able to take in order to achieve your objectives. Answer the questions and then reflect on your responses. What do they tell you about the amount of risk you can tolerate for any amount of time? If you aren't sure how to answer a particular question, check out Worksheet 13-3, which lists observations and potential conclusions that correspond to the eight risk tolerance questions, so that you can gauge or evaluate your answers.

Worksheet 13-2   **Risk Tolerance Questionnaire**

1. How would you define yourself as an investor? Pick all that apply.

   a. I'm swinging for the fences!

   b. I'm a solid base-hitter.

   c. I'm a switch-hitter.

   d. I've never held a bat.

Pick one answer for each of the following questions.

2. What amount of your portfolio could you tolerate losing in any given month?

   a. 0%

   b. 5%

   c. 10%

   d. 15%

   e. 20%

   f. More

3. What amount of your portfolio could you tolerate losing in any given year?

   a. 0%

   b. 5%

   c. 10%

   d. 15%

   e. 20%

   f. 30%

   g. 40%

   h. 50%

   i. 75%

   j. More

4. How much could you tolerate losing over five years?

   a. 0%

   b. 5%

   c. 10%

   d. 15%

   e. 20%

   f. More

5. How much money could you handle losing, in any given year?

   a. None

   b. Very minimal

   c. A minimal amount, if the opportunities appear certain

   d. A minimal amount, if the opportunities appear promising

   e. A substantial amount, if the opportunities appear certain

   f. A substantial amount, if the opportunities appear promising

6. What action would you take if the stock market dropped 25 percent from its present value next week?

   a. Nothing

   b. Sell everything I have left

   c. Invest all the cash I can raise into the stock market

   d. Borrow money to invest in the stock market

7. How many years of your financial independence or security are you willing to risk?

   a. None

   b. One

   c. Two

   d. Three

   e. Five

   f. Ten

   g. Whatever it takes (over ten)

8. Regarding your finances, what do you spend the most time thinking about?

   a. Will I have enough?

   b. How can I earn more on my investments?

   c. Could I be doing anything else smarter in regard to my personal finances?

Worksheet 13-3 Drawing Conclusions from the Risk Tolerance Questionnaire

1. How would you define yourself as an investor?

   a. Babe Ruth was the all-time home run hitter in baseball, but at the same time, he carried the record for strike-outs. An investor who identifies with a swingin'-for-the-fences mentality is likely a Babe Ruth–type of investor. When you're on, you're really on, but when you're off, you're off the charts. You have a stomach for volatility and the faith that in the grand scheme of things you'll do much better than the base-hitter type. If luck and talent are with you, you can make money as this type of investor.

   b. The base-hitter investor type isn't swingin' for the fences. She's looking for solid, consistent performance. This type of investor knows she'll sacrifice ever knowing what it feels like to hit a home run, but is willing to because she believes that slow and steady wins the race, which is true in the investment world.

   Consistent, positive growth is the most probable way to achieve financial security. You sure don't get bragging rights very often (well, at least not for many, many years), but in the end, you usually come out just right.

   c. Switch-hitters match their talent against their opponents'. If the pitcher does worse against a left-handed batter, then the switch-hitter may opt to bat left-handed. An investor who identifies with this characteristic may have difficulty staying with one investment strategy. He may always be on the lookout for a "better way."

   d. An investor who identifies with the character who has "never held a bat" has very little or no investment experience. Yet!

2. What amount of your portfolio could you tolerate losing in any given month?

It is not uncommon for the U.S. stock market, as a whole, to drop 10 percent in value in just one month. One individual stock, or the stock market of some countries, loses that much any given day.

If you're fully invested in stocks, you need to be prepared for down days, months, and even years. The more you diversify your stock portfolio the better, but only so much risk can be diversified away. You cannot diversify away all volatility, and at times that volatility can be great.

3. What amount of your portfolio could you tolerate losing in any given year?

Dropping 10 percent in value in just one year isn't at all uncommon for the U.S. stock market. In fact, the stock market commonly goes up or down as much as 1 or 2 percent per day. Too many bad days in a row totals a very bad period.

4. How much could you tolerate losing over five years?

The U.S. stock market has had only one negative five-year period of time in the last 35 years. However, for the most part, these five-year periods were actually some really good years for the U.S. stock market. It hasn't been that positive before, so don't count on it in the future.

Prepare yourself and your investment portfolio for extended down markets. Five years isn't a long time to the stock market. However, when you're living through it, a bad year period feels like an eternity.

5. How much money could you handle losing in any given year?

You shouldn't have any money invested in any stocks if you can't tolerate some chance of loss over an extended period of time. One year isn't long enough to put your money at risk and come out ahead every time.

6. What action would you take if the stock market dropped 25 percent from its present value next week?

Knowing what the "right" answer would be is difficult because the U.S. stock market hasn't lost 25 percent in a week very often. You may not really see this as a legitimate risk; however, a 25-percent drop is extremely likely to occur again and possibly several times during your investing lifetime.

The best response to a drastic drop in the stock market historically has been to raise cash and invest more, but not every time. Sometimes doing nothing is the smarter immediate reaction. Selling everything has historically not been the "right" thing to do.

7. How many years of your financial independence or security are you willing to risk?

Human beings are naturally risk averse. We don't like to lose, and the pain of losing is more motivating than the pleasure we receive from gains. So how do you know how much financial freedom you're willing to risk?

Say, for example, that you need $50,000 per year in retirement income to support your standard of living. Your portfolio is currently $500,000. Are you willing to risk losing 10 percent of your portfolio, or $50,000, if it meant you would have to work one additional year?

This question is just another way to look at your tolerance for risk. The closer you are to achieving your financial objectives, the more the definition of risk as "not being able to achieve your objective" becomes real. Does your response to this question change the way you responded to previous questions?

8. Regarding your finances, what do you spend the most time thinking about?

a. Are you questioning whether you'll have enough money for the future? Wondering whether you're saving enough? Remember that you'll need a substantial amount of capital to provide the income you may need to retire. You can use the following table to get a ballpark estimate of how much money you'll need at retirement.

Income Needed	Capital Needed
$1,000/month	$300,000
$2,000/month	$600,000
$3,000/month	$900,000
$4,000/month	$1,200,000

For each $1,000 in retirement income you need by age 65, you need to save this amount per month, presuming that you haven't begun saving for retirement in any meaningful way. (For additional information on retirement planning, refer to Chapter 11.)

Current Age	Savings / Month	Savings as Percentage of Income (approximately)
18	$48	5%
25	$86	9%
30	$131	13%
35	$201	20%
40	$315	32%
45	$509	51%
50	$867	87%
55	$1,640	can't compute
60	$4,083	can't compute

b. How can you earn more on your investments? Teach yourself and/or hire a professional. Chapter 14 can give you a great head start; other great resources for advancing your investment education include *Investing For Dummies* and *Mutual Funds For Dummies* (both published by Wiley). You can refer to Chapter 20 of this book for tips on finding and hiring the right advisor for you.

c. Could I be doing anything else smarter in regard to personal finances? Your situation can likely be improved upon; I've yet to meet the financial guru who knows every in and out of the financial world. You've already taken a great step by picking up this workbook, but to take your money know-how to the next level, continue educating yourself by reading quality books like those mentioned in this workbook and, when necessary, seek the advice of a qualified professional.

Worksheet 13-5 **My Current Portfolio Allocation**

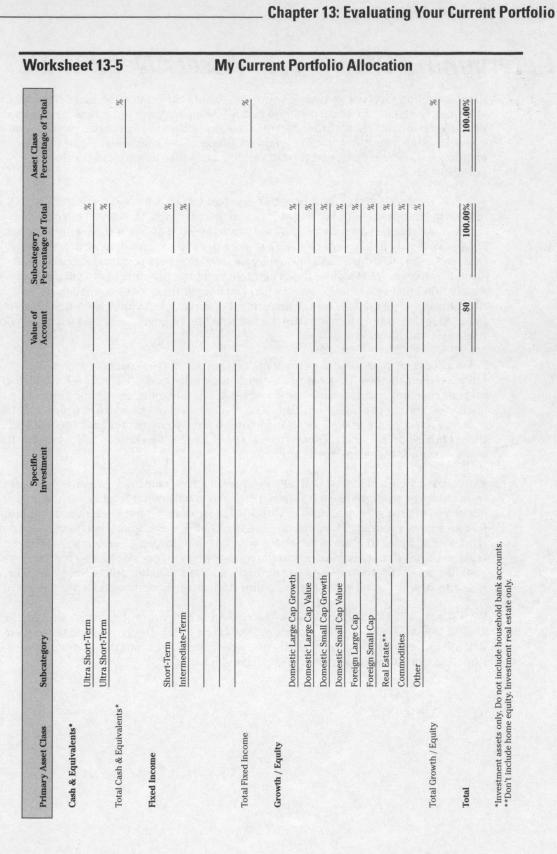

Primary Asset Class	Subcategory	Specific Investment	Value of Account	Subcategory Percentage of Total	Asset Class Percentage of Total
Cash & Equivalents*	Ultra Short-Term			____ %	
	Ultra Short-Term			____ %	
Total Cash & Equivalents*					____ %
Fixed Income	Short-Term			____ %	
	Intermediate-Term			____ %	
Total Fixed Income					____ %
Growth / Equity	Domestic Large Cap Growth			____ %	
	Domestic Large Cap Value			____ %	
	Domestic Small Cap Growth			____ %	
	Domestic Small Cap Value			____ %	
	Foreign Large Cap			____ %	
	Foreign Small Cap			____ %	
	Real Estate**			____ %	
	Commodities			____ %	
	Other			____ %	
Total Growth / Equity					____ %
Total			$0	100.00%	100.00%

*Investment assets only. Do not include household bank accounts.
**Don't include home equity. Investment real estate only.

Determining Where Your Assets Need to Be

Asset allocation involves spreading your investments across diverse asset classes in an attempt to reduce the overall portfolio risk, while maintaining or increasing expected portfolio return. In other words, one investment you own may be zigging when another one is zagging. Everything doesn't go up and down at the same time. Some investments zig, while some zag, and the net result is smoother investment portfolio performance.

You may want to just skip right over this asset allocation stuff and head straight to the interesting things, such as picking stocks and mutual funds. However, I encourage you not to make that mistake. Two significant academic studies performed within the last 20 years overwhelmingly concluded that more than 90 percent of a portfolio's long-term variation in return was explained by its weighting between stocks, bonds, and cash; in other words, it's more important that you have investments in stocks than which individual stocks you own or when you bought them. Only a small portion of the returns were explained by the investment manager's individual investment selections. Asset allocation decisions are the fundamental building blocks on which all good portfolios are designed.

Figuring out the appropriate asset allocation for your portfolio depends on your unique circumstances. To get started, check out Worksheets 13-6 and 13-7, which focus on your time horizon, tolerance for investment risk, and, of course, your personal goals. You should consider each table along with the others because in order to determine the appropriate asset allocation for your needs, you must take into account all three of these components. (Refer to your risk tolerance Worksheet 13-2, earlier in this chapter, for additional information.)

Worksheet 13-6 is a guideline that tells you how much of your total investments should be in stocks or stock mutual funds based on when you'll need this money. Think of *time horizon* as the date that you need to withdraw those dollars from your investment portfolio to support your standard of living in retirement. For example, if you're 60 years old right now and plan to retire in five years, your time horizon isn't five years. Your time horizon begins five years from now and may go for two to four decades — for the rest of your life. So, the first withdrawal you make does have a time horizon of five years. The next annual withdrawal you make has a time horizon of six years, and so on.

Worksheet 13-7 gives you the lowdown on how much of your total investment portfolio should be invested in stocks or stock mutual funds based on your responses to your risk tolerance questions (see Worksheet 13-2) regarding your maximum tolerable loss (the maximum amount of money you can handle losing).

Worksheet 13-6   Time Horizon and Equity Exposure

Time Horizon*	Maximum Equity Exposure
0–3 years	0%
4–5 years	20%
6 years	30%
7 years	40%
8 years	50%
9 years	60%
10 years	70%
11+ years	80%

When you need to spend this money.

Worksheet 13-7   Risk Tolerance and Equity Exposure

Maximum Tolerable Loss (Annual)	Maximum Equity Exposure
5%	20%
10%	30%
15%	40%
20%	50%
25%	60%
30%	70%
35%	80%
40%	90%
50%	100%

After looking at Worksheets 13-6 and 13-7, you may likely discover that the maximum equity exposure will be different depending on your time horizon and your maximum tolerable loss in a given year. If you discover a discrepancy between the maximum equity exposures for your time horizon and your maximum tolerable loss in a given year, I suggest that you select the lower of the two equity exposures.

Now, based on the maximum equity exposure that you're comfortable with and that is appropriate for your time horizon, look at what your average annual rate of return would have been if you'd invested in 1926 and stayed invested through 2000 by checking out Worksheet 13-8. This worksheet can provide you with some perspective as to what types of returns investors realized through history with these ratios between stocks and bonds.

Historical performance can't be expected to repeat itself. But the relationship to the amount of stock exposure to performance is highly correlated. If you have more stock (and therefore are taking more risk), you should receive more return over time.

Worksheet 13-8 Financial Goals and Equity Exposure (Example)

Portfolio Allocations (% Stocks / % Bonds)	Historic Returns**
80/20	8.87%
70/30	8.28%
60/40	7.92%
50/50	7.24%
40/60	6.70%
30/70	6.00%
20/80	5.31%

**1926-2000 annualized returns.*

Chapter 14

Maximizing Investment Strategies

*1*n this chapter, you discover simple strategies for implementing your investment plan with the appropriate asset allocation for your goals, utilizing traditional investment vehicles and evaluating some less conventional approaches as well.

Computing Your Current Savings Rate

Knowing what you're currently saving is an important part of making sure that you'll achieve your financial objectives (see Chapter 4). What percentage of your *gross income* (the amount of money you earn before paying taxes or anything else) are you saving? To answer this question, follow the computation in Worksheet 14-1.

Worksheet 14-1 **Computing Your Savings Rate**

1. What is your gross income per year? $_____

2. How much are you saving for retirement each year? $_____

3. Divide line 2 by line 1 to determine your savings rate.   _____%

Making Savings Happen

I don't know about you, but if I didn't have my savings and investing going out of my checking account or paycheck on a regular basis, it wouldn't happen like it should. Most people I have consulted for deal with this same issue. Most people in the United States spend 100 percent of their income — an unfortunate reality. However, you know better. You can't spend it all now and still have what you need for your future.

The first thing I'd like you to do is to establish an automatic withdrawal plan from your paycheck or checking account and set aside money each month to cover large periodic expenses that you incur, such as annual vacations, holidays, estimated taxes, real estate taxes, home remodeling, auto insurance, life insurance, and so on. Determine how much you need to cover all of your periodic expenses throughout the year and divide that number by 12 to arrive at your monthly savings requirement. Have this amount withdrawn from your paycheck or checking account every month and set aside into one or more money market accounts. When those periodic expenses arise, you'll then have the funds available to pay them.

Consider establishing an automatic escrow account for your *mandatory expenses* and a separate automatic escrow account for your *discretionary expenses.* Mandatory expenses must be paid. Discretionary expenses (or spending) occurs only if you have the money set aside for these purchases. If not, you may find yourself using your credit cards when you shouldn't. For an example, check out Worksheet 14-2. Then you can figure it out for yourself by using Worksheet 14-3.

For a listing of the best interest rates on savings and money market accounts, visit www.bankrate.com and click on the Checking and Savings Account link. ING Direct at www.INGDirect.com offers a money market account that tends to retain its spot as one of the highest yielding money market accounts going.

Worksheet 14-2 **Automatic Escrow Savings Plan (Example)**

Periodic Expenses	Approximate Annual Cost
Mandatory Expenses:	
Insurance on two autos	$1,800
Disability insurance	475
Property taxes	600
Real estate taxes	2,500
Auto replacement fund	6,000
Total Mandatory Expenses	$11,375 per year
Divided by 12 =	$948 per month
Discretionary Expenses:	
Family vacation	$3,000
Holidays	1,200
Total Discretionary Expenses:	$4,200 per year
Divided by 12 =	$350 per month

Worksheet 14-3   Automatic Escrow Savings Plan

Periodic Expenses	Approximate Annual Cost
Mandatory Expenses:	
Insurance on two autos	_____
Disability insurance	_____
Property taxes	_____
Real estate taxes	_____
Auto replacement fund	_____
Total Mandatory Expenses	_____
Divided by 12 =	_____
Discretionary Expenses:	
Family vacation	_____
Holidays	_____
Total Discretionary Expenses:	_____
Divided by 12 =	_____

Establishing Automatic Investment Programs for Retirement

You may want to consider establishing automatic investment programs to save for your retirement. Here's how you do it:

1. **Make sure that you're taking full advantage of any employer matching contribution for which you may be eligible with your company's retirement plan.**

    Contribute the maximum amount that the employer will match. If your employer doesn't make a matching contribution, skip directly to Step 2.

2. **If eligible, make the maximum contributions to your and your spouse's (if applicable) Roth IRA accounts each year, but make your contributions automatically out of your checking account each month.**

    A Roth IRA is the best retirement funding vehicle — from a tax standpoint — ever! Although you don't get a deduction when you contribute to a Roth IRA, all the earnings and withdrawals on the account are tax-free forever.

If you're single and have an adjusted gross income (AGI) of less than $99,000, or you're married filing jointly and have an AGI of less than $156,000, you can make a contribution up to $4,000 in 2007 and $5,000 in 2008. However, if you're over 50 years of age, you can invest even more: $5,000 in 2007 and $6,000 in 2008.

You can establish a Roth IRA account at most banks, through investment advisors, or my personal favorites: directly with a low-cost, no-load mutual fund company, like Vanguard (www.vanguard.com) or a deep discount broker like Scottrade (www.scottrade.com) or ShareBuilder (http://sharebuilder.com).

Making monthly contributions is much easier than coming up with the whole year's contribution at once. You can set up automatic investments directly from your checking account into your Roth IRA account. For example, if you were eligible to take this step in 2007, the maximum allowable contribution is $4,000 per person if you're under 50 years of age and $5,000 per person if you're 50 or older. Those contributions work out to be $333 per month and $416 per month respectively, depending on your age.

3. **Build your personal portfolio utilizing low-cost, tax-advantaged-passive investment vehicles, such as exchange-traded funds (ETFs) and index funds.**

You need to have investments that you can tap into if needed prior to retirement or age 59½. Also, when you retire and pull money out of your retirement account, 100 percent of that withdrawal is taxable to you as ordinary income. Capital gains tax rates are much lower. You may be much better off from a tax standpoint to pay minimal capital gains now, rather than the tax for ordinary income in the future.

Index funds are a way individual investors can own the stock market that you hear about on the news, such as the Standard and Poor 500 Composite Index (S & P 500, for short). Index funds have been available through no-load mutual fund powerhouses like Vanguard for decades. However, the range of options now available has exploded in the last few years. You can now buy an *exchange-traded fund* that invests exclusively in United States Treasury Inflation Protection Securities. Rather than buying one bond for $10,000, you can literally buy one share of an ETF, which trades like stocks, incurring a transaction fee to buy or sell shares.

You can find index funds and exchange-traded funds for every asset class imaginable. And the beauty of these vehicles is their low cost and tax efficiency. However, not all options are created equal. For more information, check out *Mutual Funds For Dummies* and *Exchange Traded Funds For Dummies*.

With the advent of deep-discount online brokerage firms like ShareBuilder (www.ShareBuilder.com) and FOLIOfn (www.FOLIOfn.com), you now can afford to make monthly purchases of exchange-traded funds. Both firms also have an online tool designed to help you identify your investing goals, gauge your investing style, and determine your risk tolerance (which you can also do in Chapter 13 in this book). By evaluating your answers to a series of basic investment objective and risk tolerance types of questions, ShareBuilder's PortfolioBuilder presents you with a model portfolio of exchange-traded funds that is designed to fit your needs and objectives. You can access this automated service for the subscription price of $12 a month, which also includes six commission-free trades to buy or sell any stock or exchange-traded fund in your account.

Based on these steps, which automatic savings programs are available to you, and how much can you direct to each of these automatic plans? Use Worksheet 14-4 to put these steps in action.

Worksheet 14-4   **Making Your Investments Automatic**

Step 1:

1. Employerís retirement plan will match to what level of income?

   _____ %

2. How much are you contributing to your employer's retirement plan?

   _____ %

3. If line 2 is less than line 1, increase your contribution as quickly as possible to the matching contribution level.

4. How many dollars per year will you be contributing to your company's retirement plan?

   $ _____

5. After you're at the maximum matching contribution level, move on to Step 2.

Step 2:

1. Are you eligible to make a Roth IRA contribution?   YES   NO

   Single taxpayers with incomes of less than $99,000 and married taxpayers with incomes of less than $156,000 are eligible to make a full contribution.

2. Contribution limits for 2007 are $4,000 for people under age 50 and $5,000 for those over 50 years of age. How much can you contribute to Roth IRA's for the current year?

   $ _____

3. How much will you save between your company's retirement plan and your Roth IRA this year? (Step 1, line 4 plus Step 2, line 2 equals your savings.)

   $ _____

Step 3:

1. How much more can you or do you need to save for retirement?

   $ _____

   (If you need assistance determining how much you need to save for retirement, refer to Chapter 11 to calculate your required annual retirement savings amount.)

2. Divide the number on line 1 by 12 to get the amount of monthly investments you need to make directly from your checking account into your personal portfolio utilizing low-cost, tax-advantaged, passive investment vehicles, such as exchange-traded funds and index funds.

   _____

Determining the Right Approach to Fund Each Goal

Your primary financial objectives (which you can set in stone in Chapter 4) may include raising money for a down payment on a home, remodeling a new home, providing for your children's college education, or retiring comfortably. Worksheet 14-5 outlines these objectives and the investment vehicles and funding strategies you should consider for each goal.

Worksheet 14-5 **Funding Strategies for Specific Goals**

Goal: **Investment Options and Strategies:**

Homes Money Market Accounts, Money Market Mutual Funds, Certificates of Deposit, and Short-Term Bond Mutual Funds

Due to the short time horizon, equity investments would not be prudent to fund for this goal.

College Your options include Education Savings Accounts, 529 Plans, and accumulating funds in tax-efficient investments in the parent's name — earmarked for child's college education.

Depending on the age(s) of your children, you may be best served by having some stocks and mutual funds. Use this table as a guide.

Time Horizon	Max. Equity Exposure
0–3 years	0%
4–5 years	20%
6 years	30%
7 years	40%
8 years	50%
9 years	60%
10 years	70%
11+ years	80%

Education Savings Accounts can be opened with low-cost, no-commission mutual fund companies. Consider their Target Maturity/Retirement date. These mutual fund assets are allocated across a broad range of investments and will shift allocation more conservatively as your target date for needing the funds draws nearer.

529 Plans issued through most states typically also have the target maturity option. If they don't, select an investment option offered by your state's 529 Plan administrator that does not exceed your maximum equity exposure limit due to your time horizon.

Index mutual funds and exchange-traded funds can be excellent, low-cost, tax-efficient investment options when saving for college in your name. Watch your maximum equity exposure.

Retirement First, pick the best options available through your employer's retirement plan and invest up to the matching contribution by your employer. Often, the investment options available to you in a company retirement plan are somewhat to very limited. Look for the best options available through the plan. You need not concern yourself with tax efficiency, so avoid using the Index option(s), if you have other good choices available that you need to round out your overall asset allocation (for example, international stock funds, small company funds, bond funds, or fixed income).

Next, continue rounding out your targeted asset allocation with your Roth IRA contribution. Once again, tax efficiency is not a concern within this account. However, you do have virtually unlimited investment options. Use your Roth IRA to complete those hard-to-fill components of your portfolio allocation, such as high-yield bonds, foreign bonds, or income-paying real estate investment trusts (also known as REITs).

Finally, complete your retirement funding requirement through your personal portfolio. This is where tax efficiency is critical. Low-cost, tax-efficient investments such as index funds and exchange-traded funds can best be used here. Your investment options are only limited by excessive costs and taxation; avoid those and you'll be doing well.

Computing Your Rate of Return on Your Investments

The best way to find out how your investments are doing is to find your *rate of return,* which is the total gain or loss on an investment or on your total portfolio over a period of time.

To find your year-to-date rate of return, compare the total value of your account today — or at the end of the preceding month — with the total value of your account at the end of last year (or since you originally invested) and then compare that rate of return to your personal objectives and the rates of return provided by similar investment options during that same period of time. Visit www.morningstar.com, a premier resource for mutual fund and stock information, for a listing of mutual fund rates of return by investment style, which you can use to compare to your own rates of return.

Worksheet 14-6   Computing Your Investment Rate of Return

1. What is your gross income per year? $ _____

2. How much are you saving for retirement each year? $ _____

3. Divide line 2 by line 1, to determine your savings rate.   _____%

Take time to compute your savings rate and the rate of return on your total investment portfolio at least once every year. This information can help you determine whether you're on target to meet your financial objectives.

Tracking Your Progress

Not only is it important to compute your savings rate and the rate of return on your investment portfolio (see previous sections), you also should keep track of your progress over time. As time passes and your financial objectives draw nearer, you will have a visual "measuring stick" you can use as a guide to determine whether you're on track. If you find yourself falling behind, you may need to increase your savings contributions. However, if you've been saving diligently, and the market has rewarded you handsomely, you may find that you can attain your objectives earlier than originally planned.

You can use Worksheet 14-7 to track your overall progress on your investments — both savings goals and total account value.

Worksheet 14-7　　　　　　　　　　**Tracking Your Progress**

1. What is the value of your account(s) currently?　　　$ _____

2. What was the value of these accounts at the end of last year?　　　$ _____

3. If the amount on line 1 is higher than line 2, your account is up.　　　$ _____

4. If the amount on line 1 is less than line 2, your account is down.　　　$ _____

5. Total the amount you or your company added to your account year-to-date.　　　$ _____

6. Subtract contributions (line 5) from the change in your account balance (either line 3 or 4) to arrive at the net gain or loss on your investments year-to-date.　　　$ _____

7. Divide the amount on line 6 by the amount on line 2 to approximate your rate of return for this period of time.　　　_____ %

Monitoring your progress on a quarterly, or at least annual, basis is essential to making sure that you stay on track with your financial plans.

Part V
Protecting Your Assets

The 5th Wave   By Rich Tennant

"You have the first case of identity theft I've ever seen where the thieves actually returned the identity because the credit was so bad."

In this part . . .

*B*ecause you face many different types of risks in your financial life, I focus on identifying those risks most significant to you and your loved ones and provide specific direction on how to minimize, eliminate, or transfer these risks most cost effectively. You can find specific details on life, health, disability, long-term care, auto, homeowner's, and liability insurance, as well as strategies you can implement immediately to protect your privacy.

Periodically, you may find that consulting with a competent, objective financial advisor is appropriate. I provide specific details in this part to empower you to know what to look for *and* what to look out for when engaging a financial advisor.

Chapter 15

Managing Risk with Insurance

• •

In This Chapter

▶ Thinking about risk

▶ Checking into insurance

• •

People are exposed to many different types of risks in their financial lives. In this chapter, I identify the major risks and suggest practical and effective ways to deal with these risks — typically that means insurance.

Identifying Types of Risk

Finance and investing textbooks define two primary types of risk:

✔ **Systematic risk** is the type of risk that is impossible to avoid completely. Examples of systematic risk include inflation, recessions, and war. You can do either very little or nothing to protect yourself from systematic risks, and no amount of portfolio diversification can eliminate systemic risk.

✔ **Unsystematic risk** is a risk that affects an isolated group of companies, industries, or countries. A company's stock plummeting after the news that the FDA declined approval of its highly anticipated new drug is an example of unsystematic risk. Diversification substantially reduces or eliminates unsystematic risks.

Systematic and unsystematic risks are the textbook definitions of financial risks, but what about the rest of the risks that you face in everyday life? *Risk* is better defined as uncertainty — the inability to *know* what the future brings. For example:

✔ Will you continue to be employed?

✔ Will your company require you to relocate?

✔ What happens if your teenager wrecks the car?

✔ What if the interest rate on your adjustable rate mortgage skyrockets?

✔ What if your in-laws have to move in?

✔ What happens if you live to be a Centurion?

✔ What happens if your child or significant other is diagnosed with a long-term illness requiring you to quit your job and stay home to care for your loved one?

✔ What happens if you wake up at age 60 and discover that you no longer want to have to work for a living, but you haven't saved enough to retire?

✔ What happens if your spouse dies prematurely?

✔ What if your home is destroyed by a flood?

✔ What if you're sued because your dog bites the neighbor's kid?

The list could go on and on. The point I'm trying to make is that life is filled with uncertainty. Some risks you may choose to bear. Others may be reduced, but the balance should be transferred to somebody else — typically an insurance company. Insurance should be purchased when you can't afford to bear the risk personally (see the section "Utilizing Insurance to Help Combat Risk" later in this chapter).

Eliminating, Minimizing, or Transferring Risk

Successful financial planning involves anticipating future events and all probable outcomes — both good and bad. Risk management attempts to eliminate, minimize, or transfer the risk of all your anticipated bad outcomes.

You can handle several risks without much hardship, if you have sufficient cash reserves on hand. For example, your teenager wrecks the car — hopefully, no one is hurt, and you have auto insurance — but you also need some cash to cover the deductible due before your insurance kicks in. You may even need additional cash to pay for a rental car until yours can be repaired. In this example, you have shouldered a certain amount of risk yourself: the deductible and the cost of the rental car. You have also transferred the majority of the financial risk to the auto insurance company.

 Establishing a safety net of three to six months worth of cash reserves, adequately insuring your home and property, your health, and your income, and remaining very aware of potential dangers goes a long way toward ensuring that you and your family won't be financially devastated when bad things happen — and they do happen. It's not a matter of *if*, but a matter of *what* and *when*.

Use Worksheet 15-1 to brainstorm on possible future events in your financial life and how these issues may be eliminated, minimized, or transferred (in other words, insured against). As you consider the bad things that can happen in your life, be reassured that you can take steps to help reduce the pain through proper risk-management techniques.

Worksheet 15-1   **Planning for Potential Risks**

Subject	Risk Management Strategy
Example: Die prematurely	Life insurance

Utilizing Insurance to Help Combat Risk

Most likely, you wouldn't even consider *not* having homeowners or auto insurance. But when do you actually have a need for insurance? Review the questions in Worksheet 15-2 and check the boxes of the situations that apply to you. If any or all of these issues apply to you, you need insurance.

Worksheet 15-2   **You Need Insurance If...**

❏ You can't afford to pay cash (in other words, *self-insure*) to repair or replace your vehicle if you're in an accident.

❏ You want to reduce your possibility of being sued. (Yes, you are exposed to liabilities, in more ways than you probably imagine — such as car accidents, a tree from your yard damaging your neighbors' house, or your dog biting the mail carrier. Each could result in a lawsuit.)

❏ You can't afford to pay cash to repair your home in the event of a fire, damaging wind, or a hail storm. If you can't afford major repairs, you definitely can't afford to replace your home if it is destroyed.

❏ You can't afford to pay cash for adequate medical care in the event of illness or injury.

❏ You need long-term medical care and aren't able to pay for it comfortably out of your own pocket.

❏ You need your income to survive.

❏ Your family needs your income to survive.

❏ You have assets to protect.

❏ You'd be more comfortable transferring big financial risks to an insurance company.

If you checked one or many of the boxes in Worksheet 15-2, you may need to consider the following types of insurance:

✔ **Disability:** Did you know that there is actually a greater likelihood that you will become disabled for a period (at least three months prior to age 65) than die? Likely, your most significant asset is your ability to earn money. So you need to ask yourself: Should I become disabled, how would I cover my living expenses? How will I be able to save for retirement? And because an overwhelming majority of disabilities are health related, can I afford the risk of being without a paycheck and possibly having increased healthcare expenses?

Protecting your income by purchasing disability insurance is one of the fundamental risk management strategies I recommend for all wage earners whose income is required to maintain their lifestyles. The two primary types of disability insurance include

Short- term: Coverage will provide income replacement protection, usually after one week of disability, and will pay for up to six months.

Long-term: This type of disability insurance kicks in generally at the six-month mark and continues until age 65.

If you happen to have disability insurance through your employer, you likely have only long-term disability coverage, and typically the coverage ranges between 60 and 70 percent of your current gross salary. So, if you're struggling to get ahead on 100 percent of your salary, how do you think your finances will work on 60 to 70 percent of what you're currently making? What if you don't happen to have disability insurance?

✔ **Life:** Under most circumstances, you need life insurance to protect your surviving family who depend on your income for as long as they'll need it. I have met very few people who have enough life insurance. In fact, the overwhelming majority of Americans are drastically underinsured in the event of premature death. Don't leave your family in this predicament!

I also recommend that a stay-at-home parent obtain life insurance, although not to protect the family from their loss of income, but rather to help offset the additional costs that it would take to replace that stay-at-home parent's services.

Example: To replace the services of a stay-at-home mom, caring for a 3-year-old and a newborn would cost $30,000 per year or more for a full-time nanny to care for the children until the youngest is in school. In addition, the children would need after-school care for several more years, and you might need a number of other domestic services too. All these expenses add up to $250,000 or more of life insurance needed on the stay-at-home parent.

Fortunately, term life insurance is actually quite affordable, presuming that you're fairly healthy. The cost of a high-quality, 20-year level term life insurance policy on a young mother may cost $300 to $400 per year — a level premium for 20 years!

✔ **Health:** Nearly one out of five Americans under age 65 has no health insurance. Over half of these people state *cost* as the reason they don't have health insurance. Almost 25 percent of uninsured people lost their health insurance when they lost or changed jobs. The unfortunate thing about insurance is that if you can't afford the premium, you definitely won't be able to afford bearing the risk yourself. (For more on health insurance, see Chapter 16.)

✔ **Long-term care:** Medicare or your health insurance policy will not pay for long-term care expenses in a nursing home or other long-term care facility. These expenses are covered in one of three ways: self pay, long-term care insurance, or Medicaid — and you have to be nearly broke to qualify for Medicaid.

Given the likelihood of an extended long-term care need, I advise you to consider purchasing long-term care insurance the day before you're going to need it. Unfortunately, you can't know what day that will be, so for practical purposes, I strongly suggest purchasing long-term care insurance between ages 50 and 65. The older you are, the more expensive the premiums. The price of the insurance goes up as you get older, and the likelihood of needing long-term care insurance increases. Coverage isn't available for anyone over 80 years of age. The insurance premiums are quite expensive, as is the cost of care. Weigh your risks wisely: Don't be pennywise and pound foolish.

✔ **Auto:** If you own a vehicle and ever let it out of the garage, you must have auto insurance. Depending on the value of your vehicle and your state's requirements, the type of automobile insurance you should carry will vary. Refer to Chapter 18 for the details.

✔ **Homeowners:** If you own a home and you have a mortgage, you must maintain adequate homeowners insurance protection. Your mortgage company requires it. However, if you happen to own your home outright, you still need to have homeowners insurance. Remember, you buy insurance to replace or repair the things that are too expensive or impossible to pay for yourself.

✔ **Liability:** You have some liability insurance protection provided with both your auto and homeowners insurance coverages. Liability insurance pays for legal fees and damages if you hurt someone or cause injury due to your negligence. In addition to the coverage available through your auto and homeowner's insurance policies, you may also determine that additional liability insurance is warranted. Refer to Chapter 18 for more information.

For a more detailed description of these types of insurance as well as an assessment of your current insurance and coverage needs, see the rest of Part V.

Evaluating the Quality of Insurance

You buy insurance to protect your income, your family, and your assets from financial ruin. However, just any ol' insurance won't do. You owe it to yourself and your loved ones to obtain and maintain the correct type and amount of coverage from a financially secure insurance company.

Insurance is worth nothing if the company isn't around to pay claims when you're in need. And you definitely don't want to waste money paying for insurance that won't pay off if the need arises because the insurer argues that your loss isn't covered.

Become an informed consumer by doing your own research. Check out the quality companies and the types of insurance you feel you need before you contact an agent. Worksheet 15-3 is a checklist of the major issues to check out and consider when evaluating your current insurance coverages or considering purchasing new policies. Throughout Part V, I get very specific about each of the different types of insurance policies that most people need to consider. This worksheet covers the basics.

Worksheet 15-3   Key Quality Insurance Issues to Consider

❑ **Financial strength of the insurance company:**

- Check out A.M. Best ratings (www.ambest.com) on any home, auto, life, or health insurance company, and only do business with the financially strongest companies. The financially strongest companies can also be extremely competitively priced. You don't have to give up security to save money.

- You can also see how Standard and Poors rates these same companies at www.standardandpoors.com; go to *Task Selector*, *Find a Rating*, and then click on *Insurance*.

❑ **Claims payment history and customer service ratings:**

- Visit your state insurance regulators' Web site or call the regulators' office and inquire about the insurance company's complaint history.

- Check out the rankings on overall customer satisfaction, claims payment history, pricing, and communications with J.D. Power and Associates at www.jdpower.com.

- Another great resource to check out a company's customer service history is Consumer Reports (www.consumerreports.org). Click *Personal Finance* and then *Insurance*. Consumer Reports online is available for a modest annual subscription price.

❑ **Price:** You can find many online resources that enable you to obtain quotes and additional information so that you can do some comparison shopping. I suggest the following Web sites:

- www.ehealthinsurance.com
- www.insure.com
- www.insurance.com
- www.selectquote.com

After you've had the opportunity to check out the financial strength of an insurance company, whether its customers are happy, and whether its price is competitive, you've greatly narrowed your selection. The only things remaining are the specific "bells and whistles" of the insurance coverages you currently own or are considering.

The rest of Part V focuses on the "bells and whistles" for each of the primary types of insurance products.

When you comparison shop, I suggest that you get quotes on comparable policies from three different sources. The three primary ways to obtain insurance quotes and products are through the following:

- ✔ **A captive agent** represents only one company, such as Allstate, State Farm, or American Family. It may seem that a captive agent may not be the best way to go; however, I have found that captive agents can be extremely competitive and provide exceptional customer service, especially for home and auto coverage. However, you won't likely want to acquire all your insurance through one captive agent. These types of companies often aren't the most competitive in the areas of life, health, disability, and long-term care insurance.

- ✔ **An independent agent** represents multiple insurers. Independent agents can do a lot of comparison shopping for you and may be able to provide you with one-stop shopping for all of your insurance needs; however, don't count on it. Shop around — even among independent agents there can be a huge difference in their offerings.

- ✔ **Buying directly from the insurance company** is another option. Don't count on any personalized attention, but you may save some money. However, I wouldn't suggest buying certain types of insurance, such as long-term care, disability, or medical insurance, without the guidance of an insurance professional.

Many insurance agents and companies out there are very interested in parting you from your money. In almost every case, insurance agents are paid only when they sell you a policy, and the more they sell you, the more money they make. Unfortunately, too often insurance agents don't put your best interest first. Above all, remember that insurance agents are sales people. In my work as a financial advisor, I've seen so many cases where people have been ripped off by an insurance agent. What's worse is that many times these agents were family members or alleged friends. Caveat emptor = Buyer beware!

Chapter 16

Exploring Your Insurance Options

In This Chapter

▶ Considering your health insurance options

▶ Thinking about long-term care needs and options

▶ Evaluating disability income protection

Can you afford the risk of not being able to pay for medical care or hospitalization, or losing your paycheck? If the answer is no, you should do everything within your power to obtain the appropriate coverage to insure you from the financial devastation of these risks. In this chapter, I tell you what you need to know to protect yourself and your family at all stages in life.

Under Age 65: Exploring Your Health Insurance Options

The majority of individuals and families have health insurance through their employers. You're likely best off with your employer's group plan than any other option that may be available to you. Group coverage is easier and much less expensive to get than private insurance. Plus, your employer may pay most or all of the cost for you, and you can't be denied coverage. However, if you change jobs, get laid off, or are fired, you can lose your group health insurance. If you find yourself without employer-sponsored health insurance, the following options may be available to you:

✔ **Individual health insurance:** Perhaps your employer doesn't offer health insurance, or you're self-employed, a student, or retired before age 65. If you're relatively healthy, you should purchase an individual health insurance policy.

Certain health conditions, such as a recent back injury or treatment for high blood pressure, may be excluded from coverage for a period of time, generally up to two years. In some circumstances, pre-existing health conditions will be covered; however, your cost for insurance can be substantially higher than it would be if the pre-existing health conditions weren't covered. Each insurance company may treat pre-existing health conditions differently and can deny you coverage altogether.

Paying the extra cost and obtaining full coverage is generally better than having a pre-existing condition excluded from your health insurance policy.

To find more info about individual health insurance, contact a health insurance broker in your area by visiting the National Association of Health Underwriters at www.nahu.org/consumer/findagent.cfm. eHealthInsurance online also provides individual, short-term, and student health insurance plans. You can obtain quotes and information at www.ehealthinsurance.com or call 800-977-8860 to discuss any current medical conditions or questions you may have. Licensed insurance professionals are available to answer questions, provide advice, and assist you in the application process.

✔ **COBRA:** A provision in the law requires almost all employers to allow their terminating employees to continue group insurance coverage for a period of up to 18 months through a program called *COBRA*. However, you must pay 100 percent of the cost of the insurance.

As your COBRA benefit period nears its end (generally after 18 months) or you get tired of paying those high premium rates for very comprehensive health insurance coverage, you need to search out group health insurance that's equal to or a better deal on your own. Generally, employer-sponsored plans (which is still who your COBRA coverage is through) have very low or no deductibles and minimal copayments. Simply by raising the deductible and copayments — bearing more of the risk yourself — you could dramatically reduce your insurance costs.

✔ **HIPAA:** The *Health Insurance Portability and Accountability Act* (HIPAA) of 1996 requires that states provide at least a minimal coverage after you exhaust COBRA benefits, as long as you haven't had any extended lapse (generally a break of 63 days or more) in coverage. Premiums under HIPAA may be two to three times what they would be for a standard rate policy. HIPAA policies are typically an option of last resort for many people without employer-provided health insurance; however, HIPAA is still better than no health insurance at all. Each state has its own HIPAA rules, so contact your state insurance department before dropping any current coverage.

✔ **Your state's high-risk health insurance pool:** If you happen to be medically uninsurable due to significant health problems, your best option may be to apply for coverage through the high-risk pool through your state, if your state has a high-risk health insurance pool available. Only 33 states have high-risk pools that provide coverage if traditional health insurance providers reject you. For more information about whether your state has a high-risk insurance pool and how it works, contact The National Association of State Comprehensive Health Insurance Plans at `www.naschip.org` or your state insurance commissioner's office. Most states have their insurance premiums capped at 125 percent to 150 percent of the cost of a standard policy.

Even if your state has a high-risk insurance pool, you may not be able to obtain insurance immediately because there may be a long waiting list.

✔ **Medicaid and other state-based healthcare programs:** If you're financially destitute, Medicaid is the nation's largest program providing healthcare services to low-income individuals and households. Each state's Medicaid income, eligibility requirements, and benefits vary. Check with your state for the specifics on Medicaid as well as other state-based programs. You can go to `www.nahu.org/consumer/healthcare/topic.cfm?catID=18` for more info.

✔ **State Children's Health Insurance Program:** This program provides healthcare coverage to children when their families don't qualify for Medicaid because they make too much money. Find out more at `www.nahu.org/consumer/healthcare/topic.cfm?catID=19`.

✔ **Federally funded community health centers:** These provide healthcare assistance to the needy. Go to `http://ask.hrsa.gov/pc/` or call 800-ASK-HRSA (800-275-4772) for more info.

J.D. Power and Associates has a very helpful health insurance plan rating tool accessible at `www.jdpower.com/insurance/ratings/health-plans`. You enter the region of the country you're located in, and a list of health insurance companies are provided, based on their ranking regarding the following criteria:

✔ Overall experience

✔ Coverage and benefits

✔ Choice of doctors, hospitals, and pharmacies

✔ Information and communications

✔ Approval processes

✔ Insurance statements

✔ Customer service

✔ Claims processing

You can also use Worksheet 16-1, which lists the health insurance options that may be available to you. The list is ranked with the more comprehensive and cost-effective insurance options at the top, ending with the options of last resort for many people. I have also included government programs that are available for those people with financial hardships.

Worksheet 16-1   Health Insurance Options

Group Coverage

❏ Are you employed and your employer offers health insurance? If so, take advantage of it.

❏ Is your spouse employed by an employer who offers family coverage?

❏ If you aren't married but have a domestic partner, does his employer offer domestic partner health insurance benefits?

❏ Are you planning to terminate your employment in the near future and you're under age 65? If you're relatively healthy, consult with a health insurance broker about your options prior to terminating your employment. You may find competitive private insurance; if not, go with COBRA.

Personal Coverage

❏ Do you currently have health insurance, but are curious as to whether you may be able to obtain better or more competitively priced coverage? Check into obtaining private health insurance coverage.

❏ Are you uninsurable due to a serious medical condition? Check whether your state has a high-risk insurance pool.

❏ Have you exhausted your COBRA benefits and can't find replacement coverage? If so, use HIPAA.

Options for the Financially Destitute

❏ Are you broke? Medicaid or other state-based healthcare assistance programs may be your answer.

❏ Do you need healthcare coverage for your children, but you don't qualify for Medicaid due to income requirements? You may want to check out the State Children's Health Insurance Program or check into federally funded community healthcare centers.

Age 65 or Older: Obtaining Health Insurance

Prior to retirement, you're likely covered by your employer's health insurance plan (if not, see previous section). However, what do you do for health insurance after retirement? Many people must postpone retirement until age 65 merely because they need to wait to retire until they qualify for the government's healthcare program, also known as Medicare. Worksheet 16-2 summarizes these benefits. You're eligible for Medicare if you or your spouse worked for at least ten years in Medicare-covered employment, and you're age 65 or older and a citizen or permanent resident of the United States. If you're not yet age 65, you may qualify for coverage if you have a disability. (Call 800-633-4227 or visit www.medicare.gov for more information on Medicare.)

Worksheet 16-2	Medicare Benefit Summary		
	Benefit	**Your Cost**	**Medicare Pays**
Part A: No cost			
Hospital	first 60 days	$992	remainder
	61–90 days	$248/day	remainder
	91–150 days	$496/day	remainder
	150+ days	100%	nothing
Skilled Nursing	1–20 days	nothing	100%
	21–100 days	$124/day	remainder
	100+ days	100%	nothing
Home Health	1–100 days	nothing (services); 20% for equipment	100% for services; 80% for equipment
Hospice	unlimited*	outpatient drugs and inpatient respite care	remainder

* Must be ordered by physician

Part B: Starting at $93.50/month premium (based on income)

	Benefit	**Your Cost**	**Medicare Pays**
Medical	unlimited	first $131 + 20%	remainder
Lab	unlimited	nothing	100%
Home Health	unlimited	20% of equipment	remainder
Outpatient	unlimited	first $131 + 20%	remainder

Part C: Medicare Advantage Plans

Medicare Advantage Plans are approved by Medicare but offered through private insurance companies. Sometimes these plans can be comparable in benefits, but more cost-effective than the original Medicare plan combined with a Medicare supplemental (also known as Medigap) policy. These plans vary greatly in cost and benefits, state by state, so you must research your plan options thoroughly before you join.

Part D: Medicare Prescription Drug Program

This program is new as of 2007. The Medicare prescription drug program allows anyone eligible for Medicare to pay extra insurance premiums and receive different levels of prescription drug coverage. For more information, visit the Center for Medicare and Medicaid Services (CMS) at www.cms.hhs.gov. This site provides online tools that can help you compare plans that are available in your area. Another great resource is the Department of the Elderly in your state of residence, because it has counselors on hand to personally assist you in finding the best plan for your needs. You may access a list of state offices at www.medicare.gov/contacts/static/allStateContacts.asp.

How do you know which part of Medicare you qualify for? And how do you know you're fully insured? Here are some guidelines:

- ✔ If you're eligible for Social Security retirement benefits, you're automatically eligible for Part A of the Medicare program (which I describe in Worksheet 16-2), beginning with the first day of the month in which you turn age 65. If you started Social Security retirement benefits before age 65, you don't need to do anything to begin receiving Medicare Part A benefits. If you're eligible for, but aren't yet receiving your Social Security retirement benefits, you must apply separately for Medicare Part A.

- ✔ If you're receiving Social Security retirement benefits, you're automatically enrolled in Medicare Part B at the time you become eligible for Medicare Part A, unless you elect to opt out of Part B coverage.

  Even though you must pay a monthly premium for Medicare Part B, this plan is extremely cost-effective for the benefits provided, so you should not waive your right to this coverage.

- ✔ To be fully insured, I strongly recommend that you consider supplementing your Medicare coverage with *Medicare supplemental insurance,* also known as *Medigap coverage,* which generally pays the deductibles and copayments not covered by Medicare Parts A or B. Medigap policies — which vary from basic (represented by letter A in Worksheet 16-3) to comprehensive (letter J) — are sold by private insurance companies to fill in the gaps in the original Medicare plan and have federal standards. Most states have now adopted regulations limiting the sale of Medigap insurance to no more than the standard policies.

  You can check out the basics of a Medigap policy in Worksheet 16-3. Review the features of each of these plans to determine what may be best for your health needs and budget. For more information about the details of the various plans in your state, visit www.medicare.gov/MPPF/Include/DataSection/Questions/SearchOptions.asp.

Worksheet 16-3 **Medigap Policy Summary**

	Benefit	Your Cost	Medicare Pays
Part A: No cost			
Hospital	first 60 days	$992	remainder
	61–90 days	$248/day	remainder
	91–150 days	$496/day	remainder
	150+ days	100%	nothing
Skilled Nursing	1–20 days	nothing	100%
	21–100 days	$124/day	remainder
	100+ days	100%	nothing
Home Health	1–100 days	nothing	100%
Hospice	unlimited*	outpatient drugs and inpatient respite care	remainder

* Must be ordered by physician

Part B: Starting at $93.50/month premium (based on income)

	Benefit	Your Cost	Medicare Pays
Medical	unlimited	first $131 + 20%	remainder
Lab	unlimited	nothing	100%
Home Health	unlimited	20% of equipment	remainder
Outpatient	unlimited	first $131 + 20%	remainder

Part C: Medicare Advantage Plans

Medicare Advantage Plans are approved by Medicare but offered through private insurance companies. Sometimes these plans can be comparable in benefits, but more cost-effective than the original Medicare plan combined with a Medicare Supplemental policy. These plans vary greatly in cost and benefits, state by state, so you must research your plan options thoroughly before you join.

Part D: Medicare Prescription Drug Program

This program is new as of 2007. For more information, visit the Center for Medicare and Medicaid Services (CMS) at www.cms.hhs.gov. This site provides online tools that can help you compare plans that are available in your area. Another great resource is the Department of the Elderly in your state of residence, because it has counselors on hand to personally assist you in finding the best plan for your needs. You may access a list of state offices at www.medicare.gov/contacts/static/allStateContacts.asp.

Preparing for Long-Term Healthcare Needs

A few decades ago, when an elderly person needed healthcare assistance, she relied on her extended family. However, society has changed — and not necessarily for the better. If you can't take care of yourself and you don't have any family members around to provide for your care, you have many other options from which to choose: home healthcare, adult daycare, assisted-living facilities, and nursing homes. Unfortunately, obtaining these services for any length of time requires a substantial amount of money.

For example, the current cost of a nursing home stay runs between $150 and $250 a day depending on what part of the country you live in. Assisted-living facilities tend to run at about half that price. Home healthcare can easily cost as much as a nursing home stay. But the majority of individuals I have met feel very strongly about staying in their homes as long as possible, so home healthcare may be a very attractive option for you as well.

WARNING!

If you or your spouse need long-term care for even a few weeks, let alone a few years, your family's financial plans may be devastated. Few people are able to *self-insure* (pay out of their own pockets) for the cost of long-term care. And don't count on the government to step in and cover these costs for you. Medicare provides a very minimal benefit. Medicaid is the only government program that provides funds to help cover long-term care expenses, but to qualify for Medicaid, you have to be nearly broke. (See the section "Under Age 65: Exploring Your Health Insurance Options" for more on Medicaid.)

Knowing whether you will need long-term care is very hard to say. The current estimate says that about one-third of men and about one-half of women over age 65 are expected to need two years or more of long-term care assistance during their lifetimes. Can you afford to pay for this type of care out of your retirement nest egg? If so, you can self-insure. If not, you have two primary options:

✔ **Take your chances.** Maybe you'll be one of the fortunate ones and not require long-term care assistance, or possibly your extended family will provide the care you need.

✔ **Buy long-term care insurance.** Long-term care insurance is insurance you purchase to help offset the cost of long-term healthcare. I feel that middle-income Americans should strongly consider long-term care insurance, at least by the time they're age 65. The odds are that if you're age 65 or older, you will need long-term healthcare assistance of some sort for at least one year and possibly much longer.

You should *not* buy long-term care insurance if:

✔ You don't have enough income to afford the premiums.

✔ You don't have many assets to protect or a desire to protect them for your heirs.

✔ You have a limited income.

You should *consider* buying long-term care insurance if:

✔ You have substantial assets and income.

✔ You want to protect the majority of your assets for your heirs.

✔ You don't want to depend on others to provide for your care or support.

If you determine that you should consider long-term care insurance, how do you know when you should buy it? The perfect time to buy long-term care insurance is the day before you need it. Unfortunately, my crystal ball isn't clear enough to figure out when that exact day will come. So instead, you have to weigh your options. The longer you wait to buy long-term care insurance, the higher the likelihood that you may be deemed uninsurable. However, the longer you wait to buy the insurance, the less money you're going to spend on insurance premiums before you *might* receive benefits.

For example: If you purchase the insurance in your 40s or 50s, you may pay premiums totaling over $100,000 before you actually begin to claim benefits — *if* you even need to claim benefits at all. But if you die in your sleep at home at age 90, then you've spent over $100,000 in long-term care insurance premiums, and you didn't need the coverage.

As you can see, you have to take on risk of some sort no matter when you purchase long-term healthcare insurance. You just have to weigh the risks and choose which option makes you most comfortable.

After you've determined the best time for you to buy long-term care insurance, I strongly encourage you to do your research prior to contacting an agent. Long-term care costs can be extremely expensive, but so can long-term care insurance. And comparing one policy against another can also be difficult. Doing your own research can make you feel more confident about your final decision. Then after you've done some legwork, contact three independent agents and consult personally with each of them prior to making a final decision. Be sure to compare the costs and benefits of each policy.

To help ease the shopping process, I recommend *A Shopper's Guide to Long-Term Care Insurance* published by the National Association of Insurance Commissioners is a great resource to provide general information about long-term care insurance. You can access a copy of this guide at `www.michigan.gov/documents/cis_ofis_ltcshop_23739_7.pdf`.

Worksheet 16-4 is a checklist of items that I strongly recommend you review for each of the long-term care insurance policies you consider. Some questions in this worksheet merely involve a yes or no answer; others may ask for a specific period of time, number of days, amount of benefits, and so on. Please complete this checklist to the best of your ability, and you'll be in much better shape to compare policies and select the one that is right for you.

Worksheet 16-4   Evaluating a Long-Term Care Policy

The policy under consideration provides for the cost of care at which of the following:

- ❏ Skilled nursing facilities
- ❏ Custodial nursing facilities
- ❏ Assisted living facilities
- ❏ Adult day care
- ❏ Home healthcare

Under what conditions will the policy begin to pay benefits?

❏ Inability to perform (preferably no more than two) specific activities of daily living, including bathing, dressing, eating, toileting, and transferring.

❏ Cognitive impairment, such as a stroke, Alzheimer's, or Parkinson's disease

❏ Certification by a doctor stating that long-term care is medically necessary, and, if so, will the policy allow for *your* doctor to provide the certification?

When will benefits begin?

❏ Is hospitalization required immediately before long-term care benefits will be paid?

❏ How long is the waiting period before benefits will begin?

How long will benefits last? (Typically, benefit periods range from two years to lifetime.)

❏ Is the policy structured to pay on a flat dollar amount per day or based on actual costs up to that dollar amount?

❏ Is there inflation protection on the benefit?

❏ If there is inflation protection available, what is the inflation rate and is it simple or compounded?

Other features to consider:

❏ Does the policy allow you — not the insurance company — to choose a doctor?

❏ Is the policy guaranteed renewable?

❏ Is there a waiver of premium in the event benefits are being paid out?

❏ Does this company offer a joint long-term care policy for couples, married or not?

Just because you've done extensive research doesn't mean that you're required to or would be best served by purchasing a long-term care insurance policy. However, you can be better able to make an educated decision about whether long-term care insurance is right for you and your family. If you need additional help determining whether long-term care insurance is right for you, I recommend consulting with an independent insurance agent who specializes in long-term care insurance or a fee-only financial advisor who charges by the hour.

After deciding that the long-term care insurance is appropriate for you, but you still aren't sure about paying the cost and want to consider ways to reduce the total cost of coverage, check out the following tips:

✔ If available, purchase a long-term care insurance group policy through your employer.

✔ Consider electing a 90-day waiting period, rather than a 30-day waiting period, before the benefits begin. This option can reduce your premiums by up to 30 percent.

✔ If you're married or in a long-term committed relationship and both of you can benefit from long-term care insurance, look into buying a joint policy for the two of you.

✔ Rather than buying a policy that provides a daily benefit equal to the cost of nursing home facilities in your area today, you may want to consider purchasing a lesser dollar amount and self-insuring the balance.

Protecting Your Income: Disability Insurance

Your ability to earn money is one of the most significant assets that you have. Expenses often increase due to disability, while income is drastically reduced. In the event that you're unable to continue to earn your income because of illness or injury for any period of time, your family's financial plans could be ruined.

Social Security includes a disability feature, but you're considered disabled only if you can't perform *any* work; you have to wait for at least five months to initiate benefits; and the amount you will receive will likely be less than 50 percent of your income.

The only way to protect yourself and your family from financial disaster is to maintain adequate *disability insurance.* Disability insurance replaces a portion of your income in the event you become ill or injured while insured. Disability insurance is very expensive because the likelihood that you may need this benefit is relatively high. The risk isn't something that you likely can bear yourself, so you must transfer the risk to an insurance company.

Disability insurance companies won't sell you an insurance policy to replace 100 percent of your income. However, they do sell policies that go up to about 70 percent of your current income. If you don't have at least 70 percent of your current income provided through your employer's disability insurance plan, you should obtain supplemental coverage bringing you up to 70 percent. If your employer doesn't provide any disability insurance protection, you should be able to purchase a private policy providing you with up to 70 percent of your income.

If you currently need all your income to provide your standard of living and achieve your financial goals, how are you going to make ends meet if you're only bringing in 60 to 70 percent of your current income? What typically happens in real life is that people have to make drastic cuts in their lifestyles. Whatever plans you may have had for retirement, for that family vacation, or for paying for the kids' college education are now unattainable — unless you obtain as much disability insurance as you can get.

One of the most significant benefits of owning your own disability insurance policy is that because you pay the premiums, the benefits you receive (should you become disabled) are tax-free. Therefore, tax-free benefits of 70 percent of your current income may be extremely comparable to 100 percent of your current taxable income. When your employer, on the other hand, pays the premium on this insurance coverage, 100 percent of the benefits you receive under this policy are taxable as ordinary income.

Disability insurance comes in two primary forms:

✔ **Short-term:** This type of disability insurance provides for benefits from the eighth day of disability up to six months of disability. Most employers don't provide short-term disability insurance benefits. And most individuals opt to self-insure for the first three to six months of disability if they're buying private policies. Adequate cash reserves are necessary to cover your living expenses in the event of disability until your insurance begins to pay benefits. (For more on how to build up cash reserves, see Chapter 13.)

✔ **Long-term:** Disability insurance of this flavor generally kicks in after the first six months of disability and typically pays benefits until age 65. Employer-sponsored, long-term disability insurance may provide what is called *own-occupation coverage* for a period of up to two years. What this means is that if you're unable to do *your* job because of an illness or injury, your disability insurance provides you with benefits. However, at the end of that two-year period of time, or in most cases from day one of your disability, the disability insurance policy pays for benefits only if you're unable to do *any* meaningful work that you're reasonably trained to do. Insurance that guarantees to pay if you're unable to perform the duties of your occupation is substantially more expensive than a policy that guarantees to pay benefits if you're unable to work at all.

I recommend that you obtain as much own-occupation, long-term disability insurance as you can afford, especially if you have a very specialized occupation that would require you to take a significant pay cut in order to work in a different capacity. However, if own-occupation disability insurance is cost prohibitive, having long-term disability coverage that provides benefits if you're unable to work at any job is better than not having the coverage at all.

Worksheet 16-5 lists questions regarding key disability insurance features and benefits that you should consider in order to evaluate your current disability insurance and any additional coverage that you likely need to obtain.

If you need to purchase disability insurance, I recommend that you use this worksheet to start your comparison shopping on the Web with sites such as www.insure.com and www.insurancefinder.com/applications/app_healthdisability.html. Also contact two or three independent insurance agents in your area that provide personal disability insurance. Compare all these policies — the features and benefits, as well as the price — and select the one that best fits your personal situation.

Worksheet 16-5   Checking Out Disability Insurance Policies

1. What company is issuing this policy?

    _____

2. How do A.M. Best, Duff & Phelps, Moody's, Standard & Poor, and Weiss rate this company? (The company or agent can provide you with this info.)

    _____

    _____

    _____

    _____

3. Is the policy noncancelable? (A noncancelable policy guarantees renewability at a fixed premium.)

    _____

    _____

4. Is the policy guaranteed renewable? (A guaranteed renewable policy guarantees that you have the right to renew the policy but the premiums may increase.)

    _____

    _____

5. Are the premiums guaranteed?

    _____

    _____

6. What are the policy's annual premiums?

    _____

    _____

7. Does the policy provide *own occupation* protection? If so, for how long?

    _____

    _____

8. Does the policy require the continuing care of a physician?

    _____

    _____

9. If I'm able to return to work on a part-time basis, will the policy continue to provide me with some sort of partial or residual benefits?

    _____

    _____

10. Do I have to be totally disabled before I would be eligible to receive partial disability benefits?

    _____

    _____

11. How is the degree of disability determined? Is it based on a loss of earned income or a reduction in hours worked?

    _____

    _____

12. How is *earned income* defined? (It should include salaries, bonuses, commissions, and any other form of earned income.)

    _____

    _____

13. How is the actual benefit determined? The immediate 12-month period preceding disability or some other calculation?

    _____

    _____

14. If I'm receiving benefits, will my benefits be adjusted for inflation?

    _____

    _____

15. Can I increase my monthly benefits in the future?

    _____

    _____

16. Can I increase my monthly benefits in the future, regardless of my insurability?

_____

_____

17. For how long are benefits paid?

_____

_____

18. What is the waiting period before disability benefits begin?

_____

_____

19. Is there a *waiver of premium rider* (if you become disabled, you no longer have to pay the insurance premiums as long as you continue receiving benefits) available?

_____

_____

20. Does the policy have some sort of rehabilitation benefit?

_____

_____

21. What is the maximum monthly benefit for which I'm eligible?

_____

_____

22. What are the policy's exclusions?

_____

_____

_____

23. Will any pre-existing health conditions that I may have be excluded from coverage? If so, for how long?

_____

_____

24. Does the policy have a Social Security rider? (If it does have a Social Security rider, a supplemental benefit is paid equivalent to the Social Security disability benefits if they're denied. In the extremely unlikely event that you actually receive Social Security disability benefits, your personal disability insurance policy won't have to pay as much benefit, and therefore your premiums will be lower than a policy without the Social Security rider.)

_____

_____

25. Additional comments and observations:

_____

_____

_____

_____

_____

Chapter 17

Figuring Out What Life Insurance You Need

In This Chapter

▶ Getting to know the ins and outs of life insurance policies

▶ Calculating how much coverage you need

▶ Comparing policies and selecting the right one for you

*L*ife insurance — in its pure form — is meant to replace your income in the event of premature death. If you're married, in a committed relationship, or have children who depend on your income, you need life insurance. If you have a stay-at-home spouse or partner caring for your home and children, you would be faced with some very substantial costs to replace those services in the event of his or her premature death. In this chapter, I illustrate how to determine how much life insurance you need, explore the types of policies available, and point out the features you should look for.

Evaluating Policies and Provisions

You have the following three primary types of life insurance to choose from, and each product has its appropriate uses:

✔ **Term:** Like home or auto insurance, *term insurance* is pure insurance in that it pays off only if you make a claim. The cost of the insurance can go up every year or remain level for a specific number of years. You can lose your insurance coverage if the term expires and the policy isn't guaranteed renewable, or if you elect not to renew if you have that option. However, term insurance is by far the cheapest form of life insurance, and the only appropriate type of life insurance for most people.

Here are a few suggestions:

• Twenty-year level term coverage is generally an excellent option for families with young children, whether or not they need a lot or a little insurance, because the insurance will be there to support the surviving family, at least until the kids are grown.

• I encourage you to consider level premium term life insurance coverage. (I'm a big fan.) For one thing, the level premium guarantees that you know exactly how much your insurance is going to cost for a set number of years. Another reason I like level premium term life insurance is that it is extremely cost-effective. I would like to see you use level premium term insurance with a guaranteed level premium for the number of years that you anticipate needing the coverage and also consider adding the guaranteed renewable rider.

A guaranteed renewable rider is a very attractive feature available with many term insurance policies and assures that you will be able to retain a term policy at the end of its initial term — if you still need the insurance — simply by paying the premiums in effect at that time. You don't have to reapply or provide evidence of insurability. This provision provides great flexibility when you're not exactly sure when you'll no longer need coverage.

- If you need coverage for only five to ten years at most, you may want to consider Annual Renewable Term (ART) life insurance because it tends to be less expensive for the first five or six years of the policy, but every year thereafter, the premiums continue to increase. The break-even point is so early in the life of the Annual Renewable Term policy that it makes no sense to buy this coverage unless you won't need it very long. In every other situation where term insurance would be appropriate, go with the level premium term insurance.

Most people I've consulted with need at least $200,000 worth of life insurance, or several times that amount, to provide for their surviving family in the event of premature death, but they can't afford spending thousands of dollars per year on life insurance premiums. They need life insurance, but they only need the coverage for a limited period of time, so in this case, term insurance is the best fit.

✔ **Permanent:** With permanent life insurance, the cost is substantially higher in the first several years of your coverage. However, the cost can't go up. The initial premium rate is as bad as it'll ever get, and the insurance company can't deny you benefits as long as you pay your premiums on time. So, if you need life insurance coverage forever — for example, if you need cash available for your heirs to pay estate or inheritance taxes upon your death — you're a good candidate for permanent life insurance. Permanent insurance comes in two primary flavors:

  - **Universal:** You may possibly need a lot of life insurance now and well into your retirement years. If this is the case, universal life insurance is likely the type of insurance for at least a portion of your life insurance need.

  - **Whole:** If you need coverage for your entire life, no matter how long you live, whole life insurance might be the right option for that portion of your life insurance need.

Insurance agents make a lot more money selling universal life, variable universal life, and whole life insurance than they do selling term insurance. This inherent conflict of interest is something that you need to always keep in mind when considering the recommendations of an insurance agent.

Determining How Much Coverage You Need

You may know the type of life insurance you need, but how do you know how much coverage is best? To calculate how much life insurance you may need to support your surviving family, check out Worksheets 17-1 and 17-2.

If you're relatively healthy, term insurance is quite affordable, so if in doubt about the appropriate amount of life insurance you need or for how long, I suggest buying as much coverage as you can afford. You can generally drop a portion of your coverage as time passes and you no longer need as much coverage as you did initially.

Worksheet 17-1 illustrates a precise way of determining how much life insurance you may need. Worksheet 17-2 that follows this example provides you the opportunity to calculate your personal life insurance needs. Complete Worksheet 17-2 for both you and your spouse or partner to determine both of your life insurance needs.

If one of you does not work outside the home, be sure to add to the monthly expenses of the surviving family the cost to replace the stay-at-home parent's financial contributions to the household.

Example: In the event of the death of a stay-at-home parent while young children are in the home, you might need to hire a live-in nanny so that your children are well cared for and you can continue to work outside the home as you have been. To hire the services of a full-time nanny, you might need to spend $25,000 to $40,000 per year, for as long as you need this level of service. Add this cost to the monthly expenses of the surviving family on line 1 of Worksheet 17-2.

Worksheet 17-1   Calculating Your Life Insurance Needs (Example)

1. Monthly expenses of surviving family $ 7,000

    Subtract: Monthly take-home pay of survivor   -   2,000

    Subtract: Monthly benefits received by survivors*   -   2,800

2. Equals: Monthly required income   =   2,200

3. Multiply: Total from Line 2 by 12 for the annual need   x   12

4. Equals: Annual amount needed   =   26,400

5. How many years before youngest child is independent?   25

6. Multiply: Line 4 by Line 5

    Total cash needed by survivors if you died today   =   660,000

    Subtract surviving spouseís benefits**   -   300,000

    Add an amount from special considerations***   +   185,000

    Subtract your current savings and investments that
    will be paid to your spouse or partner upon death   -   150,000

7. Total amount of life insurance you need   =   395,000

8. Subtract: Employer provided group term insurance   -   50,000

    Association or special group coverage   -   10,000

    Personally owned life insurance   -   300,000

9. Equals: the amount of additional insurance you need   =   35,000

* Monthly benefits received by survivors include Social Security, employment-related benefits, or similar sources.

**Calculate the present value of the stream of annual payments from Social Security or company pension received by spouse after your child is independent.

***If you want to make certain your children have money to go to college, enter that amount here.

Worksheet 17-2   Calculating Your Life Insurance Needs

1. Monthly expenses of surviving family $_____

      Subtract: Monthly take-home pay of survivor   -_____

      Subtract: Monthly benefits received by survivors*   -_____

2. Equals: Monthly required income   =_____

3. Multiply: Total from Line 2 by 12 for the annual need   x_____12_____

4. Equals: Annual amount needed   =_____

5. How many years before youngest child is independent?   _____

6. Multiply: Line 4 by Line 5

      Total cash needed by survivors if you died today   =_____

      Subtract surviving spouse's benefits**   -_____

      Add an amount from special considerations***   +_____

      Subtract your current savings and investments that
      will be paid to your spouse or partner upon death   -_____

7. Total amount of life insurance you need   =_____

8. Subtract: Employer provided group term insurance   -_____

      Association or special group coverage   -_____

      Personally owned life insurance   -_____

9. Equals: the amount of additional insurance you need   =_____

* Monthly benefits received by survivors = Social Security, employment-related benefits, or similar sources.

**Calculate the present value of the stream of annual payments from Social Security or company pension received by spouse after your child is independent.

***If you want to make certain your children have money to go to college, enter that amount here.

By calculating your life insurance needs in Worksheet 17-2, you can be assured that your family will be adequately cared for in the event of your premature death. You can also know how much life insurance you truly need, and with that knowledge, are ready to contact life insurance agents or companies and obtain just the right amount of coverage you need — no more, no less.

Determining What Type of Life Insurance Is Right for You

Worksheet 17-3 is a series of key questions to help you determine what type of life insurance is right for you.

Worksheet 17-3   **Which Type of Life Insurance Is Right for You**

1. Determine how long you need insurance protection and then find where you fall in the following table.

Type	Less than 20 years	Between 20 and 30 years	Indefinitely
Term	X	X	
Permanent			X
Universal		X	X

2. Based on the following table, figure out which type of insurance matches up with the amount of coverage you need.

Type	Tons	Quite a Bit	Not Much
Term	X	X	
Universal		X	X
Whole Life			X

3. Based on the following table, figure out which type of term matches up with the amount of time you need.

Monthly premiums for $250,000 of death benefit for a male at age:

Age	20	30	40	50	60
Annual renewable term	15	15	18	27	62
10-year level term	15	15	18	30	67
15-year level term	15	15	24	36	85
20-year level term	18	18	26	46	117
30-year level term	26	27	31	71	300
Universal life	60	87	127	200	331
Whole life	163	235	360	571	945

4. Based on your results in Steps 1 and 2, which of the following types of insurance are you leaning toward?

     a.   Term   Yes   No

     b.   Universal   Yes   No

     c.   Whole Life   Yes   No

5. Based on the length of time your survivors need coverage and the cost of insurance as illustrated in Step 3, what term or type of policy is best suited for your needs?

a.	Annual renewable term	Yes	No	Maybe
b.	10-year-level term	Yes	No	Maybe
c.	15-year-level term	Yes	No	Maybe
d.	20-year-level term	Yes	No	Maybe
e.	30-year-level term	Yes	No	Maybe
f.	Universal life	Yes	No	Maybe
g.	Whole life	Yes	No	Maybe

Say, for example, that your family needs a total of $800,000 of life insurance now if you were to die, and you want to keep $200,000 worth of coverage for your spouse when he or she reaches age 65 in 30 years. You'd like your spouse to have that coverage for the rest of his or her life. You should then obtain a total of $600,000 in term insurance — preferably 30-year-level term coverage or a 20-year-level term policy that is guaranteed renewable. Then purchase a separate universal life policy to provide $200,000 for your spouse that lasts until he or she is age 95 or stops paying premiums and depletes the cash value.

Shopping Tips and Tactics

When it comes to shopping for life insurance, the Internet has leveled the playing field. You once would've had to work directly with an insurance agent to obtain life insurance. Nowadays, you can buy directly from an insurance company via many Internet-based comparison shopping Web sites. I encourage you to do your initial comparison shopping on the Web before contacting an agent or insurance company directly. Check out online quote services such as www.insure.com, www.Insurance.com, or www.select quote.com from an estimate of the cost to obtain the type of life insurance policy that you need from a variety of competitive companies.

However, if you have any health problems or are taking any prescription medication, it is in your best interest to work through an insurance agent rather than going directly to an insurance company. For example, an agent knows which companies may be more lenient regarding high blood pressure medication. You should apply only with companies who will be most amenable to your health considerations.

If you need or may benefit from permanent coverage, you should definitely work directly with an insurance agent because permanent life insurance is actually quite complex, and you'll want to make sure that you get the professional guidance an insurance professional can provide.

Check out the general insurance-buying tips in Chapter 15 and do your initial research and comparison shopping online to become better informed about competitive rates for various policies. Then contact at least three sources and allow each company to provide you with quotes on a few different policies that may be best for your situation.

You can use Worksheet 17-4 as you comparison shop. As you question each company, be sure to consider the following:

✔ How much life insurance you need

✔ How long you will likely need this coverage

✔ How much you can afford to pay in premiums

✔ Special features or benefits, such as a waiver of premium, increasing death benefits, long-term care benefits, and so on

✔ The A.M. Best Rating (A.M. Best is one of the insurance industries' premier rating serves. For more information, visit www.ambest.com.)

Don't settle for anything less than an A.M. Best *A+* (this rating indicates excellent financial strength) rated insurance company. Going with a life insurance company that is very financially strong is critical. You don't want to risk wasting your premium dollars and your survivor's financial future on a company that may not be around to pay your claim when needed.

Worksheet 17-4		Life Insurance Comparison Checklist			
Type	*Company*	*A.M. Best Rating*	*Price*	*Special Features*	*Contact Info*

After you've done your research, the only thing left to do is to proceed with filing an application with the most attractive policy for your personal situation. Be completely honest on your application when you apply for new coverage. An insurance company isn't about to pay out tens or hundreds of thousands of dollars on a death claim without a very thorough investigation. If you fail to disclose any information asked for on your insurance application, your survivor's claim may be rejected.

Chapter 18

Insuring Your Property

• •

• •

Homeowner's and auto insurance policies are likely not the sexiest subjects that you'd want to spend your time on. However, they're two of the most critical areas that must be covered to ensure financial success. Too often, families miss very simple key elements in their homeowner's and auto insurance coverages that leave them exposed to devastating risks. Fortunately, it doesn't take much time or money to fill these voids.

Covering Your Homestead

If you're a homeowner, your house needs to be insured for a minimum of 80 percent of its value (not counting the value of the land). However, many parts of the country have seen extraordinary appreciation in home values over recent years, and if you purchased your home several years ago, your home may be significantly underinsured.

For example: You purchased a home in 1995 for $300,000. If your home appreciated an average of 10 percent per year over the last 12 years, your home is worth over $940,000. However, your homeowner's insurance may have only increased through its automatic inflation adjustments to less than one-half that amount.

You must be proactive and review your current homeowner's coverage at least on an annual basis to make certain that your insurance is sufficient to rebuild or repair your home if it is destroyed. So, what do you need to be looking for during the annual review of your homeowner's policy? Worksheet 18-1 delves into the key components required to make sure that you're fully and adequately covered.

Before you dive into Worksheet 18-1, here are a few terms you need to know:

✔ **Actual-cash-value coverage:** If you have a policy that pays the actual cash value of your home's contents, you'll get a check for what your stuff was *worth* before it was destroyed — *not* what it would cost to replace your valued items.

✔ **Declarations page(s):** This one- to two-page annual statement you receive from your insurance company each year outlines your coverages and your annual premium. Keep it with your policy.

✔ **Full replacement cost:** If your property is destroyed, the insurance company is obligated to *fully* replace or rebuild your property *without* any deduction for depreciation. Obtaining full replacement cost on your personal property will cost you only about 10 to 20 percent more than the actual-cash-value coverage. Comprehensive homeowner's coverage must include full replacement cost to repurchase all the items in your home today if they're lost, stolen, or destroyed.

✔ **Guaranteed replacement cost:** Even if the damage exceeds the limits on your policy, the insurance company is obligated to fully replace or rebuild your property without any deduction for depreciation. Guaranteed replacement policies aren't exactly what you might imagine. Insurers limit the amount that they pay out to replace or rebuild your home to usually no more than 20 percent above the amount for which your home is insured. (*Note:* If your home appreciates beyond the level of coverage, the policy won't cover that amount — even though you thought you had guaranteed replacement coverage.)

Guaranteed replacement coverage doesn't end with just the dwelling itself; you must also think about the value of the contents of your home. The contents of my "junk" drawer alone would cost more than $300 to replace. Now just imagine how much more money it would take to replace all the items throughout your home.

Even if you try to obtain guaranteed replacement coverage on your home and all its contents, you may not be able to secure guaranteed replacement coverage for certain things. For example, the majority of homeowner's insurance companies don't provide full replacement coverage for a roof damaged by hail or windstorms. Instead, the company *depreciates* it, which means that the insurance company assesses the damage and estimates the useful life of the roof prior to the storm and pays only that portion. You have to come up with the balance of the cost of a new roof. Nothing like thinking you're fully insured only to discover that you need to come up with $5,000 or $10,000 to apply toward a new roof immediately! Contact your homeowner's insurance agent and ask her specifically what items in and around your home will be replaced in their entirety or depreciated.

✔ **Liability:** This type of insurance helps protect you financially if someone is injured by you on your property.

✔ **Rider:** A rider is really a separate insurance policy that goes with your homeowner's policy to insure special types of personal property. Items like electronics, musical equipment, jewelry, and antiques are often covered only up to about $2,000 in value. You must obtain a rider on your homeowner's policy, for an additional cost, to fully insure these items. A copy of your purchase receipt and/or an appraisal may be necessary to substantiate the value of the items covered under each rider. The annual cost for this additional insurance is about $17 per $1,000 in coverage.

Worksheet 18-1   Insuring Your Home and Everything in It

1. Check with your insurer to verify these limits and enter that amount here _____%.

2. Calculate the current replacement cost of your home by doing the following:

   a. Pull out a copy of the most recent declarations page that you've received from your homeowner's insurance provider.

   b. Locate the amount listed as the property coverage for the dwelling. Enter that amount here $_____.

c. Enter the approximate square footage of your house here _____.

d. Divide the amount of coverage for the dwelling by the square footage of your home (Line b ÷ Line c). Enter the total here. $_____.

e. Talk to a couple of custom homebuilders to determine an approximate price per square foot to rebuild a home of similar quality. Be sure to let the custom home-builder know about all the expensive improvements that you've done on your home since it was initially purchased. Those granite countertops, finished rec room, and the new master suite with Jacuzzi tub have definitely increased the cost to rebuild your home.

Estimate the value of those enhancements and enter that amount here $_____ per square foot.

You can also get an estimate online at www.accucoverage.com for $7.95 or for no cost at www.building-cost.net. Enter the average result here $_____.

f. Multiply Line e by Line c to determine the replacement cost. Enter the result here $_____.

g. Contact your homeowner's insurance agent and increase the value of your dwelling to no less than 100 percent of what it would cost to rebuild the same quality home today. You will be surprised at how little your insurance premiums will increase, and you can rest assured that your home *now* really does have guaranteed-replacement coverage.

3. Take a detailed inventory of all the possessions in your home, including the contents in the basement, garage, storage shed, and so on.

You want to make sure that you're insured at a level that allows you to replace everything that you need to resume life as you once knew it before your insurance claim.

A detailed written list, including brand names, makes, models, serial numbers, purchase dates, and purchase prices, is helpful in case you need to substantiate an insurance claim. Photographs and video recordings are extremely helpful for this purpose as well. Keep this list, the photographs, and video recordings in your safety deposit box. And don't forget to update these records regularly.

Enter your guesstimate for how much money it would take to replace the contents of your home here $_____.

Yes, I know this is a lot of work. But there is no other way to prove to the insurance company that your *stuff* is worth squat without this kind of proof. Likely the easiest option is to walk through and around your entire property with a camcorder and verbally describe in intricate detail everything that is being viewed — floor to ceiling — inside drawers and closets.

Even if you try to obtain guaranteed replacement coverage on all your contents and your home, you may not be able to secure guaranteed replacement coverage for certain items.

4. Review your insurance declarations pages and your policy, answer each of the points concerning your existing coverage on your home and its contents, and contact your homeowner's insurance agent if you have questions.

Make sure that your home and its contents are properly covered according to your estimates from Steps 2 and 3. Also, ask your agent to provide recommendations regarding additional coverage or enhancements that he feels you should make at this time — Worksheet 18-2 can help with this task. (Later in this chapter, I suggest how to go about comparison shopping.)

Revisit this conversation with your insurance professional at least annually and contact your homeowner's insurance agent anytime your home (not including land) appreciates beyond 100 percent of the dwelling coverage.

Review your declarations page and insurance page to discover what the liability limits are on your policy in addition to the coverage. If you can't find that information, contact your agent.

Personal liability (each occurrence) $_____

Medical payments (each person) $_____

Although Worksheet 18-1 helps you cover the basics when it comes to making sure that you have enough homeowner's insurance, you may want to consider whether your home falls under special circumstances that may require additional coverage. In order to help you figure out whether you may need more coverage for special circumstances, go through the checklist in Worksheet 18-2. If any of these statements apply to you, you should contact your insurance agent to make sure that you're properly covered. Be scrupulously honest and extremely detailed with your current and any prospective insurance agent so that she can best help you obtain adequate insurance coverage.

Worksheet 18-2   Special Home Coverages Checklist

You may need additional coverage on your home if the following conditions apply:

- ✔ **You operate a home-based business.** If you haven't told your insurance agent about your business, you're likely not covered for any activities involving the business or your business equipment.

- ✔ **You live with someone to whom you aren't married and who isn't on the deed or title to the home.** Your roomie's possessions likely aren't insured unless he has a renter's policy. Talk to your insurance agent about how to proceed.

- ✔ **You may be exposed to water damage due to storm sewer or water backup.** I once had the mistaken assumption that because I lived on the top of the hill, my home was not at risk for flood damage. During a period of heavy rain, my sump pump malfunctioned, and I ended up with over a foot of water in my basement. My homeowner's policy did not cover any damage caused by this event. An additional coverage called *sewer backup* is necessary to provide protection under this type of circumstance. Ever since that time, I have paid a very small amount of additional premium to maintain storm drainage and sewer backup protection. You should also consider maintaining this additional coverage if you have anything of value on the lowest level of your home.

- ✔ **You live in a flood zone or are in danger of incurring water damage from other sources such as hurricanes.** Water damage from hurricanes and storm surges, as well as other types of flooding, aren't covered by homeowner's policies. For example, the massive destruction Hurricane Katrina caused was almost all due to flooding. Even those people who had comprehensive home-owner's insurance policies may not have had *flood* insurance. They lost their homes, and their insurance policies may not pay to replace them, because water damage is not automatically covered.

The only way to obtain flood insurance is through the National Flood Insurance Program (NFIP) (`www.floodsmart.gov/floodsmart/pages/index.jsp`), and the coverage isn't available in some of the most high-risk areas. Contact the NFIP or your homeowner's agent to find out more.

✔ **You're at risk for windstorm damage.** Do you live in a hurricane zone? Check to see whether your homeowner's policy has a windstorm deductible. This provision requires you to pay a portion of the damage to your property from wind created by a hurricane. Windstorm deductibles are usually 1 to 5 percent of a policy's total value. For example, if your home is insured for $300,000 and you have a windstorm deductible of 5 percent, you can be out of pocket $15,000 before the insurer pays anything.

✔ **Your home is at risk of mold damage.** Does your homeowner's policy cover for mold damage? Mold is becoming an epidemic in certain parts of the country. If you have a mold problem, you may not be able to continue living in the house or sell it, and many insurance companies are limiting the amount that they're willing to pay to fix the problem to $10,000.

✔ **You live in or near an earthquake-prone area.** You definitely should investigate earthquake coverage. In certain high-risk areas, many people have concluded that earthquake coverage is cost prohibitive. However, if you're in a high-risk area, can you afford to be without earthquake coverage? By the way, do you know one of the most significant earthquakes in this country occurred in the Midwest? Are you sure that you're not at risk for an earthquake? Can you afford to be wrong? If not, buy the coverage.

Shopping for the right homeowner's policy

If you're currently shopping for insurance for a new home, or if you haven't done any comparison shopping in a long time, you should spend a little time finding out what the marketplace has to offer. I don't advocate switching insurance companies unless you don't have a quality, competitive policy; however, you want to make certain that you're receiving quality coverage at a cost-effective price.

Also keep in mind that insurers reward loyalty. If you've been a loyal customer with the same insurance company for 10 or 20 years, you're less likely to be dropped or see a drastic increase in your premium in the event of a legitimate claim than if you'd been with the company for only one or two years.

My personal favorite place to begin my research is at J.D. Power and Associate's Web site at `www.jdpower.com/insurance/ratings/homeowners_insurance/index.asp`. This site provides an annual National Homeowner's Insurance Study and ranks companies based on customers' ratings in the following categories:

✔ Overall experience

✔ Policy offerings

✔ Pricing

✔ Contacting (interacting with) the insurer

To do some research and compare policies on your own, obtain premium quotes from different insurance companies. Be careful to compare policies with identical features and benefits. You want to look for the financially strongest companies, with great claims payments history, where you can obtain all the required and desired coverages for the best price.

Saving money on your homeowner's policy

Not looking forward to spending so much of your hard-earned cash on your homeowner's policy? Don't worry — I'm here to help you with some money-saving tips. Insurance companies often offer discounts on your homeowner's insurance if you qualify in certain categories, or you may be able to adjust your deductible to make ends meet.

If you're considering lowering your *deductible* (the part you pay before your insurance policy kicks in), keep in mind that insurance is intended to cover risks that you can't afford to bear on your own. The higher the deductible, the lower the premium. By raising your deductibles to $1,000 from $250, you may be able to reduce your premium by as much as 25 to 30 percent. Just make sure that you don't raise your deductible so high that you can't pay that amount in case of an emergency.

Ask yourself the following important questions, which may save you money on your homeowner's insurance:

✔ Are your home, auto, and liability insurance policies with the same company? And if not, would you be willing to change in order to save you money?

I don't necessarily recommend changing insurers that you have a long-term history with. In insurance, cost is only one of the major factors to consider.

✔ Do you have any safety devices (smoke detectors, fire extinguishers, sprinkler systems, alarm systems, and so on) in your home?

✔ How long have you maintained coverage with the same insurance company?

✔ Have you made any mechanical or structural upgrades to your home?

✔ In an emergency, could you comfortably afford to pay your deductible if you raised it?

If you answered *Yes* to any of these questions, contact your current or prospective insurance company to see whether you can save yourself a little bit o' money, while obtaining top quality and adequate insurance coverage. Be sure to also ask the insurance agent whether any other discounts are available to which you may be entitled.

Acquiring Coverage for Your Car

If you drive, you need to have auto insurance coverage (no contest). But just exactly which type of coverages should you have, and which ones are you required to have? The following are the key features of auto insurance (depending on your unique circumstances you may or may not need all these features; I talk about this more later in this section):

✔ **Collision:** If you're in an automobile accident, regardless of who is at fault, collision insurance provides protection to replace or repair your vehicle, subject to a deductible.

✔ **Comprehensive:** In the event of hail damage or a tree limb falling on your car (risks not involving an automobile collision), this coverage insures you. Comprehensive coverage pays to repair your vehicle, subject to a separate deductible.

✔ **Personal injury protection:** This type of insurance coverage is for medical and other expenses resulting from an automobile accident for the people specified in the policy, regardless of who is at fault in the accident.

✔ **Medical payments:** This feature provides a limited amount of coverage for you and your passengers' medical expenses as a result of an accident. The coverage pays regardless of who is at fault.

✔ **Bodily injury and property damage liability coverage:** The insurer agrees to pay damages if you injure someone or his property in an auto accident.

✔ **Uninsured and underinsured motorists liability coverage:** If you're in an accident with another driver who doesn't carry any or enough liability coverage, uninsured or underinsured motorists liability coverage allows you to collect damages that you personally experience from the accident.

Worksheet 18-3 lists commonly recommended limits and deductibles for the various coverages involved in basic auto policies.

Worksheet 18-3	Suggested Deductibles and Limits
Coverage	*Deductible*
Collision	$500 to $1,000
Comprehensive	$500 to $1,000
Personal injury protection	Deductible doesn't apply. This coverage may be required in your state.
Medical payments	Deductible doesn't apply. This feature is optional. If you and *all* your passengers have comprehensive health insurance, you shouldn't need this additional coverage.
Liability Coverage	*Limits*
Bodily injury	$100,000 per person, $300,000 per accident
Property damage	$100,000 per accident
Uninsured motorists	$100,000 (This coverage may be required in your state; however, the limit is likely less.)
Underinsured motorists	$100,000

Because states differ in regulations and because you may have unique circumstances, you may need more or less coverage than what I describe in Worksheet 18-3. For state-by-state regulations on required coverages, visit `http://info.insure.com/auto/minimum.html`. Also consider the following before deciding on what coverage you need:

✔ Increasing your liability limits and your deductibles may be appropriate for you if you have cash reserves. The additional liability coverage raises your premium; however, increasing your deductibles helps offset those additional costs. In fact, increasing your deductible from $250 to $500 could reduce your collision and comprehensive coverage premium by 15 to 30 percent. Going up to a $1,000 deductible could save you about 40 percent.

REMEMBER

You buy insurance to cover big financial risks. If you're involved in a major accident and cars are totaled, people are injured or killed, and property is damaged, the total financial impact could be hundreds of thousands, if not millions, of dollars. The liability benefits on your automobile policy help to protect you from this financial devastation. You can't afford to skimp on liability coverage.

✔ If you have a much older vehicle or drive your vehicles until they drop, a time will come when maintaining collision and comprehensive insurance coverages isn't financially worthwhile. A general guideline is to drop collision and comprehensive coverage on vehicles worth less than ten times the cost for that portion of your auto policy.

For example, in reviewing your declaration page, you see that the premium on the collision and comprehensive portions of your automobile insurance policy total approximately $220 a year. Ten times $220 equals $2,200. If your car is worth less than $2,200, you should seriously consider dropping your collision and comprehensive insurance coverages.

WARNING!

Don't drop your liability coverages under any circumstance — your old clunker can still wreak havoc in an accident. Besides, your state law probably requires that you maintain liability insurance. And like the money savvy person you are, you wouldn't want to put yourself and your family in this kind of financial jeopardy.

To review your current auto coverage, you can use Worksheet 18-4, which outlines the key features of auto policies and provides you the opportunity to indicate whether you have this coverage and how much coverage you currently have. This info becomes very useful when comparing policy provisions, recommended enhancements, and other policies when shopping around.

Worksheet 18-4	Key Features of Your Current Auto Insurance		
Type of Coverage	Limits	*Deductible*	*Annual Premium*
Collision			
Comprehensive			
Personal injury protection			
Medical payments			
Bodily injury			
Uninsured motorists			
Underinsured motorists			

The more you know about auto insurance and how the industry works, the better off you will be, and the more money you can save. The following are key factors that car insurers use to determine the price of your auto insurance and what you can do to keep it as low as possible:

✔ **Age:** If you're very young or quite elderly, your risk of being in an auto accident is statistically much higher than for middle-aged folks. You can't do anything about your age. However, some insurers may penalize you less than others with regard to your cost of insurance.

✔ **Auto insurance claims history:** Safe drivers are rewarded with lower auto insurance premiums. Your history of making claims against your auto policy will directly affect the cost of your insurance. The more you *use* insurance, the more your insurance will cost.

✔ **Commuting distance to work:** Face it — getting on the road is dangerous. The farther you drive, the higher your risk of being in an accident.

✔ **Credit history:** Insurance companies have determined that there is a direct correlation between your credit history and your risk as a driver. I guess they figure that if you're careless with your credit, then you may be careless in your driving — just one more reason why improving and continuing to maintain good credit is essential to your financial health. (For more on your credit, see Chapter 5.)

✔ **Driving record:** If you have received a traffic ticket for speeding or another form of reckless driving, you'll pay for that carelessness in higher insurance premiums.

✔ **Marital status:** Married people historically are more stable drivers.

✔ **Place of residence:** Your zip code can have a drastic effect on your cost of insurance. Certain zip codes have a history for more auto theft, vandalism, and so on, and the insurance companies are still allowed to penalize you for living in these zip codes.

✔ **Type of car you drive:** A Dodge Dart station wagon versus a Hummer or a Corvette? The latter two will pay substantially higher auto insurance premiums because those cars will cause or potentially receive much more damage in the same accident as the Dodge station wagon, and they cost a lot more to repair or replace than the older, less expensive vehicle. Also, drivers of sports cars statistically drive more carelessly then drivers of sedans. Careless driving causes accidents. Accidents result in claims. Claims result in higher insurance costs.

Don't go with the first auto insurance policy you run across or switch insurances just for the sake of switching (remember that insurers value loyalty). However, shopping around and doing some snooping around can pay off.

1. **Begin your research at J.D. Power and Associates at `www.jdpower.com/insurance/ratings/auto_insurance/index.asp`, which provides customer ratings for many insurance companies.**

2. **Have a copy of Worksheets 18-3 and 18-4 available so that you know exactly what you have and need from your auto insurance coverage.**

3. **Get at least three competitive quotes directly from some of these highly rated companies as well as one or two independent agents who represent many insurance companies and can perform some comparison shopping for you.**

    You can find an agent in your area through the Independent Insurance Agents and Brokers of America at `www.iiaba.net/agentlocator/findagent.aspx`.

Using Worksheet 18-5, you can enter all of the results from your comparison shopping. Be sure to always compare apples to apples.

Worksheet 18-5   Comparing Auto Insurance Policies

Insurer	JD Powers Ratings	Annual Premium	Notes

After you've found a policy you're happy with, buy it!

Worksheet 18-6 is a quick summary of money-saving strategies that may help you obtain the best policy at the best price.

Worksheet 18-6   Saving Money on Your Auto Insurance

Discounts

_____ Are your home, auto, and liability insurance policies with the same company?

_____ How long have you maintained coverage with the same insurance company?

_____ Do you have any safety devices, such as airbags, antilock brakes, or an alarm system?

_____ Are you over age 50 or 55?

_____ Do you use public transportation or work from home, and only drive your vehicle for personal use?

_____ Are you the only person who drives your vehicle?

_____ Are there any other discounts to which you may be entitled?

Deductibles

_____ What is the current deductible on your auto policy?

_____ What would your premium be if you raised your deductible to the next higher limit?

_____ What would your premium be if you raised your deductible even further?

_____ To what level could you comparably afford to raise your deductible?

Here are some tips to help you save money on your auto insurance:

- **Don't file small claims.** The more you use your insurance, the higher your premium rates will be. Higher premiums mean that the insurance company will make money on you. That's a good thing. If you made money on the insurance company, you must have been involved in a horrible accident. Submitting claims that exceed your deductible by just a few hundred dollars doesn't make financial sense. You won't come out ahead if you file small or frequent claims; paying for smaller losses yourself can save you money over the long term.

  The insurance company is in business to make money. Use your insurance to protect you only from devastating financial losses.

- **Don't let other people drive your vehicle.** Multiple drivers create multiple risks. More risk, more cost of insurance.

- **Wear your seatbelt.** Studies prove more people survive accidents and receive less severe injuries because they wear their seatbelts. Less injury, less insurance claim, less cost of insurance.

- **Drive the speed limit.** Speeders cause accidents. Accidents result in claims. Claims jack up your cost of insurance.

- **Take a driver safety course.** Many companies provide a discount to drivers who have taken a safe driving course.

- **Practice defensive-driving techniques.** Fewer accidents. Fewer claims. Cheaper insurance rates.

- **Continue to improve your credit score.** For more info, see Chapter 5.

- **Pay your auto insurance premium annually.** Most companies charge a service fee if you pay your premiums monthly, quarterly, and sometimes semiannually.

- **Before buying a vehicle, check out its insurance safety rating through Consumer Reports.** You can find this info at www.consumerreports.org if you're a subscriber.

Adding to Your Liability Protection

In addition to the liability coverages that you have through your homeowner's and auto insurance policies (see previous sections), you very likely should also have an *umbrella liability policy*, which is additional liability insurance added on top of the other coverages, and covers attorney's fees for claims arising from your nonbusiness activities. If you have any assets to protect, liability insurance is a must. Thank goodness it doesn't cost much.

Umbrella liability insurance is generally sold in increments of $1 million. General guidelines state that you should have one to two times the value of your assets in liability insurance. To figure out how much liability insurance you need, guestimate your net worth and then round up to the nearest $1 million.

Fortunately, the cost of this coverage is fairly reasonable. You can obtain a $1 million umbrella liability coverage for less than $150 per year. Contact the agent who provides your homeowner's and auto coverage for more information.

Chapter 19

Protecting Your Privacy

● ●

In This Chapter

▶ Implementing practices to keep your financial information safe

▶ Keeping an eye on your credit report

▶ Making Do Not Call and Do Not Solicit policies work for you

▶ Using your credit cards safely

▶ Guarding your financial information while you're online

▶ Knowing when and how often to revisit your privacy practices

● ●

*I*dentity theft has become the fastest-growing crime in America. You may think it won't happen to you, but it's happening to nearly 1 million Americans every single year — and the trend is growing. If you're a victim of identity theft, clearing your good name could take you months, if not years, and tens of thousands of dollars. And meanwhile, you can't get credit, you may not be able to get a job, and your insurance rates could skyrocket — all because of the activities of someone who is pretending to be you. You can substantially reduce this risk and protect your financial privacy by following the simple suggestions outlined in this chapter.

Keeping Your Personal Financial Information Safe and Secure

Thieves use a variety of techniques to steal private information about you and your personal finances. They may go dumpster diving, where they're actually going through all your garbage to gather personal financial information, or they may even try to scam you through fraudulent e-mails. I can go on and on about the ways thieves scheme to get your info, but instead, I want to arm you with some ways to prevent having your financial info stolen.

Worksheet 19-1 is a listing of some simple and practical strategies that you can use to protect your privacy and drastically reduce the likelihood of anyone stealing your financial information. Don't let this worksheet scare you, but do allow it to empower you to protect yourself against this growing epidemic of identity theft.

Worksheet 19-1   **Keys to Protecting Your Financial Privacy**

❏ Reduce solicitations — especially through the mail, which is only fodder for thieves. For tips on how to do so, see the section "Utilizing the Do Not Call and Do Not Solicit Policies" later in this chapter.

❏ Lock your mailbox — one quick and easy solution to keep sticky fingers out of your personal info. The postal carriers can deposit mail into the box, but no one can make a withdrawal without having the key. Consider taking your outgoing mail to the post office directly or to a U.S. Postal Service depository mailbox, which you can find just about anywhere.

❏ Have your payroll check, pension, or Social Security checks automatically deposited into your bank account so that thieves can't get a hold of any hard copies, acid-wash your name off the checks, and cash them for themselves.

❏ Shred all paperwork containing any personal information before discarding, including *any* document containing *any* of the following information:

   • your name

   • date of birth

   • address

   • Social Security number

   • account numbers

   • account statements

   • checks

   • bills

   • paycheck stubs

Prior to discarding any of these documents, keep them in a safe place, such as a locked file cabinet.

❏ Don't give out any personal information to anyone you don't know — either in person or on the phone — unless you initiated the contact or can validate that that she actually is employed by the company that she's representing. If in doubt, don't give it out the information!

❏ If possible, use a landline phone when providing private financial information over the telephone. Identity thieves can gain access to your private financial information by eavesdropping on your conversations taking place on cellular or cordless telephones.

❏ Carefully protect all user IDs, password information, and personal identification numbers. Never carry this information in your wallet and don't save this type of information on your computer or on any Web site. (For more on online safety, see the section "Protecting Yourself from Identity Thieves," later in this chapter.)

❏ Never have anything printed on your banking account checks, such as your Social Security number, phone number, and so on, that isn't required.

❏ Don't allow your Social Security number to be used as your participant number, user ID, username, or login name on anything. Frequently, group health companies use a Social Security number as your employee ID number. Call your insurers or your human resources department at work and request a new employee ID number and insurance card.

❏ If you carry a purse (or man-purse), don't let it out of your sight. Hang it on the back of your chair or place it on the floor next to your chair at a restaurant. These same rules apply to laptop computers!

❏ If or when you dispose of a computer, erase the hard drive first! You may want to use a product like Disk Wipe, which is available at `www.dtidata.com/disk_wipe.htm`.

Don't think that all thieves are strangers. In more than half of all reported identity theft cases, the thief turned out to be a coworker, family member, or friend.

Monitoring Your Credit Report

Obtain copies of your credit report from each of the three major credit bureaus and review them carefully at least once each year. Most people discover that their identity has been stolen only when they go to apply for credit and are denied. Then they obtain a copy of their credit report and discover all kinds of activities that aren't theirs.

Don't wait to be denied credit to review your credit report. Regular monitoring of your credit report and following the safety tips I share in this chapter are the best ways to protect yourself. Refer to Chapter 5 for additional information on monitoring your credit.

Utilizing the Do Not Call and Do Not Solicit Policies

You have to spend some time now to save time over the long-run, save trees, and protect your privacy. You can follow the steps outlined in Worksheet 19-2 to reduce the majority of your junk mail, telephone solicitations, and spam. Unfortunately, companies that already have your personal and private information are allowed by law to give or sell it to others unless you *expressly* tell them *not* to do so. You can use Worksheet 19-3 to express your unwillingness to let anyone give out or sell your information.

Worksheet 19-2 **Minimizing Solicitations**

❏ Add your name and phone number to the National Do-Not-Call Registry online at `www.donotcall.gov` or by calling 888-382-1222.

❏ Contact the Direct Marketing Association and get removed from their solicitation lists too. Here's the DMA's contact info for the different types of solicitations:

• Mail: Mail Preference Service, P.O. Box 643, Carmel, NY 10512; Web site `www.dmaconsumers.org/cgi/offmailing`

• E-mail: Web site `www.dmaconsumers.org/offemaillist.html`

❑ Contact the major credit bureaus and opt out of receiving *preapproved credit offers* sent to you. Go online to www.optoutprescreen.com or call 888-5OPT-OUT (888-567-8688). Or your can write the three major credit bureaus and tell them that you don't want personal information about you shared for any promotional purposes. (This step reduces the number of unsolicited credit card and loan offers coming to you in the mail and thwarts would-be thieves who'd love to get their hands on one of your pre-approved credit card offers.)

   • Equifax, Options, P.O. Box 740123, Atlanta, GA 30374

   • Experian, Consumer Opt-Out, 701 Experian Parkway, Allen, TX 75013

   • TransUnion, Name Removal Option, P.O. Box 505, Woodlyn, PA 19094

❑ Also write all companies with which you do business (your utility companies, your bank, your credit-card company, insurance companies, lenders, and so on) and specifically tell them not to sell or share your personal and private information with anyone, including their affiliate companies. If you don't proactively opt out, these companies can (and do) sell or share your personal information with others. (Refer to the sample letter in Worksheet 19-3.)

Worksheet 19-3 is a form letter that you can use to notify the major credit bureaus and all the companies with which you do business that under no circumstance do you want your personal and private information sold to or shared with anybody. Send your personal equivalent of this letter to all people and companies with which you do business who may have any of your private information. Examples are folks like the following:

✔ Your life insurance agent and his company

✔ Your local bank

✔ Your credit-card companies

✔ Other lenders you may have

✔ Any company with which you have investments

✔ Any company from which you receive one of those mandatory Privacy Policy letters or brochures at least once a year, most likely written with legal mumbo jumbo and in the tiniest print possible.

It takes some time, but you can drastically reduce the amount of unwanted solicitations, unauthorized inquiries regarding your credit history, junk mail in your mailbox, spam in your e-mail box, and computer viruses. In short, you'll be a difficult person for identity thieves to victimize.

EXAMPLE

Worksheet 19-3   **Opt Out Letter (Example)**

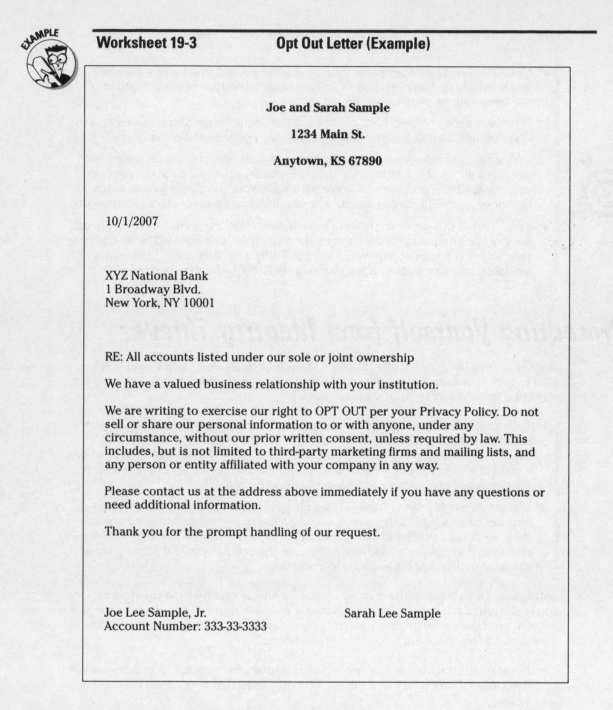

Joe and Sarah Sample

1234 Main St.

Anytown, KS 67890

10/1/2007

XYZ National Bank
1 Broadway Blvd.
New York, NY 10001

RE: All accounts listed under our sole or joint ownership

We have a valued business relationship with your institution.

We are writing to exercise our right to OPT OUT per your Privacy Policy. Do not sell or share our personal information to or with anyone, under any circumstance, without our prior written consent, unless required by law. This includes, but is not limited to third-party marketing firms and mailing lists, and any person or entity affiliated with your company in any way.

Please contact us at the address above immediately if you have any questions or need additional information.

Thank you for the prompt handling of our request.

Joe Lee Sample, Jr.   Sarah Lee Sample
Account Number: 333-33-3333

Credit Cards: Swiping Safely

Credit cards are prime targets for identity thieves because they can get the information needed and begin using your credit very quickly and easily. In order to use your credit cards for your own convenience, but still keep your financial info safe, follow these guidelines:

✔ Carry as few credit cards as necessary in your wallet — one or two should be plenty!

✔ Use your credit cards only with companies and service providers with which you regularly do business. Use cash in all other situations or secure online bill-payment options, when possible.

✔ Scrutinize each entry on your credit-card statements when you receive them to make certain that all transactions are ones that you initiated or authorized.

Online access makes checking out your credit-card accounts much easier. With just a few clicks of the mouse, you can see exactly what has been charged on your card, where, and when. You can also make your payments just as easily. Contact your credit-card companies to establish online access to your accounts.

✔ Keep a list of the entire contents of your wallet, including a copy of the front and back of each item and the company's phone number, in a safe place. Just in case your wallet is lost or stolen, you'll need to notify each company immediately. If available, ask for a freeze on your account until further notice from you.

Protecting Yourself from Identity Thieves

Identity thieves have gotten increasingly more sophisticated by using e-mail and Web sites to take your personal and financial information. The following are a few common ways that thieves may try to steal your info:

✔ You receive an e-mail saying that you have won a prize, and all you need to do to collect is complete a brief questionnaire about your personal information and request a check for a processing fee. But these scammers don't intend to send you a prize at all. (*Surprise* is a better word for it!) Instead, they will cash or acid-wash the check and continue using your private information.

✔ You get an e-mail in your inbox asking for personal information, from what appears to be a legitimate source, such as a national bank or a major corporation, needing to verify its records (for an example, check out Worksheet 19-4). However, if the inquiry was truly legitimate, the company would already know the information that it's requesting from you.

Bottomline: Don't reply to these types of e-mails! That is exactly what the thieves want you to do. And if the e-mail contains a link to a Web site, don't clickthrough to the site. Instead, send the e-mail to your spam or junk-mail folder. For more ways to avoid being scammed online, check out the following guidelines:

✔ Never open attachments or click on links in e-mails from people or companies you don't know. Don't worry — if the e-mail is truly legit, that person will contact you again.

✔ Don't fill out any forms contained in an e-mail from someone you don't know or a company you don't do business with. Never fill out forms from any pop-up ads.

Worksheet 19-4   **Fraudulent E-mail (Example)**

Dear **National City** business client:

The National City Corporate Customer Service requests you to complete the National City Business Online Client Form.

This procedure is obligatory for all business and corporate clients of National City.

Please click the hyperlink and visit the address listed to access the National City Business Online Client Form.

http://session-447667953.nationalcity.com/corporate/onlineservices/TreasuryMgmt/

Again, thank you for choosing National City for your business needs. We look forward to working with you.

***** Please do not respond to this e-mail *****

This mail is generated by an automated service.
Replies to this mail are not read by National City Corporate Customer Service or technical support.

✔ Use a combination of letters, numbers, and symbols in your online passwords. These passwords are much harder for a hacker to crack.

✔ Consider using computer software that keeps all your online password and username information in one safe, secure place. I recommend using RoboForm. Download this software from www.roboform.com and load it onto a USB jump drive so that you can remove the device and take it with you for use on other computers, such as a laptop or a shared computer. The software costs about $40, and you'll never have to remember the Web address, login information, or your passwords to log onto any Web site that you use. You simply need to remember one super-secret password to access your RoboForm information (so don't write down or tell anyone your super-secret password and don't make it obvious).

✔ When shopping online, make sure that the URL shows *https* (rather than the traditional *http*) when you're in the section of the Web site asking for credit-card or personal information needed to complete the transaction. The *s* stands for a secure site.

✔ Use antivirus software, such as AVG or Norton, and use antispam software such as Comodo AntiSpam (www.comodoantispam.com), which requires senders to verify themselves, or Mailwasher Pro, which analyzes each e-mail as it arrives and warns you if it's suspected junk mail or a virus using advanced logic and filtering. You can find out more about Mailwasher Pro at http://firetrust.com/download/mailwasher-pro.

✔ Any time you log on to a Web site, be sure to log out!

Renewing Your Privacy Protection

Unfortunately, all the protective measures I outline in the previous sections don't last a lifetime. You'd think that if you asked to have your name removed from a mailing list, you wouldn't have to make this request again a few years later. Unfortunately, that's just not true.

You have to renew these rights periodically. Table 19-1 illustrates how often you need to revisit your privacy protection and helps you keep track of when your renewal is due and when you've completed it.

Table 19-1	Privacy Update Schedule & Checklist		
Who	*Renewal Frequency*	*Date Due*	*Completed?*
National Do Not Call Registry	Every five years	_/_/_	❏
Major credit bureaus: Prescreen (opt out)	Every two years	_/_/_	❏
Major credit bureaus: Promotional offers	Every two years	_/_/_	❏
Direct Marketing Association: Mail	Every five years	_/_/_	❏
Direct Marketing Association: E-mail	Every five years	_/_/_	❏

Should you have any problems — for example, you're still receiving solicitations even after following all these steps — contact the Federal Trade Commission at 877-FTC-HELP (877-383-4357) or www.ftc.gov.

Chapter 20

Finding and Hiring the Right Advisor (If You Need One)

In This Chapter

▶ Figuring out how financial advisors work and get paid

▶ Understanding the alphabet soup of credentials

▶ Knowing when you may need to hire an advisor

▶ Discovering how to interview and select an advisor

*P*ersonal Finance Workbook For Dummies provides you with the tools and information you need to become a savvy personal financial manager. However, you may have occasions when you need to work with financial services people to obtain a mortgage or a business or school loan or to purchase real estate, securities, or insurance products. Obtaining guidance from a professional financial advisor may also be necessary and appropriate at times.

However, any swindler, idiot with a good heart, or PhD in financial planning with decades of practical and professional advisory experience can call himself a financial advisor. Fortunately, the majority of the people in financial services aren't crooks or idiots. But you need to know about the extreme differences regarding how financial advisors work and get paid, as well as how they are acquired, their training, experience, credentials, expertise, and integrity.

This chapter helps you recognize when you may need a financial advisor and empowers you to make the wisest decisions possible when searching for and selecting financial services professionals.

Identifying How Financial Advisors Work and Get Paid

One initial way to differentiate between financial advisors is by examining how they're paid, which tells you a lot about how they work and what type of work they do (and don't do).

All people in the financial services industry, which include financial planners and advisors, get paid in one of the following four ways:

✔ **Commission only:** Some advisors receive only commissions for selling financial services products such as investments, real estate, insurance products, or loans. Examples include advisors affiliated with companies like State Farm, American Family, and Edward Jones. Your auto insurance agent, the municipal bond salesman, a mortgage broker, or real estate agent are all examples of financial services professionals who are compensated on a commission-only basis.

- ✔ **Commission and fees:** Most personal financial planners are paid this way. A commonly misunderstood term used to describe this compensation method is _fee-based_. Examples include registered representatives of companies like Lincoln Financial Advisors, Ameriprise, AIG Financial Advisors, Wachovia, UBS, and Merrill Lynch. Commission and fee advisors may receive a fee for developing a financial plan for you _and_ then receive commissions when they sell you insurance and investment products recommended in your financial plan.

- ✔ **Salary plus bonuses:** Many discount brokerage firms and banks compensate their employees with a base salary plus incentive pay for bringing in new client accounts (money) into the institution. They may receive substantially higher bonuses by recommending or selling certain products and services over other options.

- ✔ **Fee-only:** Fee-only financial advisors provide advice or ongoing management and aren't registered representatives of any financial services company. They're typically self-employed Registered Investment Advisors (RIA) or employees of this type of firm. All their compensation is paid directly by you, the client. How much they charge is painfully obvious to the client.

  One benefit often cited regarding fee-only financial advisors is that they have no financial stake in the recommendations they may provide for you. They recommend only what they believe is in your best interest. This compensation method does remove many inherent conflicts of interest regarding how the advisor is paid. However, it does not ensure that the advice is rendered by an ethical or competent financial advisor.

All financial professionals deserve to be compensated fairly for the advice or products they provide, and you can find competent, ethical financial advisors working under each of these compensation methods. The only thing that should matter to you is whether you're receiving what you really need from a competent professional and at a competitive price. How do you know which advisor under which compensation model is most appropriate for your needs?

If you're looking for a house, a mortgage, a municipal bond, or auto or homeowners insurance, you'll likely need to work directly with a person who is compensated on a commission-only basis.

The most popular form of compensation for personal financial advisors and planners is currently a combination of commissions and fees. These financial advisors may be affiliated with a large brokerage firm or insurance company, or they may be registered representatives with an independent broker-dealer. They must maintain licenses to sell securities, life insurance products, and annuities. Often, the majority of their compensation comes from the sale of the products they recommend. However, they may also provide financial planning services and advice for a separate hourly fee, flat fee, or retainer fee.

Planners who charge only fees (similar to attorneys) often make a similar income as well. Attorneys typically get paid in one of three ways:

- ✔ **Hourly fee:** You pay for all the time that the attorney works on your case or spends with you. Multiply the time spent by the attorney's hourly charge, and that's how much your fee is.

- ✔ **Flat fee:** Some attorneys charge flat fees for a package of services, such as drawing up a living trust package.

✔ **Contingency fee:** You pay only if you win your case. The lawyer may invest hours or months on your case and incur lots of expenses trying to help you win your case — and if you don't, he is out his money and time. Your fee under a contingency arrangement is based on a percentage of the amount you win — commonly a third of your award is paid to the attorney.

Fee-only financial advisors charge

✔ **Hourly fee:** You pay for all the time that the financial advisor works on your case or spends with you. Multiply the time spent by the advisor's hourly charge, and that's how much your fee is. Always find out the expected cost and the maximum cost before you begin working with an advisor who charges by the hour.

Hourly-based pricing is best for:

- People who need specific advice about one or a few financial topics.

- Do-it-yourselfers who want a professional to give them his opinions.

- People who are comfortable taking on part of the legwork. They want to do as much as possible to save money, but want expert analysis and direction.

- People who recognize a need for professional advice on occasion, but don't need, or want to pay the price for, a full-time financial advisor.

✔ **Flat fee:** Some financial advisors offer flat fees for a package of services, such as analyzing whether you're saving enough for retirement and investing in the right places. Flat-fee pricing is best for people who need specific advice or services and are willing to take the gamble that the flat-fee arrangement will cost no more than it would have if they paid by the hour.

✔ **Retainer fee:** This fee isn't exactly like a contingency fee — you're definitely going to have to pay for this service, unlike in a lawsuit where you could win or lose. However, the retainer fee is often calculated based on a percentage of some sort, such as 1 percent of the assets the advisor manages for you, or some percentage of your net worth or income, or mixture of the two. Retainer fees are also computed by estimating the amount of time required to provide the services promised, based on the complexity of the case and the skills required of the advisor, for the time covered under agreement to retain the advisor.

A retainer fee is best suited for people who need, want, or can afford to transfer the responsibility of managing their personal financial affairs to a financial advisor.

Deciphering What All the Initials, Credentials, and Licenses Mean to You

Before you engage any financial advisor, you want to know a lot more about her background and experience and what her licenses or credentials mean for you.

Licenses are required by law for any financial services professionals who sell investments, insurance, or financing products. Common licenses you may see financial planners or advisors hold include the following:

✔ **Securities licenses** are licenses to sell investments and include the following:

- **Series 6:** Licensed to sell mutual funds, variable annuities, and variable life insurance.

- **Series 7:** In addition to the items covered under the Series 6, licensed to sell individual stocks, bonds, and option contracts.

✔ **Insurance licenses** are licenses to sell insurance products and are broken down into the following two categories:

- **Life and health:** Licensed to sell life, disability, medical, and long-term-care insurance products.

- **Property and casualty:** Licensed to sell auto, homeowner's, and liability insurance.

A *Registered Investment Advisor* (RIA) isn't a license, nor a credential, but a legal requirement of anyone claiming to be a financial advisor. The only way around this law is for the advisor to affiliate with a broker-dealer and become a registered representative of that broker (who must himself be an RIA). The federal or state Securities and Exchange Commissioners regulate RIAs. The advisor's business activities and records may be audited by the regulators at any time.

You may also meet advisors with a lot of initials after their names, but what do these initials tell you about their educational backgrounds and why is it important to you?

You can find no less than 70 different professional designations listed on the National Association of Securities Dealers' (NASD) Investor Education site at http://apps.nasd.com/DataDirectory/1/prodesignations.aspx. However, for your benefit, I feel compelled to narrow down the list drastically to the most significant and applicable professional designations held by personal financial planners and advisors, which you can find in Worksheet 20-1.

You should look at professional designations only as a sign of the advisor's initial and ongoing educational and examination requirements. Professional designations in no way ensure that an advisor is competent or trustworthy, but they're a start. In the next section, you can explore some interview questions that can help discover additional information you want to know about any prospective advisor, including his core competencies and potential conflicts of interest.

Worksheet 20-1   Primary Professional Designations

Financial Planning:

✔ Certified Financial Planner (CFP®)

✔ Chartered Financial Consultant (ChFC)

✔ Certified Public Accountant / Personal Financial Specialist (CPA/PFS)

✔ NAPFA-Registered Financial Advisor

Investment Management:

- ✔ Chartered Financial Analyst (CFA®)
- ✔ Accredited Investment Fiduciary (AIF®)
- ✔ Certified Investment Management Analyst (CIMA)

Insurance:

- ✔ Chartered Life Underwriter (CLU)

Tax Planning & Preparation:

- ✔ Certified Public Accountant (CPA)
- ✔ Enrolled Agent (EA)

Other:

- ✔ Certified Divorce Financial Analyst (CDFA)

Over the last few years as the financial planning profession has evolved, a number of colleges and universities now offer bachelor's and master's degrees as well as a few PhD programs in personal financial planning. A bachelor's degree in personal financial planning provides the student with a good background. However, you should focus more on someone who has also obtained one of the general personal financial planning designations (refer to Worksheet 20-1), or a master's or PhD degree in personal financial planning.

Interviewing and Selecting Your Personal Financial Advisor

When choosing a financial advisor, I recommend that savvy consumers interview a few different financial advisors to learn more about each one's background, experience, specialties, target clientele, as well as his or her listening skills and communication styles.

Worksheet 20-2 is designed to assist you in interviewing financial advisors of any type. When seeking out a financial advisor, first send this Financial Advisor Interview Questionnaire, review each advisor's responses, and then visit with two or three prospective advisors over the telephone. After you've identified those advisors who may best fit your needs, ask for a no-obligation get-acquainted meeting and meet with them in person before you make a commitment or sign any contracts.

You may obtain an electronic version of this questionnaire at `http://www.garrett planningnetwork.com/files/Financial%20Advisor%20Interview%20Questionn aire.pdf`. Consider mailing or e-mailing this questionnaire to prospective financial advisors prior to meeting with them for the first time, which saves both you and the advisor considerable time.

Worksheet 20-2   Financial Advisor Interview Questionnaire

1. Why did you become a financial planner?

_____

_____

_____

_____

_____

2. What is your educational and experiential background as it relates to personal financial planning?

_____

_____

_____

_____

_____

3. What are your financial planning credentials or designations and affiliations?

❏ Certified Financial Planner (CFP®)

❏ CPA/Personal Financial Specialist (CPA/PFS)

❏ NAPFA-Registered Financial Advisor

❏ NAPFA-Provisional Member

❏ Chartered Financial Consultant (ChFC)

❏ Certified Public Accountant (CPA)

❏ Chartered Financial Analyst (CFA®)

❏ Other (such as MBA, MS, PhD, AIF®, CDFA, JD, EA, CLU, RFC): _____

4. What are your areas of specialty?

_____

_____

_____

_____

_____

5. Please describe your most common engagement or service provided. And what is the type of client or client situation you target?

_____

_____

_____

_____

_____

6. Are you a registered representative of any broker/dealer? Are you a licensed insurance agent with any company or agency? If so, which one(s)?

_____

_____

_____

7. Are you a registered investment advisor? With the SEC? Or with what state(s)?

_____

8. Are you a fiduciary?

_____

9. How are you compensated?

_____

Fee-only, please define method of determining fees:

_____

_____

Commissions only:

_____

_____

Fee and commissions (fee-based), provide typical breakdown:

_____

_____

Other:

_____

_____

10. Do you have minimums for assets, account size, annual fees paid, and so on? And what is your typical fee or charge for an initial engagement?

_____

_____

_____

_____

11. Do you provide a written agreement detailing the total amount of compensation and services that will be provided in advance of an engagement?

_____

_____

12. Do you provide a thorough written analysis of one's financial situation and recommendations?

_____

_____

_____

13. Do you offer assistance with implementation with the plan? Please elaborate.

_____

_____

_____

_____

_____

14. Will you provide a second opinion or one-time review?

_____

_____

_____

Signature of Advisor or Planner: _____ Date: _____

Firm Name: _____

The questions in Worksheet 20-2 are designed to help you get to know a lot more about a prospective financial advisor prior to meeting with him or speaking with him on the telephone. If an advisor refuses to complete this questionnaire, that says a lot about his attitude or his schedule. In that event, continue on with other advisors who will comply with this request.

Here are a few more general guidelines as you go about your search for the right financial advisor:

✔ Some of the most revealing things you can find out about a financial advisor have to do with why he got into financial planning or advisory services in the first place. An individual that has a sincere and deep passion to serve others may be exactly the type of advisor for whom you're looking. Many financial advisors have personally lived through life events that you may be experiencing, and their personal insight could be extremely valuable to you, and it's very hard to gain through book knowledge.

✔ Another key question isn't just *how* an advisor is compensated, but *how much* that advisor will be compensated if you are to work with him. You can't compare advisors' services and prices without getting this kind of detail. And, don't forget about conflicts of interest related to compensation. If an advisor makes $1,000 recommending one strategy or investment and $5,000 recommending another, there is a conflict of interest. You should be fully aware of how this conflict can affect an advisor's recommendations, and make sure that the option that would provide the advisor more money is really the best option for you.

✔ Make sure that any advisor you choose views you as her target client. In other words, will she be proud and honored to have you as a client? If you happen to be someone who just barely makes her minimum requirements or she's made special arrangements or waived her minimums to accommodate you, sooner or later, you may find that you aren't getting the attention and personal service that you need and deserve.

✔ Many financial advisors, especially independent, veteran advisors, and fee-only advisors, require minimums. Those minimums may be the size of your investment account, your income or net worth, or the annual revenues you generate for the advisor. If you're a do-it-yourselfer or you're looking for a second opinion or one-time review, you very likely won't qualify for many of these advisors' minimum requirements. It's best to ask that up-front (when you receive their completed interview questionnaires or first speak with them) before you waste any more of your own time or theirs.

Be sure to obtain a written contract from the advisor you select, outlining exactly what the financial advisor will provide for you, how much the services will cost in total, what you must provide to get this work completed, and when you will receive the final product.

Always ask a lot of questions. Get a second opinion anytime it feels appropriate. And don't ever turn over control of your financial future to anybody and then just forget about it. You should always review your account statements and never grant custody over your money. Your advisor can have the right to place trades within your account, or even have his fee withdrawn from your account; however, he doesn't need custody of your money.

Part VI
The Part of Tens

The 5th Wave   By Rich Tennant

"Our plan is to pay for the rest of it when we pay off our college loan."

In this part . . .

A *For Dummies* book wouldn't be complete without The Part of Tens. In this part, I highlight easy ways you can trim your budget, get your finances organized, and avoid getting ripped off.

Chapter 21

Ten Easy Ways to Trim Your Budget

In This Chapter

▶ Finding ways to save a buck or two

▶ Discovering fun ways to entertain (or be entertained) on a shoestring

*W*ant some easy ways to save some money or free up some cash for more important goals? The easiest way to trim your budget or spend less money is to direct the money to where it would do you the most good before you have the opportunity to spend it. However, there are many simple ways that you can scrape up a bit of extra cash each month without even putting a damper on your lifestyle. I show you how in this chapter.

Take Full Advantage of Your Employer's Matching Contribution

Contribute the maximum amount that your employer will match in your retirement plan at work. You're basically receiving free money from your company! If your employer doesn't make a matching contribution, then you better check out the other suggestions in this chapter.

Max Out Your Roth IRA Contribution

If you have a Roth IRA and are eligible, make the maximum contributions to your and your spouse's Roth IRA accounts each year, but save monthly. For example, the maximum allowable contribution for 2007 is $4,000 per person if you're under 50 years of age and $5,000 per person if you're 50 or older. Those contributions work out to be $333 per month and $416 per month respectively.

If you don't already have a Roth IRA, you could use a no-load mutual fund company, such as T. Rowe Price, or a discount broker, such as Scottrade, to establish your Roth IRA account, because they have very low initial-investment minimums and even lower subsequent investment minimums. (For more on Roth IRAs, check out Chapter 14.)

When you establish your new mutual fund or brokerage account or if you don't already have automatic withdrawal with your existing IRA, complete an application signing up for the automatic monthly investment program. This feature sets up an automatic draft from your checking account directly into your Roth IRA account each and every month. Your Roth contribution gets funded automatically — before you have a chance to spend your income on something else.

Build Your Personal Portfolio

Start or add to your personal portfolio by utilizing low-cost, tax-advantaged passive investment vehicles, such as exchange-traded funds (ETFs) and index funds. Index funds have been available through mutual fund powerhouses like Vanguard for decades. However, the range of options now available has exploded in the last few years. You can now find index funds and ETFs for every asset class imaginable. However, not all options are created equally. For even more information, check out *Mutual Funds For Dummies* by Eric Tyson and *Exchange-Traded Funds For Dummies* by Russell Wild, both published by Wiley.

Save for Your Next Vehicle

If you know you're going to be in the market for a vehicle, set up an escrow account with a competitive money market fund or account, such as the Orange Savings Account from ING Direct by calling 800-ING-DIRECT or visiting online at www.ingdirect.com. The current yield on this account is 4.5 percent. Deposit the amount of money you need to save each month to have what you'll need to replace your vehicle when the time comes. ING Direct doesn't have any account minimums; you can make weekly, biweekly, monthly, or periodic contributions to the account in any dollar amount.

Accumulate Funds for a Specific Goal

Set aside money periodically for specific goals, such as your children's college education or a down payment on a home. If you need the money in less than five years, you should consider something like the Orange Saving Account from ING Direct (www.ingdirect.com) because it's safe and easily accessible, but pays a good interest rate. However, if you have more time available to accumulate money before you need it, consider the automatic investment options mentioned in the section "Build Your Personal Portfolio," earlier in this chapter.

Automate Your Monthly Payments

Set up automatic monthly payments directly out of your checking account to pay all your regular level monthly expenses. You can also contact your utility companies and sign up for their average monthly payment plans. Have the monthly cost automatically deducted from your checking account.

Having these expenses automatically taken out of your checking account means that you never have to worry about writing bills, purchasing stamps, or incurring late fees, saving you both time and money.

Trim the Money Tree

Next month, scrutinize each of your monthly bank statements, credit-card statements, and utility bills. What kinds of expenses appear on these statements or invoices that you can eliminate without affecting your quality of life?

For example, you may want to ask yourself some of the following questions:

✔ Are you actually using the vision package, three-way calling, and call waiting or caller ID on your cell phone plan?

✔ Can you downgrade your cable package one notch to save a little money and still get the majority of the channels that matter most to you?

✔ Are you paying for online bill payment services that you're not using?

✔ Are you paying a monthly service fee to have a checking account? (You don't have to; you can find lots of options available on the Internet and most likely in your community.)

✔ Are you paying an annual fee for your credit card? Are you getting substantial value out of paying that fee? If not, cancel that card and use one that doesn't charge an annual fee.

What other transactions appear on these statements and invoices that are of no value or very little value to you? See what you can do about eliminating them.

Other simple ways to help cut your costs include the following:

✔ **Write a grocery list and stick to it when you shop.** And never go shopping when you're hungry. (You'll always buy items you don't need.)

✔ **Eat out no more than once a week.** A family of four can easily spend $30 on one meal at a very inexpensive restaurant — even fast food. You can make that same meal, or likely a much better one, at home for about one-third of the cost.

✔ **Plant and maintain a small vegetable and herb garden.** A small garden with a few tomato plants, some green beans, basil, and oregano wouldn't take up much space. In fact, you can plant all these items in pots on your deck, patio, or balcony. By growing some of your own vegetables and herbs, you not only save money on your grocery bills, but you and your family also benefit from homegrown fun and flavor.

✔ **On the weekends, cook up a giant feast, enjoy one large meal for the family, and freeze the leftovers in individual containers.** Now you have homemade, ready-to-reheat, fabulous frozen meals for a fraction of the cost of quality processed frozen foods.

✔ **Sell items you don't use or need, and when you need to buy something, consider purchasing second-hand quality items.** Check out Craigslist at `www.craigslist.org/about/cities.html`. This online garage sale site has exploded over the nation and offers everything from housemates to horseshoes. You can sell your extra stuff that you no longer use and buy great used stuff that you need — all for a fraction of what these items would cost new. I just found a kayak I've been wanting for about 50 percent its list price; it's only four years old and in perfect condition.

Become a Do-It-Yourselfer

If you currently hire someone to mow your lawn, clean your house, or provide any other types of domestic services or basic household repairs, explore just how much money you could save by doing these projects yourself. Not only can you save a lot of money as a do-it-yourselfer, but as a parent, you're also educating and empowering your children to carry on this thrifty lifestyle.

If you're looking for a DIY resource, remember that you can find a *For Dummies* book on almost everything from sewing to remodeling your home. Just go to www.wiley.com and search for the DIY topic you're interested in discovering more about.

Entertain on a Dime

Instead of going out to dinner and a movie, consider inviting friends over for a covered dish dinner, where each person brings a dish. Also, ask each of your guests to bring two or three of their favorite movies that they may have in their own library collection, and then vote on what movie the group would love to watch together.

Utilize Your Community Resources

Before you plunk down your hard-earned money to join a gym or for various types of entertainment and activities, consider what your community has to offer — usually at little or no cost! Most communities provide access to the following:

- Community swimming pools
- Gymnasium or exercise classes
- Community center
- Local parks or jogging trails
- County libraries
- The county extension agency
- Museums and galleries
- Community colleges and universities
- Concerts
- Festivals

Take advantage of the low-cost public services you pay for with your taxes.

Chapter 22

Ten Tips on Getting Organized

- -

In This Chapter

▶ Simplifying your financial life

▶ Organizing to minimize stress and unnecessary expenses

- -

Getting your financial household in order once and for all can help simplify your financial life and minimize unnecessary stress and expenses that go along with being disorganized. In this chapter, I give you ten tips for how to get organized — and stay that way.

Establishing a System for Your Financial Records

The first thing you need to do to get organized is to set up a record-keeping system for your finances. A well-thought-out record-keeping system can save you a lot of time and money.

Refer to Chapter 2 for a listing of the financial records that you should maintain in your personal record-keeping system. Set aside a few hours over one weekend and get your financial household filing system set up once and for all.

Paying Bills the Fast and Easy Way

By paying your bills online or over the telephone, you eliminate having to write a check, possibly addressing an envelope, finding and paying for postage, and mailing the payment. It takes a few minutes to set up this type of service, but you can save at least one or two hours each month that you would have spent paying bills the old-fashioned way.

Here's how you can do it:

✔ If you use a personal computer, your best option is to utilize the online banking option through your local bank. You can set up each of the individuals or companies with which you do business or owe money. If the payment remains level and reoccurs each month, you don't have to do anything other than remember that that money will be pulled from your checking account on a certain date. If the payments fluctuate month to month, you simply need to go into your online banking account and enter the dollar amount for that payee and the date you want the payment made.

✔ If you don't use a personal computer, or you're not comfortable with online banking, your bank may offer telephone bill-payment services. This service works just like an online bill-payment service, but you can use your touchtone telephone to authorize payments instead.

For more info on these types of services, check with your bank or financial institution.

Consolidating Your Personal Investments

Rather than having investments in a bunch of different locations, consolidate all your holdings with the same discount brokerage company. By having these investment accounts all custodied with the same discount broker, you can easily track and manage these accounts.

However, you do need to have a separate account for each ownership type; for example, you may have a joint account with your spouse, an individual Roth IRA, a traditional IRA, and maybe even another account for the kids' college funds. You want to keep these accounts separate, while still consolidating with the same discount broker.

Documenting All Your Important Contacts

Do yourself and your loved ones a big favor by gathering the names and contact information for all the important product and service providers in your life on one conveniently located list.

Chapter 2 has a form you can use to list all your primary advisors. But think of all the other people and service providers that ought to be on an easily accessible list. Contacts you want to list may include some of the following:

✔ Babysitters

✔ Pet sitters

✔ 24-hour vet clinic

✔ Housesitters

✔ Handymen

✔ Neighbors

✔ Teachers

✔ Business colleagues

✔ Extended family

Utilizing Technology to Track User Names and Passwords

You likely have multiple Web sites that you visit with regularity. For security's sake, you probably don't use the same login-password combination for each site, but how can you keep them all straight? Wouldn't it be very convenient for you to open up the Web sites and go straight to your account with the click of a couple of buttons?

Well, remembering your user names and passwords really can be that easy. RoboForm sells a remarkable program that you can download to your hard drive or a USB jump drive. The software program captures every Web site you visit that requires a user name and password. The program then acts as your personal "memory" by storing your favorite Web site addresses, login names, and passwords on one single portable gadget. You have to remember only one very super-secret password to access all the information stored on this little gadget. For more information, visit www.roboform.com. The program costs less than $40 and takes only a few moments to set up. I can't imagine online life without it.

Automating Your Money Management

Utilize an online bill-payment service through your bank (see previous section on this topic) and one of the software applications for managing cash flow, such as Quicken (www.quicken.com) or Mvelopes (www.mvelopes.com) to automatically record and track your spending on an ongoing basis.

Preparing for the Unthinkable

When thinking about getting organized, imagine what it would be like for your surviving family if you weren't around. Preparing for the unthinkable is the most important thing you can do in the area of getting organized. The key topics include

- Updating your wills, trusts, and other estate-planning documents
- Verifying that your beneficiary designations are valid and current
- Obtaining enough life insurance to support your survivors
- Communicating with your loved ones regarding your final wishes

For more details on how to carry out these tasks, see Chapter 12.

Planning for the Unexpected

What if you find yourself unemployed or unable to work? You really can plan ahead and have your finances in order, just in case. To do this, you need to have the following in place:

- Sufficient emergency reserves
- Home equity line of credit
- Disability insurance

Preparing an Emergency Kit

Every household and vehicle should have a portable emergency kit. Depending on whether the emergency kit is for the house or the car, it should contain basic medical supplies, sunscreen, insect repellent, emergency medicines, flashlights, fresh batteries, a weather radio, a solar blanket, rain poncho, bottled water, high-energy snacks, jumper cables, a car charger, flares, and basic hand tools.

If you find yourself in need of any of these supplies, and you are fortunate to be somewhere where you can purchase these items, you'll likely spend substantially more money because you didn't plan ahead.

Purging Your Extra Stuff

In 1950, the average square footage of a typical family home was less than one-half the size of the average family home today, but people have still figured out how to fill their houses to capacity. To help do away with clutter so that you can stay more organized, get rid of anything that you aren't currently using and have no anticipation of using in the near future. You can easily let someone else enjoy that item and get a little cash in return. For example, you can sell your quality, slightly used stuff on Craigslist (www.craigslist.com), or if you have a whole bunch of stuff, have a garage sale. Anything that doesn't sell in the garage sale, donate to charity. Either way, you receive an economic benefit in return — somebody will either buy it from you, or you get to write off your donation on your tax return.

Chapter 23

Ten Scams to Avoid

In This Chapter

▶ Recognizing schemes that are hazardous to your financial health

▶ Smelling out potential rip-off artists

· ·

You've probably heard those infomercial offers that seem too good to be true. Well, they probably are. Believing in the hype of many get-rich-quick schemes or "super-investment" strategies can actually do the opposite of what they advertise if you aren't careful. But don't worry; in this chapter, I arm you with the necessary tools to recognize and avoid scam artists. I cover some of the hottest schemes and biggest rip-offs in the financial services world. Don't become a victim!

Investing a Tax Shelter inside of a Tax Shelter

If anyone suggests that you invest your retirement funds (tax shelter) or IRAs (tax shelter) in an annuity (another type of tax shelter), that recommendation is either going to make *him* a lot of money, or he doesn't have your best interests at heart (or both).

Another way to say this is don't invest your IRA into an annuity contract! I can think of no good reasons to do so. The excess annual costs, surrender penalties, and inflexibility never make buying an annuity contract with your tax sheltered retirement dollars a good investment strategy.

Getting In on an Initial Public Offering (IPO)

When a private company sells its stock publicly for the first time, it's known as an *initial public offering*. You may be intrigued by the opportunity to get rich quick by purchasing shares of a company the day it goes public. Unfortunately, you only hear or read about very few massively successful stories.

In most cases, investors who get in on an IPO lose 25 percent of their money by the end of year one.

Paying for Full-Cost Brokerage Advice

If you currently have a traditional, full-service, full-cost brokerage account and you have benefited sufficiently from your broker's advice, then by all means continue using that broker. However, when you make your own investment decisions, place those trades through a deep-discount broker like Scottrade (www.scottrade.com) or Vanguard (www.vanguard.com). You can save hundreds of dollars by investing in each of your own ideas in the cheapest way possible.

Accepting a Mortgage with a Prepayment Penalty

If your mortgage company insists on a prepayment penalty clause, take your business elsewhere! A *prepayment penalty clause* simply states that if you pay off your mortgage early or refinance at any time, you are smacked with potentially thousands of dollars in penalties.

I once consulted with a woman who was sold a mortgage that had a prepayment penalty. Interest rates had dropped, the woman's house had appreciated, and she needed extra cash, so she refinanced her mortgage. However, she lost about $4,500 in prepayment penalties when she refinanced her mortgage. If she had had a traditional mortgage, she wouldn't have had a prepayment penalty.

Falling for Get-Rich-Quick Schemes

So many get-rich-quick schemes are out there, just waiting for a willing victim, but they usually come out of the woodwork in one of the following packages:

- **Late-night infomercials** that, for example, boast of investing in real estate with no money down.

- **Books, videos, or software systems** promoted by money gurus.

- **Free seminars** entitled "The Secrets to Great Wealth" (or anything like that). Don't think that financial service people and companies put on these big, expensive shin-digs for completely educational or charitable reasons. They likely have motivational tapes, investment schemes, or money management services to sell; either way, they're after your business — make no mistake about it.

- **Day trading** (buying and selling stocks, possibly multiple times a day) hasn't experienced explosive growth since the technology bubble burst. But I'm sure a comeback will come soon enough — as long as people still believe that they can win big. But take note: The most respected investors of all time wouldn't consider day-trading investing — and neither should you.

✔ **The old bait-and-switch routine** can easily lure you in if you aren't prepared. For example, you may receive what appear to be tickets to an important and valuable event. All you have to do is just call the number on the cover letter to confirm your limited reservation. The seminar is advertised to be a $149 value, but is free to you and a guest. But when you sit through the "free" seminar, it turns out to be just a teaser. You would have to spend $350 to get the complete tapes and workbook "system" that was advertised, and you just wasted hours on what was literally a commercial. And most likely, if something is that hard to sell, it must not be all that desirable.

Prepaying for Membership Schemes

Think very carefully before investing in any sort of pay-in-advance membership or ownership program. Pay-as-you-go membership is often much more appropriate and cost effective for your situation.

Common examples include the following:

✔ **Vacation timeshares:** A *vacation timeshare* is a concept that enables an individual to buy the rights, along with 40 or so other people, to one week at a resort. Making money or breaking even as an investor in a vacation timeshare is extremely difficult. Most timeshare owners don't realize at the outset just how much money it can cost to own and utilize their timeshare vacation week each year. Timeshare buyers often finance their purchases through the timeshare company, and although the interest may be tax-deductible, the rates are very high. Add the cost of the timeshare (at least $10,000), plus any interest if you go into debt to buy the timeshare, plus the annual maintenance (anywhere from $600 to $1,000 for each timeshare week you buy), special assessment and taxes, and the cost of travel to and from the resort location, and you could easily afford to stay one week at an extremely nice hotel or resort, anywhere you want, anytime you want. Don't let the excitement of the moment cause you to lose sight of your most important financial objectives (see Chapter 5).

✔ **Athletic, tennis, and golf clubs:** Ask yourself why you join these clubs: as a motivator to exercise, as a social outlet, for the prestige of membership, or purely to exercise? Ask yourself whether the money you spend on these types of club memberships is worth it to you. Do you have any alternatives, such as public golf courses and community tennis courts, that can provide you with the desired benefits without the big price tag? For example, if you go to the gym to run on the treadmill, you can easily take a jog around your neighborhood for free or even invest in a treadmill of your own (which over time will cost less than your club membership).

Spending Too Much for Investment Management

Many people make the mistake of thinking that they must spend a lot of money to receive quality investment management services. That may have been true once, but it isn't true any longer. Professional investment management services have become a commodity, resulting in a drastic reduction in costs. And the availability of index funds and exchange-traded funds have also had a significant impact in driving prices lower.

✔ **Mutual funds and variable annuity subaccounts:** The annual expense ratios for these accounts shouldn't exceed the amounts found in Worksheet 23-1. If your money is invested in index funds or exchange-traded funds, pay attention to the Passive column, and if you're invested with a private money manager or in an actively managed mutual fund, then you need to look at the Active column.

Worksheet 23-1	Annual Expense Ratios
Passive	*Active*
0.20 percent for a Standard and Poor's 500 Index fund	1.00 percent for mid- to large-cap domestic stock funds
0.40 percent for small- or mid-cap index or exchange-traded funds	1.20 percent for large-cap foreign stock funds
0.60 percent for small- or mid-cap foreign stock index or exchange-traded funds	1.50 percent for small- to mid-cap foreign stock funds or emerging-markets funds
0.20 percent for domestic-bond funds and exchange-traded funds	0.70 percent for domestic bond funds
0.60 percent for foreign bond index funds and exchange-traded funds	1.00 percent for foreign bond funds

✔ **Private money managers, wealth managers, financial advisors, and so on:** Money managers hired to manage your mutual fund or exchange-traded fund portfolio on an ongoing basis often charge 0.20 percent to 1.00 percent on top of what the mutual funds and exchange-traded funds charge. So, total management expenses could range from 0.40 percent to 2.60 percent depending on the manager and the investments chosen. The high end is over six times the expense of the low-cost alternative. Try to stay at the low to middle end of this expense range. Keep in mind that your overall portfolio allocation is the deciding factor in your total cost.

✔ Also, money managers hired to manage a portfolio of individual stocks on a long-term, buy-and-hold basis should charge no more than 1.00 percent per year. And money managers in charge of fixed-income portfolios should charge no more than about 0.60 percent per year. If you're paying more than that, you should try negotiating with your current advisor and, if that fails, shop around for a new advisor!

I address only annual money management fees in this section. There are still sales commissions and surrender penalties on thousands of funds, so watch out for total costs, too. For more on getting the right advisor at the right price, see Chapter 20.

Repairing Your Credit

You may have seen advertisements by companies offering to fix your credit for an easy payment of $300. Don't waste your money! Nothing can re-establish or improve your credit other than your persistence and time. For more on your credit and how to improve it, check out Chapter 5, or you can even delve into *Credit Repair Kit For Dummies* by Stephen R. Bucci (Wiley) or *Your Credit Score: How to Fix, Improve, and Protect the 3-Digit Number that Shapes Your Financial Future* by Liz Pullium Weston (FT Press), a personal favorite.

Considering Payday Loans

Payday-loan companies are extremely profitable ventures. They give very short-term loans to people who are temporarily strapped for cash, at interest rates between 150 percent to more than 300 percent per year.

For example, you borrow $500 from a payday-loan company and plan to repay the loan in one month. At the end of one month, you owe the loan company $625. Most people have to renew their loan because they don't have the money to pay off the loan a month later. Just two months after borrowing $500, they now owe almost $800.

The abusive lending tactics rampant in the payday-loan business have caused many states to outlaw payday-loan services altogether, which is why you should avoid them as well. If you find yourself in need of cash before payday, a better option is to borrow money from traditional lenders.

Investing Like a Venture Capitalist

Venture capitalists are experienced investors and business people who have substantial resources and significant traditional financial investment holdings. They occasionally supplement their traditional financial investments with riskier, first-of-its-kind speculating. Venture capitalists can afford to lose all their investments, but can you?

Most likely not. My advice: Get rich slowly — always a more prudent investment strategy. You can find thousands of quality, publicly traded mutual funds, exchange-traded funds, and stocks in which you can invest. And you can obtain a variety of research on these traditional financial investment vehicles.

Chapter 24

Ten or So Types of Insurance You Don't Really Need to Buy

● ●

In This Chapter

▶ Saying no to limited scope coverage

▶ Buying insurance only for risks you can't afford to bear yourself

● ●

You can probably find as many illegitimate types of insurance products out there as legitimate ones. But before you buy a policy, remember this important point: You should only buy insurance to protect yourself and your property against risks that you can't afford to bear yourself.

In this chapter, I list ten types of insurance coverages that may not be worth the money for you. (Think twice before wasting your money.)

Buying Insurance to Cover Only Cancer or Another Specific Illness

Don't buy a health insurance or income replacement policy that covers just cancer. If you need health or income replacement (disability) insurance, buy a policy that covers you for any illness or injury.

Specialty policies, such as cancer insurance, can be very expensive and duplicative to your primary health insurance.

Trying to Avoid Putting Your Insurance Money Where Your Mouth Is: Dental Insurance

You buy insurance to transfer the risk of a loss that you cannot afford to bear to an insurance company. The cost of dental insurance, in most cases, will exceed the cost of just paying out of pocket for the services you need. In addition, many dental plans don't cover orthodontia — a motivating factor to acquire the insurance, in many cases. So when it comes to dental insurance, put your money where your mouth is and pay for those services on your own; skip the dental insurance.

Ask your dentist how much annual routine cleanings and other services you need typically cost. Then add up the cost of one year's worth of dental insurance for the policy you're considering and weigh your risks. Then see how much it pays of the services you need. When you do the math, you'll realize that you're very likely not seeing any savings. Remember, the insurace commpany is in business to make money — off you!

Seeing Clearly: Buy the Glasses, Not the Vision Insurance

Like dental insurance, vision insurance is another one of those expenses that you're best off avoiding. Pay for your own eye exams, glasses, and contact lenses and forget about buying vision insurance. You'll come out ahead in the long run when you self-insure.

Vision insurance is generally not worth purchasing your own private policy. If your employer provides vision coverage free of charge or at a substantial discount, go for it, but not if you have to pay 100 percent of the premiums yourself. Add these costs into your budget. Vision expenses are risks you can't afford to bear yourself, and you don't need to transfer them to an insurance company.

Saving the Premiums You Would Have Paid for Credit Life and Disability Insurance

Credit life and disability insurance, unfortunately, are a big waste of money. You're better off saving the money from the premiums and putting the funds in a rainy-day account to cover these events.

Thinking about Accidental Death and Dismemberment Insurance

If you need life insurance, buy life insurance that covers you for *any* cause of death, not just accidental death. Dismemberment coverage pays a cash benefit even if you live, but you have to lose your sight and an arm or a leg, or some unlikely combination, before it will pay off. Don't waste your money.

Trying to Come Out Ahead: Reduced-Term Life Insurance

Also sold as mortgage insurance, this type of insurance pays off your mortgage should you die before the mortgage is paid in full. It sounds good, but you can buy a term life insurance policy where the benefits don't go down over time for the same amount of money, or possibly less.

These policies typically cost about eight times the amount that a traditional term life insurance with the same death benefit would pay.

You Don't Need Home Warranty Plans

Good luck on getting the insurance company to actually pay a claim! However, when you purchase a new home, you may feel more comfortable with a home warranty. But after the first year, I'd drop the coverage.

Save your money on this type of insurance and use it instead on general home maintenance and repairs.

Extending Warranties on Electronics and Computer Equipment

Most items come with their own warranties. Of course, sales people often get a hefty commission when they talk you into purchasing extended warranties. When you buy a new appliance or electronic gadget, sales people will most likely offer you an extended warranty. These policies are hugely profitable for the sellers. If these were a good deal for you, they wouldn't be selling them. The chances are that when your equipment goes ker-plunk, you can purchase new items on your own for less than the premiums you paid to purchase the extended warranties.

Only about 2 percent of all extended warranties are ever utilized. In fact one big-box retailer reports that in one year, approximately 45 percent of its profits came from the sale of these warranties.

Saying No to Extra Coverage on Your Rental Cars

Check with your auto insurance provider because you may already be covered. If you aren't already covered, you can probably add this coverage much more cost effectively through your auto insurance company than by buying a separate policy.

Realizing that You May Not Be Insuring Your Trip: Travel Insurance

Definitely don't buy travel insurance through the company you're purchasing the trip from. In addition, this type of coverage can be extremely limited and expensive. In fact, you may even have some good coverage through your credit-card company at no additional cost. So if you're worried about becoming ill and missing your trip or the company you're purchasing your trip from going belly up, give your credit-card company a call.

Another type of travel coverage provides funds if you or one of your travel companions becomes ill and you have to cancel your trip, the airline loses your luggage, or you have a medical emergency while traveling outside of the country and have to be evacuated to a medical facility. This coverage can be very expensive and may overlap with other insurance you have. Before traveling outside the country, contact your health insurance company and confirm whether or not it provides coverage outside of the United States; many don't.

Steer Clear of Pet Insurance

Pet insurance is a profit center for the insurance company. In other words, it doesn't pay off for most purchases of the coverage. Plan for pet care expenses in your budget. Don't buy the insurance.

Index

Notes

Notes

Notes

SPORTS, FITNESS, PARENTING, RELIGION & SPIRITUALITY

0-471-76871-5

0-7645-7841-3

Also available:

- Catholicism For Dummies
  0-7645-5391-7
- Exercise Balls For Dummies
  0-7645-5623-1
- Fitness For Dummies
  0-7645-7851-0
- Football For Dummies
  0-7645-3936-1
- Judaism For Dummies
  0-7645-5299-6
- Potty Training For Dummies
  0-7645-5417-4
- Buddhism For Dummies
  0-7645-5359-3

- Pregnancy For Dummies
  0-7645-4483-7 †
- Ten Minute Tone-Ups For Dummies
  0-7645-7207-5
- NASCAR For Dummies
  0-7645-7681-X
- Religion For Dummies
  0-7645-5264-3
- Soccer For Dummies
  0-7645-5229-5
- Women in the Bible For Dummies
  0-7645-8475-8

TRAVEL

0-7645-7749-2

0-7645-6945-7

Also available:

- Alaska For Dummies
  0-7645-7746-8
- Cruise Vacations For Dummies
  0-7645-6941-4
- England For Dummies
  0-7645-4276-1
- Europe For Dummies
  0-7645-7529-5
- Germany For Dummies
  0-7645-7823-5
- Hawaii For Dummies
  0-7645-7402-7

- Italy For Dummies
  0-7645-7386-1
- Las Vegas For Dummies
  0-7645-7382-9
- London For Dummies
  0-7645-4277-X
- Paris For Dummies
  0-7645-7630-5
- RV Vacations For Dummies
  0-7645-4442-X
- Walt Disney World & Orlando
  For Dummies
  0-7645-9660-8

GRAPHICS, DESIGN & WEB DEVELOPMENT

0-7645-8815-X

0-7645-9571-7

Also available:

- 3D Game Animation For Dummies
  0-7645-8789-7
- AutoCAD 2006 For Dummies
  0-7645-8925-3
- Building a Web Site For Dummies
  0-7645-7144-3
- Creating Web Pages For Dummies
  0-470-08030-2
- Creating Web Pages All-in-One Desk
  Reference For Dummies
  0-7645-4345-8
- Dreamweaver 8 For Dummies
  0-7645-9649-7

- InDesign CS2 For Dummies
  0-7645-9572-5
- Macromedia Flash 8 For Dummies
  0-7645-9691-8
- Photoshop CS2 and Digital
  Photography For Dummies
  0-7645-9580-6
- Photoshop Elements 4 For Dummies
  0-471-77483-9
- Syndicating Web Sites with RSS Feeds
  For Dummies
  0-7645-8848-6
- Yahoo! SiteBuilder For Dummies
  0-7645-9800-7

NETWORKING, SECURITY, PROGRAMMING & DATABASES

0-7645-7728-X

0-471-74940-0

Also available:

- Access 2007 For Dummies
  0-470-04612-0
- ASP.NET 2 For Dummies
  0-7645-7907-X
- C# 2005 For Dummies
  0-7645-9704-3
- Hacking For Dummies
  0-470-05235-X
- Hacking Wireless Networks
  For Dummies
  0-7645-9730-2
- Java For Dummies
  0-470-08716-1

- Microsoft SQL Server 2005 For Dummies
  0-7645-7755-7
- Networking All-in-One Desk Reference
  For Dummies
  0-7645-9939-9
- Preventing Identity Theft For Dummies
  0-7645-7336-5
- Telecom For Dummies
  0-471-77085-X
- Visual Studio 2005 All-in-One Desk
  Reference For Dummies
  0-7645-9775-2
- XML For Dummies
  0-7645-8845-1

HEALTH & SELF-HELP

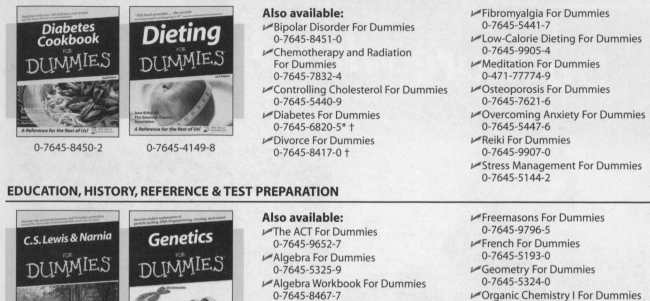

0-7645-8450-2

0-7645-4149-8

Also available:
- Bipolar Disorder For Dummies
  0-7645-8451-0
- Chemotherapy and Radiation
  For Dummies
  0-7645-7832-4
- Controlling Cholesterol For Dummies
  0-7645-5440-9
- Diabetes For Dummies
  0-7645-6820-5* †
- Divorce For Dummies
  0-7645-8417-0 †

- Fibromyalgia For Dummies
  0-7645-5441-7
- Low-Calorie Dieting For Dummies
  0-7645-9905-4
- Meditation For Dummies
  0-471-77774-9
- Osteoporosis For Dummies
  0-7645-7621-6
- Overcoming Anxiety For Dummies
  0-7645-5447-6
- Reiki For Dummies
  0-7645-9907-0
- Stress Management For Dummies
  0-7645-5144-2

EDUCATION, HISTORY, REFERENCE & TEST PREPARATION

0-7645-8381-6

0-7645-9554-7

Also available:
- The ACT For Dummies
  0-7645-9652-7
- Algebra For Dummies
  0-7645-5325-9
- Algebra Workbook For Dummies
  0-7645-8467-7
- Astronomy For Dummies
  0-7645-8465-0
- Calculus For Dummies
  0-7645-2498-4
- Chemistry For Dummies
  0-7645-5430-1
- Forensics For Dummies
  0-7645-5580-4

- Freemasons For Dummies
  0-7645-9796-5
- French For Dummies
  0-7645-5193-0
- Geometry For Dummies
  0-7645-5324-0
- Organic Chemistry I For Dummies
  0-7645-6902-3
- The SAT I For Dummies
  0-7645-7193-1
- Spanish For Dummies
  0-7645-5194-9
- Statistics For Dummies
  0-7645-5423-9

Get smart @ dummies.com®

- **Find a full list of Dummies titles**
- **Look into loads of FREE on-site articles**
- **Sign up for FREE eTips e-mailed to you weekly**
- **See what other products carry the Dummies name**
- **Shop directly from the Dummies bookstore**
- **Enter to win new prizes every month!**

* **Separate Canadian edition also available**
† **Separate U.K. edition also available**

Available wherever books are sold. For more information or to order direct: U.S. customers visit www.dummies.com or call 1-877-762-2974.
U.K. customers visit www.wileyeurope.com or call 0800 243407. Canadian customers visit www.wiley.ca or call 1-800-567-4797.